Praise for the first edition of *Shopping for Votes*

"… Delacourt lays bare a disturbing reality of modern politics. The obsession with marketing—treating politicians and election promises as products, like tubes of toothpaste—has hollowed out the soul of democratic discourse. No wonder increasing numbers of voters are staying home. When politicians treat citizens like gullible consumers, voters get turned off. Rescuing democracy from politics will start with reading this book."
ELIZABETH MAY, LEADER, GREEN PARTY OF CANADA

"… a revelation of how political marketing works. With ace investigative research and insight, Susan Delacourt lays bare the history and machinations of the branding, niche market, intuition, and gut feeling approach to viewing voters as consumers. Her unfolding of this troubling evolution in Canadian politics is rendered in clear prose, and her judgments are based in reasoned argument. *Shopping for Votes* is a must for anyone concerned about informed consensus and a democratic national vision for Canada."
JURY CITATION, HILARY WESTON AWARDS

"Susan Delacourt's *Shopping for Votes* is the most important book written on the changing nature of Canadian politics in the 21st century."
REG WHITAKER, *LITERARY REVIEW OF CANADA*

"… one of the very best books about Canadian politics to appear in many years… Ms. Delacourt has pulled the themes together in an excellently researched book that widens our understanding and deepens our depression about contemporary politics —which offers, after all, a rough mirror of who we are."
JEFFREY SIMPSON, *THE GLOBE AND MAIL*

SHOPPING
FOR
VOTES

HOW POLITICIANS CHOOSE
US AND WE CHOOSE THEM

Susan Delacourt

Douglas & McIntyre

1 2 3 4 5 — 20 19 18 17 16

Douglas and McIntyre (2013) Ltd.
P.O. Box 219
Madeira Park, BC, Canada V0N 2H0
www.douglas-mcintyre.com

Edited by Silas White
Text design by Mary White
Typesetting by Shed Simas
Printed and bound in Canada

Cataloguing data available from Library and Archives Canada
978-1-92681-293-9 (cloth, 1st ed.)
978-1-77162-109-0 (paper, 2nd ed.)
978-1-77162-110-6 (ebook, 2nd ed.)

Douglas and McIntyre (2013) Ltd. acknowledges the support of the Canada Council for the Arts, which last year invested $157 million to bring the arts to Canadians throughout the country. We also gratefully acknowledge financial support from the Government of Canada through the Canada Book Fund and from the Province of British Columbia through the BC Arts Council and the Book Publishing Tax Credit.

CONTENTS

PREFACE

The original edition of this book came out in the fall of 2013, several months after Justin Trudeau won the leadership of the Liberal Party of Canada and around the same time that Stephen Harper's Conservative government was unveiling a Throne Speech dedicated to Canadian consumers. Those two events helped set the stage for an important political shift two years later—an election that Trudeau and his Liberals handily won. Many of the same Canadians who had been wooed for a decade with Harper's extremely effective, consumer-targeted politics flocked to a very different product in the political marketplace.

In this paperback edition, featuring all-new material and interviews from the 2015 election campaign, a few more mileposts have been recorded on the long journey that Canadian politics has taken in tandem with marketing and advertising trends. Call this, if you like, *Shopping for Votes: New and Improved.* No matter what was said in the immediate aftermath of the 2015 election about a new era of politics, the Liberal victory was built in no small part as a result of—and a reaction to—the fusion of politics and marketing that came before it: the story told in this book.

Shopping for Votes was originally written as a result of a search for a new metaphor. In over twenty years covering federal politics in Canada, I had run out of ways to tell readers how political life resembled the world outside the Ottawa "bubble." Once, it was easy to tell my readers that politics was like a courtroom or a university classroom. The architectural edifices of their institutions, in all their solemn grandeur, are certainly similar. But as time wore on, it was increasingly difficult to argue that the political players were in pursuit of higher knowledge or a considered judgement.

For a while it worked to think of Parliament as one big work-place, or political parties as families. Then those metaphors fell short as well. Where, besides the most dysfunctional offices or families, could people yell past each other all the time? Sports and theatre comparisons ran their course, too. Enough with knockout punches and performance critiques.

And soon, like many others, I started to recognize the creep of shopping language into the political marketplace: brands, products, selling and buying. It was also hard not to notice that the parties paying the most attention to marketing trends were more successful than those resisting marketing's influence on politics. The politicians who were speaking in shopping language were clearly winning. So I decided to try to unravel this comparison, to see where it started and yes, to see what price we were paying for mixing consumerism with democracy.

Like the original edition of *Shopping for Votes*, what readers will get in this book is more of a story than a study. As much as polit-icos love to use marketing language, they also love to talk about the need for a "narrative." Here, then, is a new and updated narrative for how we look at our political culture in Canada, complete with bars of soap, cans of tomatoes and of course, generous helpings of beer and doughnuts.

INTRODUCTION

DOLLARS AND CHANGE

In the final week of Canada's 2015 election, Conservative leader Stephen Harper and Liberal leader Justin Trudeau were conducting two very different styles of campaigns. Harper, in keeping with his decade-long pitch to consumers' pocketbooks, was talking to Canadians who voted with their wallets. At stop after stop, he tried to persuade his audiences that Trudeau and his Liberals would take hard-earned money out of the pockets of Canadian taxpayers. Standing in front of a bright red sign emblazoned with the warning *The Cost of Liberal Tax Hikes*, Harper counted out dollar bills to the old-fashioned chime of a cash-register bell. One of these cash-register-themed events in the final week of the campaign included guest appearances from former Toronto mayor Rob Ford and his former councillor brother Doug. The Fords, who had run Canada's largest city for much of the time Harper was in power, liked to see themselves as pioneers in their view of citizens as "taxpayers."

"I'll tell ya, Rob came up with this phrase, but nothing I can remember in a federal election is any more important than respect for taxpayers," Doug Ford told the crowd in his warm-up speech before the main event. Trudeau, meanwhile, with his Liberals soaring in the polls, was out on the streets. As Trudeau's campaign bus rumbled through Southern Ontario that final week, small and large towns were forced to close roads to handle the crowds that the Liberal leader was attracting. The rooms booked for Trudeau appearances were too small to hold the burgeoning audiences. In Winnipeg, the same day that Harper was appearing in Toronto with the Fords, Trudeau walked the length of a lineup stretching for several city blocks, shaking hands with the hundreds of people who had turned up to see Canada's next prime minister. Trudeau, too, had a bright red sign on hand for his events. It read, *Real Change Now*. This is how a momentous election for Canada was ending: cash registers versus crowds; dollar bills versus change.

Sitting in his new office a few months later, which had been vacated quickly by Harper after the October 19, 2015, vote, Prime Minister Justin Trudeau talked about how his election campaign had been an attempt to pull Canadian political culture away from the cash registers and put it back on the street, among the people. Sure, Trudeau said, Canadians often think of themselves as consumers. But not all the time. "They don't want to be consumers of politics," he said.

Yet consumerism has had a profound impact on Canadians' lives, including their civic life, as the story in the following chapters will show. Trudeau's own father Pierre led the country through some of the earliest and groundbreaking forays by politics into the worlds of advertising and marketing. Harper grew up in that world, too, in the suburbs of Toronto where Pierre Trudeau's brand of politics left an enduring mark.

Ideologically, Trudeau and Harper may have been opposites in the 2015 election campaign, but as political salesmen, they were both heirs to Pierre Trudeau's legacy and to the prime ministers with their teams of advertising, polling and marketing strategists who came after him. Throughout the past half-century or so, trends in the consumer marketplace have repeatedly found their way into politics, from musical jingles to "branding" to sophisticated data analysis of the customer base. Has this been good for politics or democracy? The evidence is decidedly mixed.

In Harper's decade in power, the fusion of politics and marketing was complete and pervasive. It was a time in which Canadians began to sort their voting preferences as they did their coffee choices—the world of the "Tim Hortons voters." Harper did some of his most memorable work in front of cash registers. His promised vote-attracting cuts to the goods and services tax were first announced at a Mississauga electronics store, for instance, during the 2005–06 election campaign. He would return to that store in 2007 to proclaim his GST-cut vow as a promise delivered. In 2009, Harper skipped a summit of world leaders at the United Nations to speak instead behind the counter of Tim Horton's headquarters in Oakville, Ontario, delivering an ode to the doughnut chain that had become shorthand for the double-double-drinking suburbanites that all the political parties were wooing. The Speech from the Throne in 2013 was specifically dedicated to improving the lot of Canadian consumers.

Harper's Conservative government would repeatedly reach out to citizens with all the cash-register bells and whistles of the consumer world: "boutique" tax credits, snappy marketing slogans on legislation, as well as advertising—lots and lots of advertising. In their ten years in office, the Conservatives' public spending on advertising was estimated at about $750 million, and that didn't include the undisclosed additional millions in party donations spent on political advertising against Trudeau and a couple of ill-fated Liberal leaders who came before him. It all meant that between 2006 and 2015, Canada was governed by a prime minister and a party that talked to Canadians as consumers or "taxpayers" first.

Here was the irony, though. For all this effort to reach Canadians through their wallets or at the cash registers, public interest or engagement with politics was also at an all-time low during Harper's decade in power. Voter turnout had plummeted to around 60 percent by the 2011 election, membership in political parties declined and cynicism about the democratic system was rampant. So although the political world had been adopting all the methods that marketers used to sell merchandise to people, much of the public was simply not buying the product.

Something shifted in this political culture in the 2015 campaign, though, which stretched from early August to late October. Voter turnout went up—at least seven percentage points over the turnout in 2011, to more than 68 percent. The country hadn't seen a turnout that high in twenty years. Nearly eighteen million ballots were cast, a surge of almost three million more than the ballots cast in the previous election. The increase was attributed to higher engagement from young people and indigenous Canadians, and maybe even an election that captured voters' imagination.

It had been a campaign filled with conversations that went beyond mere value for the dollar, and into values of the heart and head. Canadians and their politicians talked about whether the country was a welcome place for refugees or Muslim women who wanted to wear the niqab to citizenship ceremonies. A political party, the winning one, would fly in the face of twenty-year-old political orthodoxy around budgeting in Canada and campaign with a promise to increase taxes and the deficit. Trudeau, the new prime minister, was not even a fan of the word "taxpayers."

"Unless you say 'service-receivers' at the same time as you say 'taxpayers,' you're only [giving] half the equation," Trudeau said in that post-election conversation in his office. "The idea of 'citizen' involves both benefits and responsibilities, and I like that a bit better." It would be tempting to see the 2015 election, then, as a page closed on the story of how Canada's politics got all mixed up with marketing, and how citizens became consumers or "taxpayers." But time and cultural shifts can't be rolled back, especially the kind of shifts described in the pages of this book. "Marketing? Social media? They're just ways of connecting with people, and if you're someone who gets people, you'll get marketing and advertising, too," Trudeau said.

Trudeau's old friend and chief adviser, Gerald Butts, also said in a post-election conversation that politics needs to talk to people on their own terms. "The idea of being a consumer has become such a fundamental way of being that it's absorbed into who we are," Butts said. "You can lament it, you can applaud it, or you can celebrate it, or you can hate it. It is what it is. Whether you're trying to win an election, convince someone to go to your university, or sell them a tube of toothpaste, at the end of the day you have to take into account how they see the world and themselves within it."

How the voters came to see themselves this way is the story of this book. It's a story that unfolds in three parts. Part one, "The Pitch," spans the years from the postwar period to the 1970s, when Canada became a consumer society and Canadian political practitioners began to realize they could borrow tools and wisdom from the marketing world. In many ways, this was an age of innocence and discovery. If we could find a way to people's hearts through the tools of the marketplace, what could possibly go wrong? The second part, "The Bargaining," spans the 1980s and 1990s, when tension started surfacing between the consumer market and the political world, along with debates over where to draw the line between the two realms. Part three, "Sealing the Deal," takes us into contemporary Canadian politics and culture, where the fusion of marketing and civics appears to be nearly complete. The victory of Trudeau and his Liberals built upon that twenty-first-century reality in new and interesting ways.

Through each aisle of this three-part shopping trip, we'll see patterns and common threads: the traffic between political marketing techniques in Canada, the United States and Britain. We'll meet the people in the polling and marketing industries who helped build the bridge between civic and consumer culture. We'll see ongoing ambivalence on the part of our politicos over whether to treat citizens as educated or sedated consumers. We may well want to throw up our hands and conclude these are forces that have been too powerful to resist, on either side.

It would be tempting to blame politicians or the plotters in the political "war rooms" for this reality, and certainly, as we'll see, modern methods of advertising and marketing are as fundamental now to Canadian political operatives as old-fashioned speeches and town hall meetings were to their historical predecessors. But in the pages to follow, ordinary citizens may also recognize their own complicity in their transformation into consumers of Canadian democracy. Politics and for that matter shopping are exercises in giving the people what they want. The 2015 election has not ended that story, but has opened up a new chapter in the saga of how we and our politicians, of all stripes, have been shopping for votes.

THE PITCH

LET'S GET CANADA SHOPPING

Never mind what you may have heard about Canadians being hewers of wood and drawers of water. Forget all those endearing and enduring rural symbols that are supposed to bind the country together—the beavers, the moose, the Great White North. Canada is now a nation of shoppers, doing their hunting and gathering on store shelves. The economy depends on it.

True, Americans are bigger shoppers than Canadians, with consumer spending accounting for somewhere between 60 and 70 percent of gross domestic product in that country since 1980. But Canadian shoppers are also an economic force, with consumption representing 52 to 58 percent of our GDP during those same decades.

So when politicians say that they are focused on the economy, what they often mean is that they are focused on getting Canadians to buy stuff. Jean Chrétien, campaigning to become prime minister for his first term in 1993, delivered this as a blunt home truth. "When people go to the city and they see some cranes or construction they feel good, and they go and buy either a house, a cottage or a car," Chrétien told CITY-TV while on the election trail. Translation:

feeling good about Canada's economy means Canadians will get in the mood to buy big-ticket items. Or they may go to Tim Hortons, or a big-box store, or, in more recent years, they may shop online. If it is the job of Canadian politicians to keep the economy rolling, it's the Canadian citizenry's job to keep lining up at the cash register.

This partnership between consumerism and the citizenry has been building since the early years of the twentieth century, long before Chrétien wanted to make Canadians feel good about construction cranes or Stephen Harper wanted to make people feel warm about Tim Hortons. But if we want to understand why politicians have come looking for our votes in the shopping aisles, perhaps we should do a whirlwind tour of how citizenship became so all-consuming.

The Hudson's Bay Company is the perfect place to start. For a couple of centuries, it operated as a series of trading posts, expanding across the vast northern wilderness, providing places for hunters and trappers to exchange fur for manufactured goods. If all those wilderness symbols of Canada speak to you, the canoes and moose and such, this version of The Bay is your kind of shopping. By the end of the nineteenth century, though, early Canadians were showing up at The Bay with money, not pelts. Canada was officially born with the 1867 Act of Confederation and in the first years of its nationhood, the era of big department stores was also beginning. The first Eaton's store in Canada opened in Toronto in 1869, two years after Confederation, and in the next couple of decades, Hudson's Bay department stores arrived in the cities rapidly growing across the country, especially across the West. So just as we were becoming a country, we were starting to shop at the big-time retail outlets.

And some of the identity of this new, modern nation was being defined within the pages of the department-store advertising, and especially in the glossy catalogues, which would become bibles of the new consumer nation. Millions of Canadians who came of age in the last century will remember the department-store catalogues as a cultural marker in their lives. As the *Toronto Star*'s Jack Brehl wrote in 1969, "In Scotland, the children were raised on porridge and the shorter catechism; in Canada, on cornflakes and [the] Eaton's catalogue." The catalogues announced the arrival of the seasons: spring/summer, fall/winter and the much-anticipated Christmas season, with pages stuffed with pictures of the newest toys. These bulky volumes, printed by the millions even in the early years of the twentieth century, could paper over rifts in the new Canada in a way that politicians and other institutions could only envy. Rural Canadians could pore over the same wares that urban citizens were seeing on display in the downtown aisles and windows of Eaton's or Simpson's or The Bay. A francophone child in Quebec could pine for the same dolls as her English-language counterparts in British Columbia. The catalogues' reach far exceeded any newspaper of their time, and they painted a happy picture of life in early Canada: a consumer paradise, filled with shiny new merchandise.

Were Canadians interested in politics in those days? Certainly global and domestic politics had an effect on their lives. Two world wars and one depression brought political events literally to their doorsteps—boys and men went off to war, many didn't come back, and households faced daily rationing and shortages. Canadian women joined the workplace during the wars and earned, over the course of the twentieth century, the right to vote, to run for Parliament and to be appointed to the Senate. Politics mattered, with an importance driven by people's interests in larger forces shaping the times—nationalism, communism, fascism and rapid urbanization. Voter turnout at federal elections hovered around 65 to 70 percent for the first half of the century. When the Second World War ended, politics appeared to matter even more, with election turnout climbing to almost 80 percent in the early 1960s. But Canadians were also busy setting about the serious business of shopping their way into a new future, filled with new children, new homes, new inventions and new, consumerist preoccupations.

The Canadian Dream

Two of the most beloved Christmas-movie standards were made in the immediate aftermath of the Second World War, and though they were Hollywood productions, they reflected a lot of the hope that ordinary people in Canada were feeling about the future, too. *It's a Wonderful Life*, released in 1946, starred James Stewart as George Bailey, a man who becomes the town hero by devoting his life to the Building and Loan Society, helping new immigrants and young families buy their first homes. In a heated argument with Mr. Potter, the cynical bank owner, Bailey elegizes home ownership as the paragon of good citizenship: "You're all businessmen here. Doesn't [owning a home] make them better citizens? Doesn't it make them better customers? … Just remember this, Mr. Potter, that this rabble you're talking about: they do most of the working and paying and living and dying in this community. Well, is it too much to have them work and pay and live and die in a couple of decent rooms and a bath?" A year later, the big Christmas movie of 1947 was *Miracle on 34th Street*, in which Susan, the little girl who doesn't believe in Santa Claus, gets her fondest wish—not a doll or a skipping rope, but a real, live home in the suburbs.

Canadians, like their American neighbours, were caught up in the postwar passion for home ownership and expected their governments to share that desire. A National Housing Act was forged in 1944, giving the federal government the leading role in Canada-wide housing programs. The Central Mortgage and Housing Corporation was created on January 1, 1946, to administer the new housing legislation, and to get to work building all the houses that returning war veterans, new Canadians and the baby boom generation were going to need. By the end of the 1940s, the CMHC also got in the business of building social and rental housing, recognizing that not everyone in Canada was going to vault into immediate home ownership. Urban renewal came next, with the CMHC starting to administer grants so that derelict, downtown areas could be razed and new city-project homes could be built. Regent Park in Toronto was the first such project in Canada.

How were Canadians paying for these new homes? Some, clinging to the frugality of the Depression and the war years, were paying with their own savings or with generous grants that the federal government was providing for war veterans and other deserving folks. Between 1945 and 1947, nineteen thousand loans were approved under the act and more than seventy-six thousand homes were built in 1947 alone. In 1954, borrowing money to buy homes became even easier for Canadians, when the federal government made an expansive and far-reaching change to the National Housing Act, allowing banks to give mortgage loans.

The new "baby bonus" cheques, rolled out in 1945, also helped with postwar Canadian household finances. This program was no small step in the evolution of the Canadian consumer state. It was, in effect, a product in itself, which arrived as a gift on the doorsteps of every Canadian parent just like the department-store catalogues. It was Canada's first universal social program. It established a direct connection between the government and its consumer-citizens—a monthly, tangible assurance that the state was as interested in their material circumstances as they were. For Prime Minister Mackenzie King, it was a "micro-targeted" program to accomplish macro-economic and political goals. It would keep Canadians purchasing things after the war, it would encourage people to have children and it would fend off threats to the Liberals coming from the rising strength of the left-wing Co-operative Commonwealth Federation and from within Quebec. Baby bonuses united all Canadians, regardless of politics or language, as consumers in the modern, postwar state.

In the first wave of this program, parents received five dollars a month for each child aged five and under, six dollars a month for kids aged six to nine, seven dollars for children aged ten to twelve, and eight dollars for early teens, aged thirteen to fifteen. Those cheques could prove handy, in a time when Baby's Own Tablets (for teething, digestive problems and "fretfulness") cost a quarter and a frilly Easter blouse for a young girl could be had for $1.98 at Clayton's in Toronto. The total annual cost to the treasury for the initial program was estimated at between $200 million and $250 million.

In May 1945, a Gallup poll on the new baby bonus found that a whopping 95 percent of respondents were aware of the program and, in the main, of the view that the money would be spent wisely—not wasted on beer and popcorn, for example. Gallup asked, "In your opinion, are a large number of Canadians likely to use this money for other purposes, or are only a few likely to use it improperly?" Of the 95 percent who said they were aware of the baby bonus, 56 percent said the money would be spent on food and clothing and other necessities for child-rearing. Another 30 percent, though, said the money might be squandered elsewhere. About 9 percent were undecided.

In their emergence as consumer-citizens, Canadians began to make more demands—not just for goods, but for rules and standards over how they were getting them. In 1947, still in the shadow of the Second World War, the Consumers' Association of Canada was launched—by hundreds, then thousands of Canadian women. The association's first motto was "in unity, there is strength," and it boasted 250,000 members by 1948.

The association's first big battle was a fight over margarine. Yes, margarine. Thanks largely to pressure from dairy farmers, margarine had been banned in Canada since 1886. The ban had been lifted during the First World War when butter was scarce, but the prohibition was still active at the end of the Second World War. In 1948, thanks in part to the advocacy of the new consumers' group, Canada's Supreme Court lifted the ban. In the 1940s and 1950s, the Consumers' Association would go on to fight for information labelling on clothing, safety and moving guidelines for refrigerators, disclosure of charges on consumer loans and an end to deceptive "red-stripe labelling" being used to sell fatty bacon to unsuspecting shoppers. The red stripes on the see-through plastic packaging made it look like the bacon inside had more meat than was the actual content. In the grocery stores, Canadian shoppers drew the line in the 1950s when it came to promising meat and delivering fat.

At the same time, feeling their power, Canadian consumer-citizens were also starting to look to government to provide them with more goods and services. First came the baby bonuses, then the new houses, and then a rising demand for a national health-care program and old-age pensions for everyone. Medicare was introduced in Canada in 1957, thanks to the success of the first public hospital insurance program in Tommy Douglas's Saskatchewan. The Canada Pension Plan, meanwhile, came along in 1965 as a compulsory universal retirement-savings system.

In the new and emerging Canada of the postwar era, the dream was of an ever-expanding middle class, secure in its access to the basics and striving, shopping, for more. And the government was happy to be seen as the agent of dream fulfillment, delivering cheques to the doorsteps of the houses it was helping Canadians to buy—on credit, more and more.

Charging Ahead

The word "consumerism" actually only came into common usage in the years after the Second World War, along with the idea that it was a cause to be championed. Though shopping was seen as mostly a female preoccupation in the early days, an interesting thing happened to the Consumers' Association of Canada by the 1960s—it had transformed itself from a women's-only organization into one that welcomed men as well. Almost simultaneously, the group began a six-year mission to establish a Consumer Affairs ministry within the federal government. That goal was achieved in 1967, and its first minister was the up-and-coming politician John Turner. The mission of this new ministry was "to promote the integrity and viability of the market system in Canada," through vigilance on orderly, efficient, healthy competition and movement of capital between business and citizens.

Into this mix came another important consumer tool—credit cards. Individual department stores and gas stations had been extending credit accounts to individual customers before the 1950s, but it was the Diners Club that first paved the way for the ubiquitous credit cards stuffing Canadian wallets today. In 1950, Hamilton Credit Corporation head Frank McNamara went out for dinner with some friends (including one of the Bloomingdales, of New York department-store fame). At this dinner, McNamara and his friends were talking about how some clients were getting themselves into trouble by lending their credit accounts to neighbours in trouble and then finding themselves unable to pay. At the end of dinner, ironically, McNamara realized he'd forgotten his wallet. Embarrassed, he called his wife to bring him some money, and as legend has it, he vowed that it would never happen again.

The Diners Club card was born—the first card that could be used in multiple locations. It started out small: just a flimsy piece of cardboard with about a dozen accepting locations written on one side. And it took a few years to catch on. But by 1958, Diners Club had some competition, from the newly formed American Express Company and BankAmericards, which then rapidly started expanding the credit-card market in the United States.

In Canada, the first credit cards arrived on the scene in 1968. Chargex cards on simple plastic with blue, white and gold horizontal stripes were offered to bank customers in good standing, but also carried a whopping 18-percent interest charge. Canadians loved them though, and it wasn't long before MasterCharge, with its distinctive overlapping circles on its card, came in to compete with the Chargex and American Express cards, too.

Consumer debt was steadily climbing—from $835 million in 1948 to $11 billion by 1969. In 1948, consumer credit amounted to 7.5 percent of Canadians' disposable income. By 1969, it was up to 21.5 percent. By the early 1970s, it was estimated that more than ten million credit cards were in the wallets of Canadian consumers and Canadians were actually outpacing Americans in their use of consumer credit.

Drivers of Democracy

"Fordism" is the name given to the type of economy that Canada was building in these decades. The term, coined by cultural analyst Antonio Gramsci, described the pervasive, mass-production methods of automobile maker Henry Ford and his assembly lines. After the Second World War, mass production emerged to accommodate jobs and goods for the burgeoning population. Fordism was about more than cars. It was about building a world in which people were paid well for low-skill work so that they could afford all the consumer products that their work was churning out. Still, the car stood at the centre of this economic and cultural revolution. As any chronicler of the postwar era knows, the automobile changed everything. In 1945, only 1.1 million automobiles were registered in Canada. In 1952, car registrations had doubled and by 1961, there were 4.3 million cars in a nation of 18 million people. Or, if you prefer, you could look at it this way: when the Second World War ended, one in ten people had a car in Canada; by the dawn of the 1960s, roughly one of every four Canadians had a car. Four was also, probably not coincidentally, the size of the famed "nuclear family"—a mom, a dad and two kids, one of each gender, which also happened to be the ideal of the 1960s.

The car would indeed change Canada in fundamental ways, going far beyond the jobs it provided in the auto sector or the fuel costs it incurred for the daily commuter. Cars changed the actual land-scape of Canada, with the arrival of multi-lane highways, driveways, garages and parking lots, not to mention the drive-in restaurants, motels and movie theatres. A whole new way of looking at the world, from the window of the automobile, ushered "car-chitecture" into the design lexicon, and buildings and signs were created to catch the eye of passing motorists. The McDonald's golden arches were a classic example; so too, for that matter, was the Tim Hortons sign, with its own oversized, bold, brown-and-white design. Cars made the suburbs financially possible, indeed attractive, for the increasing numbers of people working and living in urban areas.

As Richard Harris notes in his book *Creeping Conformity*, a chronicle of how Canada's suburbs were built, "The automobile allowed men, especially, to live much further from work and encouraged suburbs to spread at lower densities. Instead of twenty-five-foot lots, forty- and fifty-foot lots became the norm, larger still around smaller cities and in affluent suburbs." Don Mills, in Toronto, was one of Canada's first real suburbs, the brainchild of financier E.P. Taylor, who commissioned the design of quadrants and cul-de-sacs that would distinguish the future geography of most suburbs. Taylor acquired the necessary two-thousand-plus acres of land from North York from 1947 to 1952. More than fifty builders would work on the homes to fill the new suburb, and the first home opened on Jocelyn Crescent to much fanfare in 1953.

Don Mills, just outside downtown Toronto, became the exemplar for a brave new world. In 1954, CBC's *News Magazine* travelled across the country to document the housing situation at mid-century, noting approvingly the rise of planned suburbs such as Don Mills. "A key word to Don Mills—community," the narrator said, lauding the way that the neighbourhood had been designed to put stores, schools and homes within walking distance of each other, and all of this fewer than ten kilometres from the city centre. In March 1955, *Chatelaine* devoted a whole issue to "How to Live in the Suburbs," featuring stories such as "Is the Coffee Party a Menace or a Must?" and "How to Furnish a New Home Without Panic Buying."

Although the original intent of the suburbs was to create instant neighbourhoods and community, front porches became increasingly uncommon, with inward-looking suburbanites favouring back decks or basement recreation rooms instead. And of course, in a nod to the rising dominance of the automobile, driveways and garages became distinguishing, prominent features of the suburban landscape.

It's worth reflecting on what the car and the suburbs did to Canada's existing political architecture as well. Canada's Parliament, like most Western democratic legislatures, was designed in a time when people lived and worked in the same riding or electoral district. So voters could expect their local MP to understand the breadth of their day-to-day concerns, whether they were related to their homes or their jobs. But a whole new commuting class of Canadians meant that many voters (mainly men) spent a large part of their day out of their home riding. Their political views may have been informed by the places where they worked, but their votes were cast in the places where they lived. A factory employee with strong union views, for instance, may have been inclined to vote for the NDP because of where he spent his day, but found himself voting in a riding where the Conservatives had historically held sway. A businessman working in a downtown office all day could find himself leaning toward Conservative policies, but cast his ballot in a riding where the Liberals had created jobs or opportunities.

This new commuter class was a boon for radio, too, which provided news, sports and information to all those Canadians driving back and forth to work each day. Sixty-two new radio stations opened in Canada between 1945 and 1952, meeting a demand that was fed in part by the new commuters. Cocooned in their automobiles, they became a captive audience, ripe for advertising or political persuasion. By 1962, there were over two million car radios in Canada. The surge in car ownership, in fact, rescued radio from potential extinction. Though radio had been the second-largest medium in Canada up until the early 1950s, just behind newspapers, the arrival of television meant that radio lost its position as the central entertainment unit for the whole family. This would fundamentally change the nature of and the market for radio: it went from family audiences to an audience made up of individuals, most of them in their cars, listening at peak times between seven a.m. and nine a.m, and again, to a lesser extent, between four p.m. and six p.m.

Rather than try to be all things to all people, radio stations looked for niche markets and target demographics. The radio dial was divided into specialized channels: mellow music and commentary for commuters, rock and roll for teenagers, country music stations for those whose tastes ran in that direction. This fragmenting of the market was a foreshadowing of changes to come in the political market, too, several decades later.

In the meantime, television took over as the mass-market medium. Canada's own television industry officially launched in 1952, with the opening of the CBLT station in Toronto and CBFT in Montreal. Canadians close to the US border with strong antennas had been able to pick up American channels for several years by this point, but these two new CBC stations were home-grown. Just a year before, in 1951, the Massey Commission had handed down its report on Canadian culture, warning that measures had to be taken to protect Canada from the mass-market culture of our neighbour to the south.

"We benefit from vast importations of what might be familiarly called the American cultural output," the Massey Report stated. "Of American institutions we make the freest use." In the movie theatres, the commission stated, the problem was most acute. "The cinema at present is not only the most potent but also the most alien of the influences shaping our Canadian life. Nearly all Canadians go to the movies; and most movies are from Hollywood. The urbane influences of Carnegie and Rockefeller have helped us to be ourselves; Hollywood refashions us in its own image."

The first Canadian-made TV broadcasts were done live from the studios in Montreal and Toronto. Viewers were treated to piano performances from Glenn Gould and singalongs from staffers or puppet shows for children. On the debut evening of Toronto's TV channel, news announcer Lorne Greene informed citizens solemnly that the notorious Boyd Gang had escaped from Toronto's Don Jail. TV brought the political life of the country into people's living rooms as well. In 1955, for the first time, Canadians could follow along on television as ceremonies were held to mark the opening of a session of Parliament.

Although those first made-in-Canada TV channels reached only 10 percent of the Canadian population when they first went on the air, TV rapidly expanded across the country in just a few short years. By the end of the 1950s, there were forty-eight TV stations up and running in the country, beaming grainy black-and-white programs into the homes of roughly 75 percent of the Canadian population. Advertising revenues rose by a staggering 1,400 percent in this decade, making the ad business into a lucrative career for creative, educated, ambitious types—the kind who might be attracted to politics, too.

Better Lives Through Science

After the Second World War, Canada was also caught up in the worship of science, evidence and systems—fuel for the politicos who were keen to bring that same discipline into their often unpredictable world. Military service during the war had elevated the virtues of drills and organization; it was no accident that politics had borrowed heavily from armed forces lingo to do its own organizing, complete with battles, troops and campaigns. Science transformed people's homes in the second half of the twentieth century, too, including bringing plastic dinnerware into the modern housewife's cupboards, and the design of kitchens and bathrooms began to resemble clean, sterile laboratories. Science could solve every problem, but it created some, too.

Malcolm Wallace, principal of University College, put it this way in his submission to the Massey Commission: "Most of the changes which have transformed our daily lives, our standards in matters of government and education, our hopes for the future of man, and indeed those general ideals which serve as lanterns to mark our path—all these changes have originated in the dominating role which science has come to play in our lives. No such fundamental change has ever before been recorded in so brief a period of human history. Science has taught us to increase human productivity of goods to an incredible extent; we not only enjoy comforts and conveniences hitherto undreamed of, but power to create a new Eden on earth. As a matter of fact we have chosen to indulge in the most expensive of all luxuries—recurring world wars. Our discovery of the atomic bomb would seem to guarantee bigger and better wars in the future."

The atom bomb, of course, loomed large in the collective global imagination after the Second World War, with the United States and the Soviet Union engaged in their own Cold War nuclear arms race. Canadians were following every twist and turn in the tension of mutually assured destruction, and the federal government built the "Diefenbunker," in Carp, Ontario, near the capital, to house the prime minister and cabinet in the event of a nuclear attack from the Soviet Union. Canadian schoolchildren were watching films that demonstrated to them the superiority of democracy and the dread of communism. One measure of a truly free society, Canadians were told, was the freedom to choose and the freedom to shop. In Eastern Bloc countries, people lined up for everyday staples, but in free and democratic nations, people could browse plentiful wares in the store aisles. Shopping wasn't a chore, then, but a high democratic privilege.

People liked the idea that science could even shape minds and allow people to choose their own destiny—which before then had been shaped by geography or genetics. Sigmund Freud's ideas of the subconscious mind and the idea of a "self" had taken hold by the mid-twentieth century in Europe and North America. Psychoanalysis, Freud's pioneered method of putting people in touch with their deeper selves, was a growing method of therapy in Canada, with the founding of the Canadian Psychoanalytic Society in the 1950s. But it was in fact Freud's nephew, Edward Bernays, who put Freud's

16

ideas into use in the commercial and then political sectors, to work arts of persuasion on the masses. It was Bernays who coined the term "public relations" as a gentler term than propaganda and Bernays who also dreamed up some of the tools that are still in the arsenal of the PR professional today—press releases, for instance. Bernays's clients in the early twentieth century included the United Fruit Company and President Woodrow Wilson. Bernays, who has been called the "Father of Spin," could also be called the great-grandfather of modern consumer-citizenship. Where Freud operated on the more democratic principle that minds should be opened, Bernays shaped his methods around mass minds that would remain closed.

"In almost every act of our daily lives, whether in the sphere of politics or business, in our social conduct or our ethical thinking, we are dominated by the relatively small number of persons... who understand the mental processes and social patterns of the masses. It is they who pull the wires which control the public mind," Bernays wrote in his book *Propaganda*, a title evidently chosen before that word had somewhat darker connotations.

Before Bernays made that observation, there had been tension in the advertising world between styles of marketing. On the one hand was the "Barnum approach," from Phineas T. Barnum, the renowned circus master, who was famed for using outrageous stunts to grab the public's attention. Barnum would become known for his immortal phrase "There's a sucker born every minute." Still, his approach to mass persuasion was admired and studied north and south of the forty-ninth parallel. In Canada, magazines such as *Saturday Night* and a trade journal, *Economic Advertising*, pointed to Barnum as a master of publicity. Even the respected economist Harold Innis, conducting his studies of advertising and communications, looked to Barnum for clues to mass persuasion.

On the other hand was the Powers style, so named for John E. Powers, advertising manager of Wanamaker's, an early US department store, which was focused far more on educating consumers with clearly marked prices and short, concise ad copy. Where Barnum sought to provoke or even shock his audiences, the earnest Powers sought to inform. "To the extent that the Barnum style played to the gullibility of its audience, there was a degree of condescension in its view of humanity. The public were rubes, at best co-authors of their own illusions. Powers was more inclined to see the public as customers. Customers, seen within the intellectual framework of classical economics, had interests of their own that they sought to maximize in every commercial transaction. They were not to be misled, but assisted in the formation of their purchasing decisions," advertising professor and author Russell Johnston writes in his book *Selling Themselves: The Emergence of Canadian Advertising.*

It bears keeping that Barnum–Powers distinction in mind as we wind through the ins and outs of political marketing in subsequent chapters. Just as commercial advertisers had widely different views of the consuming public, so too have political marketers had varying views of consumer-citizens. Call it optimism versus pessimism, or reality versus cynicism. Both sides have been able to claim some vindication for their views over the years, often looking to emerging research in psychology to bolster their impressions of their audience.

In Canada, the scientific discipline of psychology found its roots as the study of "mental hygiene" and of eugenics—the pseudoscience devoted to the idea of "improving" races either physically or mentally. After the Second World War, however, when psychology had proven useful—in the selection of officers or even in espionage—psychology found its way into Canadian schools, both for testing students and as a separate discipline at universities. Fledgling market-research companies, still mainly based in the United States, were increasingly attracted to the idea of psychology as a way to track and predict consumer behaviour. The Canadian Psychological Association, founded in 1940, saw its ranks swell from about 150 members to more than 700 in 1955.

As was the case in the United States, the 1950s and 1960s saw psychologists becoming celebrities in their own right, the most famous in the US being Dr. Benjamin Spock with his child-rearing advice. In Canada, Dr. William Blatz was known as the "Canadian Dr. Spock" for his work on child development and his "security theory." Another famed Canadian psychologist of the time was Samuel Laycock, from Saskatchewan, who came to early prominence when a criminal lawyer named John Diefenbaker asked him to conduct psychological tests on a seventeen-year-old boy scheduled to hang for a crime. Laycock pronounced the lad a "low-grade moron" and the death sentence was commuted.

Perhaps not surprisingly, given so much change in Canadians' lives in such a short time, there was also a lot of skepticism about these new-fangled notions behind psychology and advertising. Canadians may have been swept up in their new suburban lives and shopping centres, but they were by no means the brainwashed masses that Bernays may have envisioned. In fact, whether it was the paranoia of the Cold War or just shopping fatigue, by the end of the 1950s Canadians appeared to be already growing wary of all the advertisements saturating their lives. In the United States, Vance Packard published his blockbuster bestseller *The Hidden Persuaders*, showing all the ways in which advertisers were using "strange and rather exotic" arts of psychology to lure unwitting consumers to buy more things.

Canadian advertisers were paying attention to this emerging skepticism about their methods, and they worried that the overall credibility of the industry was imperilled. Moreover, there were fears that the government would step in and regulate the industry for them. And so the Canadian Advertising Advisory Board (CAAB) was born in 1957—a joint effort of the Association of Canadian Advertisers and Institute of Canadian Advertising.

This board would prove to be essential in protecting the integrity of advertisers, all through a voluntary code with three basic tenets:

truth, fairness and accuracy. The code, still in existence today, spells out all kinds of forbidden ad practices for the commercial sector: no lying about prices or guarantees, no false claims about science or competitors, and so on. Attack ads, which would become a staple of the political world, are strictly frowned upon by the businesses that subscribe to the ad-standards code. "Advertisements must not, unfairly, discredit, disparage or attack one or more products, services, advertisements, companies or entities, or exaggerate the nature or importance of competitive differences" the code states.

So even if Canada was turning into a consumer society in the immediate postwar period, at least it would be an educated consumer society. In *Chatelaine* around this era, the Magazine Advertising Bureau frequently published notices encouraging shoppers to be discerning critics of the ads they were seeing. One read, "If you tried to buy everything that was offered, your money wouldn't last long. So you become a smart shopper. You choose which things you are going to buy. Isn't it nice to have choice? Isn't it good to see so many people trying to please you by turning out ever-improving things?" No one had to read too far between the lines to see the Cold War subtext there: choice equals freedom, and freedom equals happiness, and isn't that better than life in the cold, grey communist countries?

Canadians weren't just embracing choice on the store shelves, either. The 1960s would present Canadians with a whole buffet of personal-life choices they hadn't been free to make before. The 1960s saw the laws changed to make it a lot easier to get divorces, meaning that men and women were no longer stuck for life with the commitment they made at the wedding altar. Women wanted the right to choose when to conceive children, too, and along came the revolutionary invention of the birth control pill, known simply as the Pill, to accommodate that desire. It was approved for general sale in Canada in 1961, though it would take another eight years for chemical birth control to be fully legal in this country. Nonetheless, for the thousands, then millions, of women who took the pill, it opened up their reproductive lives to all-important choice. That same virtue would fuel the drive to make abortion legal and accessible.

All of these huge societal changes were creating the conditions for a Canadian consumer state, which would have profound implications for politics and citizens' relationship to their government. The choice and freedom they saw in their shops they demanded of their political culture, and vice versa. Even by the 1960s, Canada had all the textbook attributes of a consumer culture: increasing availability of consumer goods, the expansion of shopping as a leisure pursuit, political organization by consumers and ever-growing pools of credit and debt. Those conditions would only deepen over the subsequent decades, turning Canada into a consumer nation and Canadians into consumer-citizens.

The proof of that reality? As the twenty-first century dawned, Industry Canada decided to take a sweeping look at consumer trends in Canada. One finding stands out. A focus-group study asked each of the participants: When do you consider yourself a consumer? When you're shopping? When you're watching TV? The answer: All the time. Coming through fifty years of the postwar spending spree—including the advent of cars and television, rapid expansion of shopping choice and wide availability of merchandise—Canadians said they were consumers 24-7, and that they saw their entire world as a series of consumer choices. As we'll see, much of Canada's democratic culture, from politics to government, has encouraged and obliged this view of consumer-citizenship.

And how would this consumer-citizenship be felt in Canada's political and civic culture? Well, it started with advertising.

SOLD LIKE SOAP

Hard as it may be to believe these days, a Canadian soap company once thought politics would help sell its wares. In the late nineteenth century, David Morton and Sons slapped a picture of John A. Macdonald on its bars of N.P. Soap. And for good measure, the soap-maker also created sales posters featuring Canada's first prime minister holding a three-pound bar of the product, casting a bemused smile above his likeness on the packaging.

About a half-century later, in *Canadian Forum* magazine, a bible of the country's left wing, a writer named Philip Spencer argued, "In this day and age, until we've learned how the technique of selling soap works, we'll go on making a mighty poor fist of selling socialism to the lower middle and working classes, the younger voters and the women."

It's an odd partnership, politics and soap. But it's an enduring one, lasting long past the days when politicians used to stand on soapboxes at local rallies. For decades now, it seems that whenever we want to talk about the gritty business of politics and advertising, we're tempted to reach for the soap metaphors. Perhaps it's a way of washing our hands of the whole business. Canadian political marketing expert Alex Marland, of Memorial University, found that as far back as 1952 US Democrats complained that early TV ads by the Republicans reduced politics to something sold "like hair tonic or soap."

"The art of selling politicians like soap on TV" was the headline for a 1980 *New York Times* feature on the ways in which the techniques of consumerism and psychology had infiltrated the American political system. Ronald Reagan, a Hollywood actor, literally did sell soap in the years before he became a politician and ultimately president of the United States from 1980 to 1988. Ads featuring Reagan, shilling for Boraxo hand soap, still live on YouTube, where the then B-list actor is seen in 1960s spots extolling the virtues of "waterless hand cleaner." A couple of decades later, installed at the White House, Reagan saw himself, if jokingly, as the actual soap for sale. Ducking his head into a meeting of the powerful ad executives creating his "Morning in America" campaign pitch, Reagan reportedly said, "I understand you guys are selling soap. I thought you'd like to see the bar."

Perhaps it's fitting, then, that one of the earliest examples of negative political advertising in Canada came in the form of a radio soap opera, the serialized drama format originally sponsored by household cleaning product manufacturers. During the 1930s, the Conservatives engaged the services of the J.J. Gibbons advertising firm, which came up with a subversive idea—why not use fiction, on the radio, to tilt Canadians' views away from the Liberals? And so, at some expense, the Conservatives rolled out six radio dramas, the first lasting fifteen minutes, the rest thirty minutes each, featuring the homespun wisdom of "Mr. Sage." Listeners to CRBC, the precursor to the modern CBC, were told that Mr. Sage was "an old political observer," as well as a "friend and neighbour," who had some pointed views about Mackenzie King and the Liberals.

Mackenzie King, irked that this political fiction was not billed as a Conservative party production, would put in place the legislation that led to the creation of CBC radio as an ad-free medium in 1936. King had always envisioned radio as a way to connect Canadian citizens to their nation—and not to advertisers. In a speech at the Canadian National Exhibition in 1927, King had asked, rhetorically, "May we not predict that as a result of this carrying of the living voice throughout the length and breadth of the Dominion, there will be aroused a more general interest in public affairs, and an increased devotion of the individual citizen to the commonweal?" Graham Spry, founder of the Canada Radio League, had similar views about radio's civic potential, saying this new medium in Canadian households "should make the home not merely a billboard, but a theatre, a concert hall, a club, a public meeting, a school, a university."

So even in the early twentieth century, Canadians had misgivings about mixing advertising with public institutions—mixing soap and politics, you might say. It was no doubt linked to that older ambivalence about advertising itself—the Barnum vs. Powers debate, cited in the last chapter—and its potential to treat consumers as dupes. Would political advertising be a tool of education about the political process, its people and policies? Or would it just pander to public ignorance? In the Canadian political sphere, parties had been using advertising agencies as far back as the 1800s to help design the posters, billboards and ads they placed before the voters at election time. These too were often blunt appeals to citizens' consumerist demands. During the height of the 1891 election, for instance, John A. Macdonald's campaign ran newspaper ads featuring the slogans "Wages higher!" "Employment plentiful!" and "Living cheaper!"

It was the Second World War, however, that really attached Canadian political leaders to the notion of advertising as an essential tool of government. At the outbreak of the war in 1939, Prime Minister Mackenzie King set up a Bureau of Public Information, which reported directly to him. The bureau's mission was to stay on top of the mood and opinion of the electorate, employing all the latest tools of the emerging research into psychology and advertising.

With about one hundred people on staff, the bureau produced a constant flurry of patriotic propaganda in the forms of radio broadcasts, films and posters to keep Canadians supporting the war effort. Advertising had formally become an arm of government.

John Davidson Ketchum, a University of Toronto psychology professor and pioneer in bringing market research methods to government, had some reservations about using hard-sell techniques from the ad world to shape opinion on something as important as a war. In a report titled "Ballyhoo in Wartime," Ketchum wrote, "A Victory Loan is still launched like a new brand of soap flakes; a wounded fighter gets the same buildup as a Hollywood starlet." There again was the soap refrain: wartime duty and sacrifice were being sold to Canadians like a cleaning product.

Canada's Mad Men

Any fan of the TV series *Mad Men* will know that the serious cultural clout of the advertising agencies arrived in the 1950s and 1960s, at the dawn of the television age and during the great expansion of the consumer economy. In the political world, the ad men first arrived in the halls of power in the form of "public relations" experts. In August 1953, the *Wall Street Journal* reported that a man named Walter Williams would be getting an office at the White House with the duty of "selling" the president. An anonymous White House official put it in terms that any businessman could understand: "We all suddenly realized we were busy manufacturing a product down here, but nobody was selling it." That distinction—between making a product and selling it—would be an important clue to understanding where the economy and culture of North America was headed in the final half of the twentieth century. The people who understood this evolution in the commercial world would have an advantage, and the same would also turn out to be true in the political world.

Canada doesn't have a geographical equivalent to Madison Avenue, but the big ad firms in the 1950s and 1960s were concentrated mainly in downtown Toronto. And it did have its "Mad Men"—bright, creative minds plying their arts in the consumer marketplace and the political market, too. At the time, Toronto was home to around 700,000 citizens—1.1 million if you counted all the surrounding suburbs that now make up the Greater Toronto Area. The CN Tower had not yet been built in the 1950s, nor had most of the skyscrapers. The Royal York, on Front Street, was the most imposing building on the skyline, and the subway, with its first 7.5 kilometres of tracks rolled out in 1954, was still brand new. Throughout its construction, Torontonians sang along with a catchy tune that was written just for the occasion and played in constant rotation on the radio: "Yes, we're gonna have a subway in Toronto. We've got to get the working man home pronto."

It was the 1957 federal election that gave the Canadian ad men their first serious entree from downtown Toronto directly into the inner political-strategy circles. The Conservative party, with its new leader John Diefenbaker, had assembled a backroom operation for this election that put two private-sector marketing experts at the top of the organizational chart—a first in Canadian political history. Those two men were Allister Grosart and Dalton Camp. Grosart was a fifty-year-old Toronto advertising executive who had worked with successive provincial Conservative governments in Ontario. Camp, then thirty-six, was an ad executive and gifted copywriter who had extensive experience in Conservative politics, especially in his home province of New Brunswick. Both men viewed politics as something separate from advertising, believing that while the two worlds shared some traits, not everything learned in the consumer marketplace could be transferred to the realm of higher public service. Camp would write in later memoirs of his constant efforts to reassure politicians about the "strange new circumstances, mostly unpleasant," that advertising imposed on politics.

Grosart, meanwhile, had penned a memo for the 1953 federal election with explicit warnings about respecting the distinction between ads for products and ads for politicians, which naturally mentioned soap (well, detergent). Some of Grosart's warnings, read through the prism of twenty-first-century political salesmanship, now look quaint, and show us just how far things have moved from more than sixty years ago:

> The commercial product analogy must not, however, be carried too far. Experience proves that many of the successful techniques of product merchandising are not applicable in the political field... We do not have the endless "second chances" which are heavily relied on in a long-term product campaign. We have less control over our field force and no reliable daily "sales" reports to guide our market tactics. We are denied most of the "shock" techniques of commercial advertising... We must therefore choose carefully between product techniques but we cannot afford to ignore the vast store of knowledge of how public attitudes react to believable quality claims and can be motivated to the desired mass action. As we pick and choose we remember, for example, that we do not sell the benefits of a correspondence course or the Encyclopedia Britannica as we would detergents or cigarettes.

Camp had chosen the advertising business because he felt it would give him self-sufficiency from the whimsical ups and downs of political life, when a person could be in favour one day, out of favour the next. His first job was at the J. Walter Thompson ad agency in Toronto, where he learned the trade by writing ads for Wrigley's gum. He quickly rose up the ladder of the Thompson firm and was promoted to creative director within two years of his arrival. He then leaped to Locke Johnson, a rival agency in Toronto. While there, Camp got his big break in 1952, when he took a leave of absence to help run the New Brunswick Conservative election campaign. The Conservatives hadn't been expected to win, and Hugh John Flemming, the leader, had misgivings about why advertising was even necessary. But Camp, installed at the Lord Beaverbrook Hotel, was determined to prove him wrong.

He hired Jack Fenety at the CFNB radio station to read one-minute commercials, which Camp would hammer out on a typewriter before the broadcast. He commissioned a young cartoonist named Duncan Macpherson to draw four cartoons for the Tory campaign. (Macpherson would go on to become one of the leading political cartoonists in the country.) He also poured his writing gift into opinion columns, strategically placed in paid-advertising space in the papers. They appeared under the pseudonym "L.C. House," which was a play on the "Let's Clean House" slogan for the Conservative campaign (it wouldn't be political advertising without some reference to soap or cleaning, after all). Clearly, New Brunswick's voters were in a housecleaning mood. Flemming pulled off a surprise victory and Camp was given a large part of the credit. Once Flemming was premier, Locke Johnson was given the New Brunswick tourism account—thus establishing a pattern that would be repeated whenever Camp helped Conservatives win provincial and federal elections in decades to follow.

In 1957, the federal Progressive Conservative party was also dreaming of an unexpected, come-from-behind victory. The Liberals had been governing Canada for most of the century and had a hammer-hold on power after the Second World War—from the final years of Mackenzie King's rule and then, after he stepped down in 1948, under Louis St. Laurent. The Liberals not only presided over the institutions of power—they *were* the institutions of power. They ran their election campaigns as they ran their governments: in low-key, bureaucratic fashion. Political science professor Paul Fox described it this way: "The Liberal government aims at operating noiselessly, like a respectable mammoth business corporation which fears nothing more than making people aware that it is there." It also helped that Canada's citizens were awash in their new consumerism, shopping their way into seeming complacency about political affairs in the 1950s, content to leave them to the "organization men" in the Liberal party.

But in 1957, the Conservatives, with the help of the ad men, were about to use what they were learning about consumer-citizens to shake up the way political campaigns were run in Canada—permanently. Under the direction of Camp and Grosart, the Conservative campaign was organized entirely around John Diefenbaker, the leader. Leaders had always been important in political races in Canada, but Camp and Grosart, the ad men, used their skills to make the leader the "product" as well. Local campaigns featured Dief prominently. "On Monday, June 10, make a date with Diefenbaker" the signs read, then went on to name the local Tory candidate as a secondary aside. Camp and Grosart fashioned advertising that played up the image of Diefenbaker as an energetic, populist visionary. Campaign posters had a big, black slogan, "It's Time for a Diefenbaker Government," with the Progressive Conservative party in tiny print in the bottom corner. Meanwhile, the Liberals were running a steady-as-she-goes campaign, which was clearly proving to be a misread of the consumerist, advertising-age times. Where St. Laurent was awkward and television-averse, for instance, Diefenbaker's oratory seemed to soar in the broadcast media.

As John Duffy describes it in *Fights of Our Lives*, a book on pivotal Canadian elections in history, this 1957 campaign was essentially a showdown between institutional politics and consumerist politics:

> The Liberal show was suffused with the production values of the House of Commons: ministerial speaking tours; the stately, even remote figure of a prime minister; and the low-key deflation of opponents' charges through irony and a gentlemanly smile. It was all very Question Period. The Tory effort and its architects anticipated the future generation of private-sector political hit men, TV-pundit strategists, and million-dollar pollsters. Its style

was Madison Avenue North: single-minded promotion of the pitchman, relegation of secondary players to the shadows, and abandonment of the brand itself in favour of the spokesperson.

Camp used many ad techniques in the 1957 federal election that had proven successful in the upset New Brunswick win— playing up the leader, playing down the party and presenting the campaign as an opportunity for Canada to "clean house." One of the more vivid pitches was a full-page newspaper ad, depicting the Peace Tower as a guillotine, with the headline "Black Friday." Another featured a large photo of Diefenbaker, with quotes from favourable newspaper articles and the slogan, again: "It's Time for a Diefenbaker Government."

Camp was particularly proud of the way in which the 1957 Conservative ad campaign had cut down the excess verbiage of previous election pitches. Rather than pummel the populace with dense, full-page ads loaded with text, as the McKim agency had done in 1953, Camp boasted that he'd been able to organize an entire election ad campaign with fewer than one thousand words of copy. As well, Camp had cleverly imported a tactic from consumer advertising into the political world—customer testimonials. Many of those words in his ad copy were not his, but excerpts from positive press reviews of Diefenbaker: "A Canadian with a spirit of true Canadianism" or "He has a first-hand knowledge of the trials and problems, the hopes and dreams of ordinary people."

The advertising approach to politics clearly wowed the customers, who were in a mood to toss out a Liberal government seen to be too arrogant and plagued by scandal. On June 10, Diefenbaker and the Progressive Conservatives won a minority government, which they would convert into majority rule a year later. Turnout for the 1958 election was nearly 80 percent—the highest-ever turnout figure in the history of the Canadian federation. Populism and pitchmen had sent Canadians flocking to politics in droves, it seems.

Camp, meanwhile, went back to the ad business, setting up his own firm, Camp and Associates, in 1959 with his brother-in-law Norman Atkins. Their first accounts were tourism contracts for the New Brunswick and federal governments, followed quickly by similar tourism accounts from Nova Scotia, Manitoba and Prince Edward Island. Camp, as a gifted writer, had a talent for advertising copy. That talent would be used for corporate clients, too, including Labatt's, Inco and Telus, as well as the Clairtone Sound Corporation, founded by Peter Munk, who would go on to run Barrick Gold.

"Over the years of Diefenbaker's ascendancy and decline, my Toronto office—otherwise and ostensibly an advertising agency—became a clearing house, talent bank, hiring hall and recruiting office for the Tory party... From there, forces were deployed to fight provincial campaigns in Newfoundland, Nova Scotia, New Brunswick, Prince Edward Island and Manitoba," Camp wrote in his book *Points of Departure*.

All this advertising know-how and electoral success was obviously bad news for the beleaguered Liberal party and its new leader, Lester Pearson. The strongest hopes for the Liberals' revival were concentrated in Toronto, home to that burgeoning ad business and a young radio salesman named Keith Davey. Davey, when he wasn't selling radio ads, was living at the beating heart of the Liberal party revival, as part of what was known as Cell 13, a clubby backroom group of high-achieving Toronto Grits with lofty ambitions for the future—their own, their party's and the country's. They were meeting weekly, first at the King Edward Hotel, then at the Board of Trade, to plot the Liberals' return to power. This being the 1950s, these ambitious Grits were attracted to all the things that were shaping consumer society: television, science, psychology and yes, advertising. All of them had witnessed how the advertising smarts of Camp and Associates had clobbered the plodding institutionalism of the Liberal party in the 1957 and 1958 elections. Davey, for his part, was also highly influenced by Theodore

White's book *The Making of the President*, which documented the slick style of campaigning that brought John Kennedy to power in 1960. Davey carried that book around as a bible, keen to import its lessons to Canada. His biggest import, eventually, would be Kennedy's pollster himself, Lou Harris.

The Liberals' chosen ad firm in these days was MacLaren Advertising Co. Ltd., which would bring its knowledge of the consumer marketplace into the world of politics. MacLaren knew its soap, too—the company had been putting together television ads for Macleans toothpaste, which boasted that it would make Canadians' teeth "irresistibly white." MacLaren also held the lucrative contracts for General Motors and Canada Dry. The ads for these firms' products were aimed at Canada's burgeoning middle class and the typical families of the time, and featured well-dressed men and women extolling the virtues of their new cars or ginger ale, the latter being an excellent mixer for the cocktails it seemed everyone was downing around the clock.

MacLaren also had significant input into the political soapbox of the time. The Liberals established a public relations committee in the 1960s, with heavy input from MacLaren, to help design winning political strategies that would ultimately seal the importance of PR in the business of politics. It was partly through MacLaren's influence that the Liberals arrived at the idea—then revolutionary, as well as controversial—of picking ridings where they could win and concentrating their efforts mainly in those places.

Efficiency experts had been around the manufacturing world for decades, helping companies come up with labour-saving ways to churn out more profits. Why not apply the rigour of scientific observation and statistics to political prospects? Rather than mass-marketing their political campaign, treating all ridings as the same, the Liberals would target their efforts at the places where they could make gains. It was smart politics, undoubtedly. But it also put political contests into the same territory as business: a search for maximum profitability at minimum expense. In this case, though, profit was measured in votes, not dollars.

In a 1961 progress report to the National Liberal Federation, the MacLaren ad firm offered assurances, almost apologetically, that it was respectful of the distinction between the often wacky world of advertising and the serious business of Parliament, especially as it pertained to Liberal leader Lester Pearson. "While Mr. Pearson's behaviour in caucus and in the House may be beyond the frame of reference of an advertising agency, we will mention that vigorous, outspoken leadership are preferred characteristics of a leader," the report stated. Like Allister Grosart and his 1953 memo, the ad firm was trying to say that selling soap and selling politicians was not exactly the same thing.

The report then explained why Liberals should direct their efforts only toward ridings where winning prospects prevailed. "No money should be spent on hopeless ridings," it said, flatly. As well, MacLaren argued there was no sense throwing money at ridings where Liberals were going to win anyway. "At MacLaren, we are satisfied that we know pretty well now which ridings are most likely to show a return on advertising investment." This wisdom was being culled through "market research" and early, rudimentary polling efforts. MacLaren also advised that the ads have a different look and feel from commercial advertising: "The ads should not be pat, professional and slick-looking"—counsel that all political parties would follow for decades to come. People didn't seem to mind slick sophistication from the people selling them cars or TVs or gadgets, but they liked their politicians to look like reluctant amateurs in the marketing game.

Keith Davey, in the meantime, was amassing market research on the images of Pearson and Diefenbaker, and his files were starting to bulge with reports on the comparative "pictoral appeal" of the leaders. One marketing report noted that people were fond of photos that showed Diefenbaker in "folksy" scenes—sitting in a classroom or holding a fish, for example. Pearson, on the other hand, seemed to evoke more positive responses in "more dignified" surroundings—in Parliament, for instance.

In 1962, MacLaren was also out testing future election slogans for the Liberals—yet another sign that the ad firm was starting to shape the actual party message, if not the party itself. The firm tested ten different slogans and found that Canadians, probably in spill-over thrall from John Kennedy's Camelot, were most impressed with phrases that talked of "vision" and a "new frontier." MacLaren highly endorsed the phrase "Take a Stand for Tomorrow." It also advised the Liberal party to be a little selective and strategic about where it placed its advertising. TV ads should be the priority, MacLaren advised, followed by mainstream newspapers. The third-ranking homes for campaign ads should be radio, weekly papers and the ethnic or cultural media. Don't even bother with billboards or magazines, the ad firm counselled. Indeed, the 1961 draft of a Liberal campaign budget reflected this kind of thinking. With $1 million in its coffers, the Liberals set aside $450,000 for TV ads, most of which was to be spent on ninety commercials of one minute each, in prime time, on all stations. Another $264,000 was budgeted for newspaper advertising, as well as about $200,000 for radio commercials and a little over $80,000 for weekly newspapers.

It would take until 1963 for the Liberals to wrest power from Diefenbaker's Conservatives, in what was, in essence, a faceoff between the emerging, ad-savvy politics of both teams. Davey, still in the thrall of US-style politics, put out an "election colouring book" featuring nasty drawings and remarks about the Conservatives, and enlisted a Liberal "truth squad" to dog Diefenbaker on the election trail. Dalton Camp, meanwhile, decided to run as a candidate himself in the 1963 election—unsuccessfully, as it turned out. Like many of the best people in the ad business, it seems, Camp's talents were more suited to supporting than leading—more useful in the backrooms than on the stage. Lester Pearson became prime minister in the spring of 1963, kicking off a reign of Liberal power that would stretch for another twenty years.

In power, the Liberals' attachment to advertising and imagery would only deepen. When Pearson went on TV to do a broadcast of "The Nation's Business" in May 1965, Davey wanted to know how the audience was reacting. A select group of citizens in Hamilton and Toronto was asked to watch the show and then give their reactions in telephone interviews afterward. Though 2,000 people were invited to participate, the survey eventually winnowed down to 189 respondents, who offered their critiques of Pearson's performance, on everything from his trustworthiness to the question of whether he was wearing makeup. More than 60 percent thought Pearson had "things under control," for instance, while 39 percent were "somewhat bothered" by Pearson's voice. Forty percent did not believe he was wearing makeup and 93 percent thought he "looked in excellent health."

The southwestern Ontario city of London was often used as a test market for new consumer concepts and products. It was mid-sized, situated in the middle of Canada and had a large middle class, so Londoners were seen as good arbiters of potential success or failure in the commercial world. London was the site of Canada's first McDonald's restaurant, the first downtown enclosed mall, the first Kmart, the first automated bank tellers and the first debit cards. At one point in the 1960s, Keith Davey and the MacLaren ad agency even surveyed the good citizens of London to determine what would make the perfect Liberal candidate—the idea being that you could apply consumer-preference test methods to politics, too.

So London was a natural place for Liberals to trot out an idea aimed at capturing consumer-citizens' hearts in the 1960s. In 1967, the new consumer and corporate affairs minister John Turner gave a speech at the University of Western Ontario in London in which he sketched out plans for a guaranteed annual income for Canadians, to be financed by tax increases. *The Globe and Mail* columnist Dennis

Braithwaite caught the speech and wrote a column headlined "Beware of Grits": "I wish someone would explain to John Turner and all those ambitious chaps who are seeking our favour that it's a new ball game today. We don't want any more handouts, thanks a lot. We just want to keep a little of our own money, so that when we save a little, or get a raise or pull off a deal, the rewards will be real and tangible, not an illusion and a mockery."

Another person also noticed the speech with disfavour: Colin M. Brown, an insurance executive at London Life, one of the city's major industries. Brown was perturbed at the way in which politicians were monopolizing the media to put only their own positions across—he believed that Canada's hard-working citizens deserved a say, too. On April 14, 1967, Brown took out a full-page ad in *The Globe and Mail* protesting that the Liberal government appeared to be on its way to turning a budget surplus into a projected deficit of $3 billion within the following five years. The ad reprinted the Braithwaite column as well as some excerpts from other financial commentators. Brown, for his part, wrote, "All federal political parties, in their race for votes, seem to be prepared to make Canadians, in all walks of life, the heaviest taxed people of the world." He ended the ad with an appeal for donations, to finance more and similar ads: "If you share my alarm, your support is welcome."

Apparently, Brown had many allies. His son, Colin Jr., would recall bags and bags of mail landing at his dad's office or on the doorstep of their London home, many with cheques. In this way, an organization called the National Citizens Coalition was born—an organization that would prove instrumental in the creation of a future Canadian prime minister. But let's not get ahead of ourselves here.

It would take a couple more decades for the NCC to start making a real impact on Canadian politics. In the meantime, shopping was still growing as a national sport. The Yorkdale shopping centre in Toronto had opened to wild public favour, with spots for more than six thousand cars and expectations of $100 million a year in retail sales. Canadians were starting to agitate for evening shopping and retailers were keen to oblige.

Still, thanks largely to the increasing presence of women in the workforce, it was believed, retail sales were down. Canadians had spent 64 percent of their income in retail outlets in 1957, but that had dropped to 52 percent in 1967. Approximately 33 percent of married Canadian women were working, and they were finding it difficult to get shopping done on their lunch hours, according to a study commissioned for the national Retailers Institute.

By this time, the Liberals were also looking to the Toronto ad firm Vickers and Benson for some of their big projects. The firm, founded in 1924 by Rex Vickers and Don Benson, was an elite ad agency, catering to some of Canada's corporate giants. It had been among the first to get into TV advertising, with a sixty-second spot produced in 1952 for a Ford dealer and shown on the fledgling CBC TV. In 1967, Vickers and Benson was given the contract to do the publicity surrounding Canada's centennial year. The agency's work in the commercial sector found its way into this project, too, specifically in musical form. Bill Bremner, then the president of the firm, had come to know a musician named Bobby Gimby through his previous ad work for Eaton's. Gimby told Bremner that he had written a song for Canada's one hundredth birthday, and he showed up at the Vickers and Benson offices wearing a cape and waving a regal staff. As soon as the diminutive Gimby started belting out the tune—"Ca-na-da, we love thee"—the ad guys knew they had a pop anthem on their hands.

Al Scott, then the vice-president of Vickers and Benson, told the story to a magazine called *The Canadian*. "The government brass in Ottawa had already settled on a centennial hymn and an anthem," Scott said. "But I knew neither would work. Canadians tend to be complacent patriots. And the sophisticated city slickers in the newspaper business have almost made it a sin to express enthusiasm about our nation. What we needed was a grabber. A stirring flag-waver that would make everybody feel, 'Gee, this is a real good opportunity.'" The Gimby anthem exceeded all hopes. By the time the centennial year ended, nearly every schoolchild in Canada had memorized the lyrics. More than 250 school choirs actually recorded the tune, and Gimby himself became known as the Pied Piper of Confederation, travelling to hundreds of Canadian communities, pumping up patriotism for the centennial year.

Still in the glow of Expo '67 and Canada's centennial year, the Liberals turned in 1968 to find a new leader—one who would also come to symbolize the heady, youth-fuelled spirit of the times. Pierre Trudeau, a hip, bilingual bachelor, was chosen to replace Lester Pearson at the party's 1968 leadership convention. Almost immediately, this cerebral, very private intellectual became a consumer product himself—a sex object for swooning female fans and a consummate performer at mass rallies. Canada's emerging consumer society had been handed a leader who was a politician and a fashion. Turnout at this election, though not at the Diefenbaker high of 1958, was still a healthy 75 percent.

The Big Blue Machine

With Trudeaumania in full force and the Liberals with a comfortable hold on power in Ottawa, the Conservative advertising men were plying their trade mainly in Ontario, where their party appeared to have "natural governing" status. Ontario had been led by Conservative regimes since 1943—all the way through the postwar boom in Canada's largest province.

Camp and Associates was going strong, but gradually, over the years, as Dalton Camp got more involved in politics and journalism, his brother-in-law Norman Atkins assumed greater control over the advertising end of things. And when the new Ontario Conservative leader Bill Davis came calling in 1971 for the ad men's help, it was Atkins who oversaw the operation. The product of that work would be dubbed the Big Blue Machine—the Conservative advertising and strategy team that vaulted Davis into a fifteen-year-long dynasty in Canada's largest province. Some of the machine's methods would be imitated by successive generations of political operatives of all stripes.

The Big Blue Machine came up with the idea of an ad "consortium" to oversee political operations. Rather than dole out work to just one ad firm, they would assemble a group of sharp ad minds from a variety of agencies. Atkins called his group, fittingly enough, Ad Hoc Enterprises, though it was more often simply called the "media group" or the "creative group." Their efforts in the early 1970s reflected the expansiveness of the time; it seemed no expense would be spared, no method untried. It all felt a little American, too, including the red-white-and-blue colour scheme they embraced for the Davis campaign. They brightly painted and decorated the Greyhound buses they had rented, an artistic inspiration that the bus company would adopt for its own purposes later, proving that good ideas were travelling back and forth between the private and public realms. Ad Hoc enlisted the services of a cameraman to meticulously follow Davis on his travels and film man-in-the-street interviews with the Ontarians he encountered. These film clips, which resembled nightly news segments in style and format, would become standard fare of election advertising. The ad guys, led by Atkins, also went to some lengths to surround Davis with old-time political razzle-dazzle—lots of streamers, buttons and stickers. They even commissioned a song for the 1971 campaign, called "Keep on Goin'," which was used as background music in commercials but could also be jazzed up to a Dixieland-style tempo for the big rallies.

"The Tory advertising campaign unfolded by Norman Atkins in the early days of the [1971] election campaign was the most spectacular political sales job the country had seen," Jonathan Manthorpe wrote in his book on the Ontario Conservatives, *The Power and the Tories*. "It was highly sophisticated in its organization and the material it produced, but there was nothing subtle about the message. It was Davis, Davis, Davis. Davis in living, breathing colour. Davis barbecuing hamburgers. Davis, his back to the camera, walking pensively on the beach by his cottage in the evening sunlight. Davis among crowds of supporters. Davis walking through woods with his wife, Kathy. Davis with his family. Davis, Davis. Davis." The narration for these ads was supplied by a professional announcer, and Atkins's ad team deliberately played down the politics, mentioning the Ontario PCs only in a flash of small print at the end of the commercial spots.

The slick professionalism of the ads caught the Ontario Conservatives' opponents off guard, and they complained that US-style politics had arrived in Canada, that Davis was being sold "like a can of tomatoes." Actually, that last part was true. Leading up to the 1971 campaign, in addition to Camp and Associates, Davis had retained the services of a thirty-two-year-old sociologist named Martin Goldfarb, who was just starting his own public-opinion consulting business.

Canada didn't have many of its own polling gurus yet. Although the federal Liberals had been using polls for about a decade, the Liberals' pollster of choice up to 1971 had been an American. Goldfarb, as the 1970s dawned, was slowly building up his political clientele and was still calling himself a "researcher" or "sociologist"— not a pollster. He was doing psycho-social research for Newfoundland premier Joey Smallwood and Manitoba Liberal leader Izzy Asper. For Davis, Goldfarb was conducting what he called "sensitivity sessions" with small groups of ten to fifteen people each, trying to explore what the voters wanted or needed to hear from the Ontario Conservatives. Today, we'd call these "focus groups."

In an interview with Canadian Press in May of 1971, Goldfarb rather flamboyantly—and infamously—compared the selling of politics to the sale of tomatoes: "It's a matter of choice. There may be twenty cans of tomatoes on the shelf and the consumer has to choose one. Well, it's really the same in the voter marketplace."

Davis saw the article and phoned Goldfarb. "Tomatoes?" the premier asked incredulously. Goldfarb brushed off the wounded feelings. It wouldn't be the last time that he encountered a politician who felt slighted by the product comparison.

Despite his early work with Davis, Goldfarb would end up where his political heart really rested, with the Liberals. These were days when advertising and marketing traffic, not to mention friendships, spanned party differences. Liberals and Conservatives were intensely competitive, but they didn't let that stand in the way of business or socializing, for the most part. And they also shared an approach to this new business of selling their political wares like soap (or tomatoes), aided by the rising dominance of TV. The people who understood that voters were far more easily moved by images, their emotions, and their feelings about leadership would be at the vanguard of political salesmanship in the coming years.

But just as people had grown skeptical and wary in the 1950s of over-saturation from commercial ads, North Americans were stirring in these decades to the reality that hard-sell techniques from the private sector were invading the political sanctum. Joe McGinniss, a journalist at the *Philadelphia Inquirer*, decided to follow closely the 1968 presidential campaign of Richard Nixon to see what was being bought and sold among voting Americans. The result was a milestone in the chronicles of political marketing history: his book, *The Selling of the President*. With the co-operation of Nixon's image consultant, Roger Ailes, McGinniss was treated to an inside view of the packaged world of Republican politics, circa 1968. Ailes had been a producer of *The Merv Griffin Show*, and micro-coached the Nixon campaign into the television age. Nixon, after all, had probably been the first politician burned by TV, when his five o'clock shadow and sweating countenance helped make him the loser in TV debates with Kennedy.

In *The Selling of the President*, McGinniss minced no words. He wrote that Nixon relied on television "the way a polio victim relied

on an iron lung." The cover of the book was made to resemble a ciga-
rette package, with a figure of Nixon at the centre of it. "Overnight,
it made Theodore White's campaign book seem wan and dated,"
Dwight Garner wrote in the *New York Times*, where the McGinniss
book rocketed to the bestseller lists. But like the 1961 Ted White
book, called *The Making of the President*, it would also be an accurate forecast of the style of politics to move north of the forty-ninth
parallel in the coming years.

At the Big Blue Machine, Norman Atkins initially rejected criticism that Canadian politics was getting Americanized. Welcome to
the television age, Atkins would say. "TV does it. It's not American.
It's a product of TV. It's the leader-oriented society… The leader is
important. Trudeau proved that was right."

The leader-centrism style had been a fixture of the Conservative
campaign approach going back to Diefenbaker's election. But in
the 1971 election in Ontario, it became systematized—and marketing-friendly. Atkins was the brains behind a system that helped
centralize the advertising message among the local campaigns, to
make them more leader-dominated. It would turn out to be a tem-
plate for many election campaigns at the federal level in future. The
result was called the "Candidate Service Centre," run by another
ad executive with offices not far from Camp and Associates.
Conservative riding organizations were urged to send in their pro-
posed advertising material for an "upgrade" and assessment by the
experts in Toronto, and then they would be sent back all kinds of
red-white-and-blue paraphernalia prominently featuring the leader.
Customized posters, proclaiming the candidate's support for Davis,
would also be tucked into the return package to the ridings. It was an
unsubtle way to ensure that all campaigns revolved around the leader,
and thus all candidates owed their election success to him. Politicos
learned a valuable lesson: you could achieve a kind of control over
your caucus through advertising that you couldn't through charisma,
charm, discipline or any other traditional tool of leadership. All you

needed was a unified message, with everyone speaking from the same script, with the same pictures.

The Big Blue Machine's methods attracted many admirers, including Richard Nixon's Republicans in the United States, who flew to Canada to observe the machine in action. It was one of the few times that Canadians were imitated by American politicos rather than vice versa. In the *Wall Street Journal* in the 1980s, a Republican pollster was quoted as saying of the Big Blue Machine that its operatives were "very good at retail politics—identifying their vote and getting it out—probably better than most organizations in the US."

Rival Liberals paid the Big Blue Machine the immense compliment of imitation. History would repeat itself—just as the federal Liberals saw and watched the success of the Diefenbaker campaign and put it to use in the 1960s, so too would the Liberals go on to borrow some of the Big Blue Machine's methods in the mid-1970s.

Red Cap Nation

Trudeaumania faded in the early 1970s. Hobbling along with a minority government after the 1972 election, Trudeau himself was emerging in the public eye as a haughty, even aloof character—a far cry from the populist leader he'd appeared to be when he first vaulted into power. In the spring of 1974, Pierre Trudeau's Liberal minority government staggered to an end and the country was plunged into an election. At this point, the Liberals' affection for advertising was turning into ambivalence; the 1972 ad campaign had been a bit of a disaster. The team from MacLaren had come up with the slogan "The Land Is Strong"—a slogan that became more of a punchline than an effective sales pitch for the Liberals. Keith Davey had also fallen out of favour with Trudeau and the inner circle; a cloud fell over his reputation because his legendary organizing skills had failed to win majorities for the Liberals. Trudeau was also permanently wary of professional backroomers and of the whole Toronto Liberal crowd.

At a dinner at 24 Sussex in 1973, he'd told them he wasn't sure why they were involved in politics—where was the fire in their bellies?

For all these reasons, the 1974 election loomed with only lacklustre Liberal enthusiasm in the advertising hub of Toronto. Although Davey had been put in charge of the national campaign committee, and some bridges had been rebuilt between Trudeau and Toronto, things were not going all that well in the city most pivotal to the Liberals' fortunes. And that was where Jerry Grafstein, a long-time Liberal supporter and a good friend of Davey's, came to play his part in the fusion of Liberal politics and advertising.

Grafstein, a lawyer, was part of the new guard of Toronto Liberal partisans, a skilled and sophisticated thinker about consumerism and the media. Grafstein had served as a special adviser in the establishment of the Department of Consumer and Corporate Affairs when it was set up in 1967. He was also one of the founders of the CHUM Radio empire, and in 1972 he co-founded the wildly successful upstart station CITY-TV with Moses Znaimer. Grafstein also founded *The Journal of Liberal Thought* in the 1960s.

So if any Liberal understood the new media and advertising landscape of the 1970s, it was this Toronto Liberal. And for the 1974 campaign, he was chosen to be in charge of ad strategy. Grafstein, who had been watching the success of the Big Blue Machine, knew exactly what he had to do—set up a consortium of the best minds in the ad business. And because of his experience with CHUM and CITY-TV, he knew who these people were. He collected them from MacLaren and from Ronalds Reynolds, also a leading ad firm of the time. Rounding out what came to be called the Red Leaf consortium was a man named Terry O'Malley, then thirty-eight years old and already seen as one of the most creative minds at Vickers and Benson.

A proud native of St. Catharines, Ontario, O'Malley had grown up playing hockey and spending his idle hours glued to AM radio broadcasts from Buffalo. He was mesmerized by the world that opened up to him through his table-model Addison radio—through its broadcasts, O'Malley was plugged into a consumers' paradise where you could get Converse running shoes, Double Bubble and Bazooka gum, and Milk Duds. He didn't know then that through those ads, he was also seeing his future.

Through the Harvard Club of Buffalo, O'Malley won a scholarship to the Ivy League university in Cambridge, where he got a degree in English literature. When he returned to Canada, he thought he had his whole future mapped out: he was going to teach at Ridley College in his hometown of St. Catharines. He even had the requisite corduroy jacket with the elbow patches, as well as the pipe. But a tag-along trip to a girlfriend's interview changed his life. While she was applying for a job at the Kodak Company on Richmond Street in Toronto, O'Malley wandered into the MacLaren advertising firm next door and, without much of a sales pitch, landed a $50-a-week job for himself as a copywriter. Just twenty-four years old, he was immediately swept into the mad mad world of 1960s advertising, where his bosses downed bottles of rye before noon, a blue cigarette haze permanently hung in the air and every firm had its own in-house bar for round-the-clock socializing.

O'Malley was neither a heavy drinker nor a smoker. A big pail of candy sat on the desk in his office, and visitors were invited to graze freely. He loved sports, especially hockey and baseball. He was also shy, preferring to express himself at his Underwood typewriter rather than in public speaking. He would show up for meetings with a bundle of sharpened pencils and notepaper, scribbling and free-associating slogans while the clients stated their needs. When it came time to hammering out the slogans at the typewriter, O'Malley would always come up with them in multiples of five, and number twenty-seven would always be called the "Frank Mahovlich" one.

For his first few years in advertising, O'Malley moved around from agency to agency. But in 1964, he landed at Vickers and Benson, where he stayed for the rest of his career, dreaming up some of the ads that are emblazoned into Canadian marketing memory.

Some of his favourites were the ones he did for the Dairy Bureau of Canada, casting butter as a sensuous indulgence ("Just Butter It") and cheese as a friendly meal staple ("Show your cheddar more warmth; take it out of the fridge more often"). In the political realm, O'Malley penned the slogan "a leader must be a leader" and helped cast Trudeau to the public in the famous gunslinger pose that became one of his iconic images. The big difference between writing ads for products and writing ads for politicians, O'Malley found, was the speed and urgency around the political campaigns. They had a "finish line" and a score. The ad campaigns O'Malley wrote for products and the private sector, meanwhile, could afford to take a more leisurely route into the public psyche.

Like many creative folks, O'Malley found it hard to describe how he came up with so many marketing home runs, but he did subject his ideas to what he called the "Teddy and Eddie test"— always imagining how his old St. Catharines buddies, Ted and Ed, would respond to the ads he was creating. The trick in advertising, as politicos were learning, was to reach the people who didn't care about what you were selling. Keith Davey believed that O'Malley was unquestionably the most talented ad man in Canada. The two men had met at Harry Rosen's while Davey was being fitted for one of his trademark pinstriped suits and quickly struck up a bosom buddy friendship, fuelled by their mutual love of baseball.

O'Malley was the creative brain behind the Carling Red Cap beer campaign in the mid-1960s, which helped seal the position of Vickers and Benson as one of the pre-eminent ad firms in Canada. The beer had been suffering a market decline, and O'Malley came up with the idea to turn the remaining loyal patrons into populist heroes, a nation unto themselves. In essence, the man who had been helping politicians behave more like brands was infusing a brand with a political identity. Red Cap drinkers, O'Malley decided, would be a collective society of their own with a leader, an anthem and a salute.

As O'Malley described it, "It was as though it had a life of its own. The first spot would be the launch, and it would be the initial gathering of Red Cap drinkers, a speech from the president, the singing of the anthem, and the concluding salute: an extended right arm, thumb up, with the left hand over the heart… We took about half the office staff down to Maple Leaf Stadium and, through… camera trickery, made the stadium appear full. Nick Nichols, whom we had made the president, spoke from the pitcher's mound in rousing political style."

The ads were an immediate hit—university students sang the song and did the salute at football games, while newspapers and magazines did long features on the ad campaign. Vickers and Benson started work on a second campaign, featuring real people and their participation in the Red Cap Nation—shades of the Tim Hortons "True Stories" ads that would come three decades later. Red Cap Nation also blazed a trail for beer-and-patriotism ads that would prove popular later in the twentieth century. The nation-gripping Canada–Russia hockey series in 1972 was also a Vickers and Benson production. The firm came up with the name "Team Canada" and even designed the Canadian team's jerseys with their bold red-and-white maple leaf. Again, they were ahead of themselves. Later in the decade, hockey would also become interlaced with politics and patriotism—part of a larger fusion between democracy, commercial brands and sports.

Vickers and Benson also won the advertising account for McDonald's Restaurants in Canada—a task that included hiring people to play the clown-like mascot, Ronald McDonald. One day, as O'Malley was passing by the receptionist's area of the office, he looked over at people coming and going near the elevators. Keith Davey was stepping off one elevator, while one of the Ronald McDonald actors, in full costume, was getting on another, on his way to an assignment. To O'Malley, this brief visual said everything about Vickers and Benson. "I said to myself, 'That's us!'" O'Malley recalled. Could there be any more vivid picture of this ad firm's place at the nexus of consumer and political culture in Canada?

Yet even as the politicos and the TV-commercial characters were passing each other in the corridors of the ad firms, they were still inhabiting different worlds. Political ads were getting slicker, image-wise, but they retained a certain earnest optimism about Canadians' interest in matters of state. The goal of the advertising, for the most part, was to provoke citizens into civic-mindedness. The idea was to make citizens like their politics, and their politicians, a little better. Still, the 1974 campaign would mark a turning point for the Liberals—when Trudeau and the party stepped into a modern campaign heavily steeped in TV, emotion and slick marketing methods.

Gone were the earnest efforts of the 1972 campaign to engage the intellectual Trudeau in a "conversation" with Canadians; Trudeau would be more removed from the fray—an image more than a personality, in what was dubbed a "peek-a-boo" campaign. "The leader's campaign was a cunning, neo-traditional mixture of old-fashioned optics with modern media management," Stephen Clarkson wrote in his book *The Big Red Machine*. "Instead of creating a campaign themselves, the ad men simply highlighted the effort being made by the leader on his tour." The Liberals took out a full-page ad in Saturday newspapers across the country, with the headline "Issues Change from Year to Year. The Ability to Lead Does Not." The entire appeal was focused on strength, leadership and stability in uncertain times—under an elusive, distant leader. (Canadians with more recent memories might find strong parallels to the Stephen Harper campaign of 2011, also focused on turning a shaky minority into a "strong, stable majority government.")

Under Grafstein's direction in the 1974 campaign, the Red Leaf consortium came up with advertising intended to endear Canadians to Trudeau and have them vote with their emotions, much in the same way that advertisers wanted to capture their clientele. The free-time film commercials, overseen by Jerry Goodis of MacLaren, depicted a "loving" and "beautiful" Trudeau. Goodis himself called the ads "straight propaganda, featuring ordinary Canadians in fedoras and glasses, ethnics, country people, kids—films full of uglies and one beautiful guy."

The larger fight of the 1974 election, though, was about very consumerist concerns—wage and price controls. The Conservatives, under leader Robert Stanfield, were insisting that controls were necessary in these times of rampant inflation and rampaging gas prices. The annual inflation rate was ballooning over 10 percent and food prices had been rising even more rapidly. The Liberals were arguing that wage and price controls weren't necessary; Trudeau famously mocked the Tories with his "Zap, you're frozen" line on the campaign trail.

In radio ads, Liberals argued that wage and price controls were a failed experiment, internationally. "The United States tried wage and price controls and ended up with spiralling costs and a huge bureaucracy," said one of the ads, drafted by Vickers and Benson and read by Trudeau over the airwaves to Canadian consumer-citizens. "The UK tried them and faced rioting labour unions. As a slogan, wage and price freeze may sound good, but it just does not work. What is needed is a mechanism where a government can roll back prices that result from profiteering or gouging. That's the approach that was in our budget. To implement this Liberal idea for a stronger Canada, I ask for your support on July 8." Liberals also argued that if Conservatives and New Democrats were serious about addressing the concerns of Canadian consumers, they would have voted for the budget, which had contained sales-tax cuts. Politics meet shopping.

"Why did they vote against a budget which was reducing sales tax—taking sales tax completely off clothing and shoes and other goods?" yet another radio ad asked. "Ask yourself that when you buy your next pair of shoes, and you know you're paying two dollars or three dollars more, or four dollars or five dollars more for your dress or your suit—more than you would have paid if they hadn't voted against our budget. The Liberal budget would have meant lower prices on clothing, footwear and other essentials. The Liberal budget would have helped you cope with the cost of living."

With a combination of playing to the fears of consumers and slick, modern campaigning, Trudeau won his majority on July 8, 1974. He thanked Davey with a framed editorial cartoon from the campaign, which Trudeau dedicated to the man "who made the sun shine." Grafstein would go on to run the Red Leaf consortium for the better part of the next two decades. The whole idea of ad consortiums, in fact, first dreamed up by Norman Atkins, would become a staple of modern Canadian electioneering.

No matter how successful these early ad consortiums were at playing politics, the election campaigns themselves couldn't sustain a business. Canada was not then, and still isn't today, a country that sustains a full-time political consulting profession. When all the streamers had been put away and the TV ads were off the air, the ad guys had to make a living with private-sector clients. "My profession is advertising and my hobby is politics," Norman Atkins was fond of saying. Some of the spillover effect would be immediate: ad firms that did a good job for the party in power would be rewarded with government business once the election was over. "It paid to be in with the government," Jonathan Manthorpe wrote in his book on the Big Blue Machine. "Large amounts of money were spent each year by most of the government ministries on advertising, and these accounts were seldom tendered for. Awards were made, not on the basis of who could do it most cheaply, but on which firm's approach the minister liked the best. If a company had a proven ability to work with the Conservatives during an election campaign, then why should they not be equally easy to work with on government business?"

Camp and Associates held the lucrative contract for Ontario's tourism advertising all the time that Bill Davis was in power, for instance, and Brian Mulroney, once he attained federal office in 1984, would do the same thing. As Mulroney recalled in his book *Memoirs*,

"After a victorious campaign, Dalton K. Camp and Associates would lay claim to the government advertising account, and the caravan would move on. Dalton and his brother-in-law Norm Atkins made a great deal of money in this way, hitting the jackpot when I won federally; and the Government of Canada gave them the advertising contract that enabled them, some time later, to sell the company at a handsome multiple." Meanwhile, the folks from the Red Leaf consortium would get their share of federal Liberal business, too, in between elections.

The cost of being a consumer in Canada continued to escalate in 1975, the year after Trudeau's Liberals had won power by promising not to legislate controls over wages and prices. On a scorching day at the end of June, Finance Minister John Turner handed down a budget that added an immediate ten cents to the price of a gallon of gasoline at the pump, and another five-cent increase for August. One twenty-seven-year-old resident in the model suburb of Don Mills staged his own intriguing form of consumer revolt at an Esso self-serve station, refusing outright to pay the 71.9-cent price until Parliament made the increase official. "I'm not going to be gouged anymore than I have to be until Parliament passes a law to back up the new excise tax," Wayne Halse told the *Toronto Star*. He gave his name and address to the attendant and told him to bill him for the additional fuel costs when the law was passed.

The government, perhaps naively, still seemed to believe that citizens could be rallied away from spending and into a collective project for the national good. All it needed was the right kind of persuasion. In the fall of 1975, the Vickers and Benson team was summoned by Jim Coutts to help in a "special, confidential project." Through a PR blitz, the government hoped that all good Canadians would come to the aid of restraint. In the memos outlining the need for this program, the Prime Minister's Office cast the inflation problem as a threat to national stability in the same dimensions as the FLQ terrorist crisis of a few years before. Moreover, the Liberals were in a big political bind—only a year earlier, they had campaigned against wage and price controls. Their only hope now was to recruit the country into a voluntary thrift program. And by now, they realized that if you were trying to get to the hearts and minds of Canadian voters, you had to go the advertising route.

Ottawa's goal was to curb inflation at its current 12-percent rate, to work toward an inflation rate of 8 to 9 percent, to curb inflation without killing jobs, to control government spending and to use the market system to reverse the inflationary trend. The Liberal government turned to Vickers and Benson "to communicate in such a manner as to enlist the intelligent and emotional involvement of the Canadian public." In essence, it was asking the ad firm to persuade Canadians to be less like consumers, and more like citizens; to be more like Powers than Barnum. It was a far cry, in other words, from the exhortations to spend that Canadians would get in the economic meltdown of 2008. In the 1970s, government still believed it could use advertising to discourage consumerism.

"Trudeau must clearly establish that the time has come for all Canadians to make their choices between those things they need and those they don't. Canada must be put first... [Citizens'] self-interest will lead to national failure," Vickers and Benson recommended in its ad plan. And, in a foreshadowing of populist politics to come later in the century, Vickers and Benson also said that restraint, like charity, would have to start close to home. "Since MPs' salaries appear to be paramount in the public's mind, consideration should be given to immediately adjusting them downward."

O'Malley and the team brainstormed slogans to be placed on signs—"Reality before dreams" and "Needs before desires"—and mused whether they could place them in stores. What about a national Pioneer Day, to reacquaint Canadian citizens with their not-so-consumerist past? Perhaps Canadians could rein in their spending through posters asking, "Do you really need it?" But advertising couldn't solve this problem. Trudeau, amid turmoil in his government—Turner had abruptly resigned—was forced to go on TV on Thanksgiving and announce that he was legislating wage and price controls. While the political implications of this move were profound and far-reaching, it was also a significant milepost along the route to consumer-citizenship in Canada. Not even advertising, a tool of the marketers, could curb Canadian citizens' enthusiasm for the consumer marketplace.

3

SCIENTIFIC SHOPPING

For several months in 1940 and 1941, *Canadian Forum* magazine ran a rather unusual series of stories, in which a man named Philip Spencer argued that socialism could be sold to Canadians like any other household product. *Canadian Forum*—a bible for the left wing, not known for embracing the free marketplace—was an unlikely vehicle for this kind of thinking. But Spencer argued that politicians could learn something from advertisers about researching the "customers" of democracy, whom he called Mr. and Mrs. Jones.

"Plain and fancy research is part of the everyday routine of the advertisers. Surely, when socialism claims it can produce results infinitely more beneficial to the public than individualist economy—surely socialism should use this means of tapping the mind of Mr. and Mrs. Jones too," Spencer wrote in the October 1940 issue of the magazine. "When the goodies of socialism are as apparent as the benefits of orange juice, then socialism will be at hand!"

The mysterious Philip Spencer may have been the first modern political marketing champion in Canada and the first spokesman for consumer-citizenship. (The name was a pseudonym, and after these articles it never appeared in the pages of *Canadian Forum* again.) He was also a good twenty years ahead of Joe McGinniss and the Nixon presidential campaign in making the connection between politicking and product-selling. Forget politics as a form of educating the masses, Spencer said—if you want to reach people where they live, you needed to appeal to their emotions and impressions. "Until we know what people do and think and read, until we have developed a strategy that is really relevant to the readers of *Popeye* and the listeners [of] Charlie McCarthy, we can't hope to make socialism the loud, imperative and compelling shout that it should be," he wrote.

In subsequent articles, readers of *Canadian Forum* were treated to the findings of a "political consumer survey" Spencer had conducted among the good citizens of Toronto, trying to gauge whether socialist ideas were compatible with their lifestyle habits. He found that lower-income people preferred the comics and sports pages of newspapers and that the only way to reach women was through women's magazines, where they were engaged in their own "cozy chats about baby's diet and how [they] stopped middle-aged spread." On the radio, he said, drama and variety shows were far more popular than news or public affairs broadcasts. Slipping a little editorial commentary into his findings, Spencer pronounced it "nasty" that young people and the lower classes who should be voting for the CCF (the forerunner of the New Democratic Party) were far more interested in "escapism."

Spencer said disinterested voters presented a special challenge to politics; that they would require much different tactics or entreaties from the socialists. He was making the case for polling and rigorous market research as a way to tailor political appeals to the consumer tastes of voters. Advertisers, first in the US and then in Canada, had been using market research with increasing frequency and sophistication for a couple of decades already. The University of Western Ontario had become the academic hub of consumer-survey research through its Department of Business Administration, established in 1927. But in the realm of politics, polling had been used only sparsely by Canadian political parties when Spencer was writing his articles in the 1940s.

The Liberal party had close ties to Cockfield, Brown and Company, which was the first advertising agency to do extensive market research. Throughout the Second World War as well, Mackenzie King's government had been exploring ways to gather public opinion, relying on research methods advocated by psychology experts such as John Davidson Ketchum from the University of Toronto. Although the original purpose of this research was to mobilize support for the war, King's Liberals, presumably, could hardly fail to notice a possible political payoff, too. Meanwhile, the Gallup organization and a survey firm called Canadian Facts were conducting preliminary surveys of the Canadian political landscape.

However, it would be a couple more decades until Canadian political parties really caught the polling bug and, no doubt to Spencer's regret, it wouldn't be the socialists who first saw the wisdom of using market research to sell politics to the masses. Political market research did begin in earnest, though, at the site of Spencer's "political-consumer" survey—Toronto, which was also home to the ad business.

"Young Marrieds"

On May 15, 1959, Toronto was experiencing an unseasonable chill, including some late spring flurries, which forced the cancellation of the Friday night Toronto Maple Leafs baseball game. But the economy was heating up. Canada's burgeoning auto industry had turned out more than eight thousand cars in the previous week, while prices for everyday goods were climbing—a result of an overall recovery in the North American economy.

Canada's consumer boom had fully arrived by this point, and with it, a radical shift in the everyday circumstances of the typical Canadian family. Children born in the 1950s were growing up in homes very different from the ones lived in by those who were born in the late 1940s. With the rise of convenience products, shopping for the home was replacing working in the home as a primary pursuit—not just for women, but for men, too. In the *Toronto Daily Star* on this chilly Friday, readers were treated to the occupational annoyances of Canada's cashier of the year, Connie Burridge: "Men are the worst offenders in piling things up, she says. And of course it delays the service. Cashiers are fond of people, usually women, who departmentalize their piles. All the meats together, all the vegetables together, all the frozen foods together. And of course anything that is 'two for thirty-eight,' for example, together. Secret of not getting rattled is not to look up on a busy night, she says. 'If you don't lift your head and see that crowd waiting to go through, you'll be all right.'"

Also in this section, on what was commonly called the newspaper's "women's pages," were stories about how to avoid buying bad meat and how to use your new electric mixer to make a quick pie crust, as well as ads for fur storage, bridal gowns, corsets and dress-coat sets. Canada was in a postwar buying boom and citizens were surrounded by fellow shoppers and ad pitches. Automotive giant General Motors, in its own *Star* ad appearing that day, attempted to cut through the noise with some reassuring words for frazzled consumers. Makers of superior products didn't need to boast, GM said. "On every side, nowadays, the average Canadian is faced with a baffling array of claims and counterclaims... Statistics, figures and comparisons are bandied about, sometimes carelessly."

And on that same Friday, at Toronto's CKFH radio station, Keith Davey was making a presentation on how to capture audience and advertisers. CKFH, known today as "The Fan," began as a sports and news station owned by famed hockey announcer Foster Hewitt (hence the "FH" in the call letters). The station was on the rise, looking for a solid foothold in the growing radio marketplace. The secret, Davey said in his presentation, was to tap into the demographic group with the biggest buying power—"the young marrieds."

He rattled off some statistics: in Toronto, 35 percent of the entire population, 457,000 people, were between the ages of twenty and thirty-nine. Almost all of them were married and in the midst of growing their little families. Annually, Davey said, this group spent $217 on home furnishings, $697 on automobile costs, $1,011 at grocery outlets, $159 at drug stores, $310 on clothing and $901 on "general merchandise." Moreover, Davey said, these "young marrieds" were fuelling demand for new homes—twenty-three thousand were built in the Toronto area the previous year.

Davey said that these young consumers needed a radio show to fit their abiding, if quotidian, interests. How about a "motoring show," as he called it? (These days, we'd probably call it the "afternoon drive.") On their way back to their shiny new homes, filled with shiny new merchandise, these people were looking for a soundtrack to match their middling tastes and pursuits, Davey said: "Be sure to avoid any irritating or excitable music, and this includes 'way out' jazz."

Davey, as a "young married" himself, no doubt made a compelling case to his fellow employees at CKFH. He was in his early thirties, living in Don Mills with his own young family and had a happy-warrior outlook that kept widening his circle of friends. Radio sales may have been Davey's day job in the late 1950s, but his real passion was politics—specifically, Liberal party politics.

And in this endeavour, the charming Davey was also highly attentive to the emerging field of demographics—could it do for his Liberal party what it did for building radio audiences? His enthusiasm for demographics and statistics was further elevated when he read Theodore White's 1961 book *The Making of the President* and began to dream that a prime minister in Canada could be created the same way.

White, in that book, recounted one of the early contests between Kennedy and his Democratic challenger, Hubert Humphrey, in the Wisconsin primary. Although each candidate spent roughly the same amount of money, approximately $150,000, they spent it in radically different ways. Humphrey poured his resources into old-fashioned advertising, relying on the help of volunteers. Kennedy, however, had pollster Louis Harris on staff, and, as White put it, "Harris' polling of twenty-three thousand Wisconsin voters was not only the largest ever done in a single state but invaluable in informing his candidate of moods." Humphrey himself would tell Harris that the comparison between the two campaign approaches was like "a corner grocer running against a chain store."

The shopping metaphor was entirely apt. Though Harris had specialized in political polling since beginning his career and founding his own firm in the 1950s, it was the corporate and commercial sector in the United States that first embraced polling as the growth elixir. George Gallup, the grandfather of political polling, got his start in the United States at the Young & Rubicam advertising firm in the 1930s and spent the 1940s doing survey research for Hollywood. Pointedly, Gallup refused to work for political parties, arguing it would compromise the independence of his polling. So when Gallup did do research on the democratic issues of the day, he financed his surveys with his commercial work. The pattern was set early—pollsters would make their main money in the private sector, but their reputation in the political realm. The same had been true in the advertising world.

Davey's career path, however, would take the opposite route— politics would become his business, while advertising and public opinion would be his passionate hobby. In later years, people would often mistakenly believe that Davey had had a lengthy career in advertising. Within a year or two of that presentation to CKFH on the chilly May day, Davey was sent to Ottawa, installed as the national organizer of the Liberal party for leader Lester Pearson and given a free hand to explore how politics could benefit from a more rigorous understanding of Canada's demographic, consumer realities. In this, Davey became a Canadian pioneer in merging politics and the market research world. And his work would start with the introduction of polling to the central Liberal campaign apparatus in Canada.

With his well-thumbed Ted White "textbook" in hand, Davey almost immediately set about recruiting Kennedy's pollster, Lou Harris, to come and do some work for the Liberal party. Harris ran his own polling firm, called Penetration Research, based in Bronxville, New York. But he set up a Canadian subsidiary to do his surveying north of the border and sealed the deal with the Liberals when he promised to personally do the analysis of the numbers.

The Liberals, many of whom were keen Canadian nationalists, were well aware that having a pollster from south of the border might send the wrong signals about their own patriotism. But this American invasion was too hard to resist for Canadian political marketers in training, who were seized with the desire to put the modern methods of science and organization used in the commercial world into the dusty old world of politics. Davey himself, in his autobiography, *The Rainmaker*, described polling as the tool with the power to turn baser political tactics into the more exalted "political strategy."

"Most people knocking on doors during campaigns have a difficult time sorting out strategy from tactics. They become consumed with the tactical side of campaigning which, of course, is a very significant component. Far more important, of course, is the overall strategic game plan. In the final analysis any campaign comes down to the major issue, whether it is a personality or a policy... Having determined the best issue, then that becomes the issue of the campaign. Polling is extremely useful in making this determination."

Even though polls had been kicking around in Canadian politics for a couple of decades, the 1962 election was the first real faceoff between modern political polling methods. In the *Financial Post* in April of that year, journalist Richard Gwyn wrote that Canada was about to have its "first scientific election." He described the public opinion surveys and statistical analysis as "completely new weapons" in the political arsenal. As Gwyn saw it, this would be the campaign in which the imprecise arts of politics would be challenged by "the skills of sociologists, statisticians, advertising experts, pollsters and mass-communications experts."

The "science" in that election was mainly on the Liberal side, and it clearly wasn't sufficient. Conservative Prime Minister John Diefenbaker, who had famously said that "dogs know best what to do with polls" and "polls are for dogs," still put his trust in the old-fashioned, populist arts of politics. (He never forgot that the Gallup organization had put the Liberals fourteen points ahead on the eve of the 1957 election that brought him to office.) Conservatives were able to hang on to power in the 1962 election, despite all the fancy poll-work and science that Davey was trying to bring to the Liberal side. Part of that victory was owed to a much more complicated electoral dynamic. A newly formed New Democratic Party had arrived on the scene in time for the 1962 campaign, strongly backed by organized labour and fed by western, rural populism and a demand for Medicare. But a year later, with Davey still investing tens of thousands of dollars in repeated national polls by Harris, the Liberals finally wrested power from the Conservatives.

Harris's firm would continue to supply the Liberals with polling material and insights into the minds of voters through the 1960s— even if some of these insights were also gained through extensive work in the United States. Periodically in its reports, Penetration Research would acknowledge its Americanisms for its Canadian Liberal party readers. "Through years of pounding out hundreds of reports for candidates scattered through the fifty United States, our typewriters have become habituated to spellings such as 'labor,' 'connection' and 'defense' and to such locutions as 'the government is'; we will attempt to correct these mannerisms, but habit dies hard and we apologize for the slips that will undoubtedly clutter the report," the writers noted in one of their 1960s-era surveys on the political climate in Ontario.

Lou Harris's firm also had some blunt convictions about the limits of voters' interest or enthusiasm for matters of state, just as Philip Spencer had warned readers of *Canadian Forum* a couple of decades earlier. Repeatedly in its reports to the Liberals in the 1960s and 1970s, Penetration Research would stress the pre-eminence of "bread-and-butter" issues in the minds of citizens. Consumer concerns would always trump weightier matters, Harris's analysts kept telling the Liberals, despite what the media or the political class maintained to be priorities.

"Nor is there any hint of the frequent suggestion from the press, pulpit and soapbox that university educational opportunities and facilities must be expanded to meet the challenge of the Russians in science and technology," an October 1960 study said, when the US and Soviet Union were in the midst of the space race. In other words, the opinion leaders might be seized with science and the Cold War, but ordinary working folks, the young marrieds, just wanted their consumer needs met, maybe with some mellow, non-excitable music on their afternoon commute home to the suburbs. There were echoes here of Spencer's findings in 1940s Toronto and foreshadowing, too, of what would become a political-polling truism for decades ahead: matters of high politics hold little interest for ordinary Canadians. (In tone and intent, it's not all that different from the populist rhetoric that ran through the Mike Harris "Common Sense Revolution" in Ontario in the 1990s or the federal Conservatives' conviction in the 2008 and 2011 elections that Canadians cared more about pocketbook issues than pointy-headed debates about the environment, parliamentary democracy or Afghan detainees. It's probably the kind of advice that went into Stephen Harper's decision to skip the UN meeting in 2009 and head to Tim Hortons instead.)

A decade after Davey had embraced polling in earnest as a basic implement in the Liberal campaign toolkit, this notion of Canadians as selfish consumers, above all, had solidified in findings of the

Liberals' American pollsters. Here's a July 1971 bit of analysis from Penetration Research, passed along in what was titled "A Survey of the Political Climate in Canada":

> The other side of the coin is unemployment, or jobs. This is unquestionably the top issue in the nation today. A great number of Canadians regard themselves as living in hard times and this concern dwarfs their concern about everything else. Sometimes we tend to forget that human beings are basically and instinctively selfish. Those in the press and in government tend to talk to each other to the exclusion of the masses. In the process, such people often convince themselves that what they regard to be important is what people generally regard to be important. A major finding of this survey is that foreign policy, Canadian unity, relations with the US, Constitutional reform, pollution and other such matters are not at all the big issues, any of them. All other issues are secondary to the wish for better times in Canada, and this issue is more important today than it has ever been in the nine years we have been conducting surveys of public opinion in this nation.

Davey, despite his sales background, believed there was a distinction between selling a product and selling a politician. For him, politics was more like sports, or at times a religion. But for the man who would become one of Davey's chief allies in the Liberal inner circle, Martin Goldfarb, there was valuable political information in how Canadians behaved in the consumer marketplace. He'd been the one, after all, who in 1971 made the link between selling politicians and selling tomatoes. In that same article, he said that this newfangled polling business could be crucial in reaching as much as 10 percent of the electorate, whose vote swings could determine the fate of an election. At the time, 10 percent was considered a large figure—most Canadians' loyalty to their chosen political parties was long and deep, often going back generations, and they didn't tend to use election campaigns to "shop" for another preference.

The Anthropologist

Martin Goldfarb had grown up with his two brothers in a tiny apartment over a grocery store that his parents operated on Dundas Street West in Toronto. He had graduated with a bachelor's degree in anthropology and then a master's degree in sociology from the University of Toronto. For a while after graduating he taught high school, but then he started doing some survey work on the side with MacLaren Advertising. He saw this moonlighting job as the perfect outlet for his anthropology training and started to apply many of the analytical skills he had learned at university to his work. Within five years, he'd given up teaching to dive into market research full time, operating his business first out of his own home, then in a small office at Bathurst and Lawrence in Toronto.

Martin Goldfarb and Keith Davey had met while working on Paul Hellyer's 1968 Liberal leadership campaign, which they lost to Pierre Trudeau, and had come to be friends and political allies. When Davey was put in charge of a royal commission into the state of Canada's media in 1969, he hired Goldfarb to do the research surveys.

Davey wanted to make Goldfarb the official Liberal party pollster in the 1970s, but he had to overcome some hurdles first with Trudeau. The prime minister hadn't appreciated Goldfarb's tomato comparison. He was also ticked off by an article that Goldfarb had written in *Maclean's* magazine, outlining how Trudeau could be beaten at the polls and how he was contributing to a "moral breakdown" in Canadian society. This was after the infamous "fuddle-duddle" furor, in which the prime minister had been caught uttering a four-letter word in the House of Commons. The first meeting between Goldfarb and Trudeau, arranged by Davey, didn't go well at all. Trudeau had the *Maclean's* magazine in front of him. He asked Goldfarb if he stuck by his words. The pollster did: "You can't say f— off in public."

Goldfarb also had some blunt views about how Trudeau was hand-ling Quebec, believing he had put the wrong people in charge. After a short, frosty conversation about whether Trudeau needed any more of this kind of advice, the pollster was asked to leave.

Somehow, though, Goldfarb overcame this initial hostility from Trudeau and went on to enjoy a long and influential career as the official Liberal party pollster. Between 1970 and 1980, Goldfarb's firm raked in $1.3 million in government contracts on top of its work for private-sector clients. In 1984, Goldfarb would be called "Canada's most influential private citizen" on the front cover of *Saturday Night* magazine. So cozy was the relationship between the Liberals and their pollster, in fact, that "government by Goldfarb" became an accusatory cry on the Conservative opposition benches in the 1970s and 1980s. "Government by Goldfarb" became a form of political shorthand in Canada for a while for any government accused of taking its marching orders from pollsters.

Goldfarb believed that people revealed themselves with their choices, whether they were consumer choices or political choices. Anthropologists study material culture for clues about civilizations; so should political researchers. "A brand is a promise you make consistently over time. What's the promise? That's the essence of a politician," Goldfarb stated. Throughout his time as the Liberals' pollster, Goldfarb would apply what he was learning in his market-ing research to the marketing of politics. Like all pollsters, he would make his money in the private sector—a lot of money, in fact—but earn his reputation in the political realm. The knowledge he was building, information gleaned from people's attitudes toward the pol-itical and commercial markets, would form the emerging profile of a Canadian consumer-citizen, from the 1970s all the way through to the twenty-first century.

Much of Goldfarb's work was also being used at the time by Terry O'Malley and the gang at Vickers and Benson, thus solidify-ing the politics-advertising-polling triumvirate that fuelled much of the Liberals' political successes. It was Goldfarb's data that helped Vickers and Benson come up with the pitch for butter as a sensuous product for the Dairy Bureau. Goldfarb also did the research for the ad agency's accounts with corporate giants Ford and the Bank of Montreal.

One of Goldfarb's larger successes in the corporate sector came with his client Wonderbra. The Canadian manufacturer was creating undergarments that boasted of camouflage and restriction—"foundation" clothing, as it was called. Goldfarb, however, went off on a little field-research expedition, to San Francisco, where he took careful note of the city's more liberal attitudes to nudity and strip clubs. Nothing about the temper of the times convinced Goldfarb that women were interested in more restriction. He persuaded Wonderbra to turn its thinking upside down: freedom was in the air, he said. Wonderbra created something called "Dicey"—the "no-bra bra," which was a runaway success and much mimicked by competitors. What does underwear have to do with politics? Goldfarb, the anthropologist, saw the connection: "They wanted freedom. They did not want government to impose restrictions on how they behaved and this was a way of expressing it."

Goldfarb, plugged in as he was to the private sector, was a big fan of focus groups, those small gatherings of citizens who would agree to be interviewed, usually behind a one-way mirror, so that their reactions could be scrutinized in depth. Researchers would lure citizens into participating in these focus groups with small cash incentives and refreshments. Focus groups, relying heavily on people with time to spare, can rarely claim to be representative of the busy population, but they can suggest typical responses. The commercial world had come to appreciate this style of research because it was a way of gauging intangibles that straight polling could not measure: emotion, gut response and the like.

It was through focus-group research in 1980 in Marin County, California, for instance, that Goldfarb collected some stunning news for the Ford Motor Company: most participants had never been in a Ford car and didn't even know anyone who had owned one. "It was an absolute shock to the corporation," Goldfarb told the *Chicago Tribune*. Ford responded with an ad campaign specifically for these strangers to the brand: "Have you driven a Ford lately?"

In the political realm, Goldfarb applied the same approach, convinced that understanding hopes and fears of citizens was more useful than gauging vague political support. Rather than ask whether Liberals were simply losing strength in the 1970s, he would probe the emotions behind the numbers. Were Canadians afraid of inflation because of the dent in their wallets or the threats to their jobs? In turn, Goldfarb could then counsel the Liberals on how to tailor their rhetoric to match these more deep-seated sentiments among the electorate. Goldfarb didn't invent Trudeau's "just society," but he liked the way it worked as an indelible, over-arching "brand" for the party throughout the 1970s. His research told him that Canadians were looking for fairness in this decade, whether it was fairness in store pricing or fairness in hiring practices. Pierre Trudeau's "just society" spoke to a value that travelled from the grocery aisles to the ballot box.

There's an old saying in advertising from Leo McGinneva, a US marketing expert, that revolves around knowing what you're trying to sell. When customers go to a hardware store to buy a drill bit, he said, "They don't want quarter-inch bits. They want quarter-inch holes." What he was saying, in essence, is that consumers are buying the *idea* of a product. Successful marketing rests in understanding people's motives and wants, beyond the mere transaction. This is what Goldfarb was supplying to the Liberals with his research, and why it was useful to the public and private sectors. People who were looking for freedom in their undergarments might also be looking for freedom in their political dialogue. People who wanted choice in the grocery aisles would want choice in their political options, too. This would be especially true of checked-out voters, who were often more informed about their consumer choices than their political ones.

Politics, as always, was several steps behind the consumer world in terms of market research in the 1970s—probably because the politicians were still operating under the idea of their craft as something separate from the less lofty world of commercialism. It was fine to let the ad guys sell the political brands at election time, and maybe even throw them some work in between campaigns, but the marketing experts remained just outside the inner circle of power.

"Emotional Commitment"

By the 1970s, Canada's advertising community was getting deep into the idea of consumer research, and "positioning" was the hot new fashion. Products had to be "positioned" against their competitors in the marketplace. Shopping malls were proliferating across the country and Statistics Canada, in a 1973 report, found that stores in these convenient, multiple-merchandise centres, with their ample parking, generated 30-percent better sales per square foot than traditional stores. In Toronto, the giant Eaton's Centre opened in 1977—a six-storey, two-block-long marvel of steel and glass that immediately became a shopping and tourist mecca. It even had a ceiling sculpture of Canada geese in flight, so shoppers could feel a tinge of patriotism as they browsed through the merchandise. Commercials on TV were getting slicker, with video replacing film and colour taking over from black and white, and the old sixty-second ad was being pared down to a speedier thirty seconds. At the same time, advertising-savvy political aides were trying to coach their bosses in the art of the "thirty-second clip," which politicians would continue to see as a necessary but lamentable decline in public discourse.

For someone like professor-turned-politician Ed Broadbent, for instance, clip-friendly speaking became part of his on-the-job training. Broadbent came to politics from academia. He had been a professor at York University and his early speeches were dry, complex historical lectures—not exactly crowd pleasers for the blue-collar audiences in his Oshawa riding. But he would get the hang of things. In 1977, Broadbent told *Toronto Star* reporter John Honderich, "I had an instinctive inclination to speak in sentences that included colons and subordinate clauses and always qualify en route. Now I put the conclusion first." After the Throne Speech that fall, Broadbent was disciplined enough to distill his reaction into seventeen quotable words for the media: "The failure of this throne speech lies in the absence of specific suggestions dealing with the economy."

Television arrived in the House of Commons that same year, 1977, forcing all Canadian politicians, front bench and back bench alike, to reckon with issues of packaging and image. Patrick Gossage, then press secretary to Prime Minister Pierre Trudeau, chronicled the development in his diary, which he published as a book, *Close to the Charisma*, in 1986. "Just to make sure we don't get away with anything, television was launched in the House of Commons this week. Show business has now penetrated the sanctum of Canada's most exclusive club. The regime is terrified," Gossage wrote in a November entry. By January, terror had given way to grudging acceptance. "One image-polishing exercise is working well," Gossage wrote. "We are finally doing something about the performance of ministers in the House, now that their every finger-up-the-nose is televised for the nation to laugh at."

Gossage and some TV-savvy folks even prepared a videotape to shock and mock the Liberal cabinet ministers into paying more attention to their image. "The result was hilarious and devastating. It was a compilation of fast cuts of bad-taste ties, horrible checked jackets ([Eugene] Whelan's the worst) and childish behaviour by ministers as a colleague spoke." Ottawa tailors suddenly started doing a brisk trade in new suits for ministers, and Trudeau himself took more time in the Commons to better "frame" his replies for the camera lens.

The Liberal ad guys, meanwhile, were all too aware of how TV was changing the message, if not the entire political medium. In a

May 1978 speech at the Four Seasons Hotel in Toronto, the party's man in charge of advertising, Jerry Grafstein, laid out all the ways in which TV was transforming the political business—making it far more concentrated on emotion, character and leadership. He said that the mass media and the mass public were looking for the same thing: "emotional commitment."

"I believe there is a common factor—I call it the EC factor, the Emotional Commitment factor—in the mass mind," Grafstein said. "Politicians are constantly searching for that factor—the emotional commitment by the largest mass of our citizenry. So the political battle is not a battle so much for ideas as it is for minds. It is a psychological battle for the conscious as well as the conscience. It is the creation or promotion of symbols, or a group of symbols, distributed to attract the widest number of individuals in the society that the politician serves. Those symbols can be policies and programs or best, pictures to reflect ideas."

There were two prescient observations in Grafstein's speech. He said that eventually, political messages and societal values would be transmitted through non-political media, such as TV sitcoms. What if, for instance, he said, Canadians got their ideas about cultural tolerance from shows such as *King of Kensington*? Additionally, Grafstein predicted, television would prove to be the most persuasive and powerful medium for those citizens who have checked out of political debates. "The less educated, the more uncommitted, the undecided, the less partisan, the non-party people rely more on TV than any other mode of public persuasion. Those whose 'software systems' or 'codes' are not fixed or simply don't care are persuaded the most," Grafstein said. "It appears that television, if it has any persuasive power, persuades those most who care the least about the particular issue."

As Canadians were becoming more enamoured of those flickering images on TV, they were also becoming more fickle consumers. Martin Goldfarb saw the 1970s and 1980s as a time of disloyalty and abandonment of the big brands. "People abandoned known product lines and sought out generic brands because of cost, quality and competitiveness," he wrote in his 2010 book *Affinity*. Consumers, thanks to the omnipresence of advertising, had become "more savvy, more tough-minded," he believed. And as always, he saw the link to Canadian political culture. This was a time, he said, when old loyalties to parties began to unravel and more Canadians became "floating" voters, switching their allegiance back and forth in successive elections. That unravelling of loyalty became apparent as early as the 1974 federal election, when post-vote analysis turned up a significant amount of party-switching since the previous election. About 70 percent of Canadians who cast a ballot, voted the same way in 1974 as they had in 1972. Another 20 percent had switched their vote between parties. (The other 10 percent were either newly eligible voters or people who had chosen not to vote in 1972.)

This analysis turned up another interesting fact about voting behaviour in the 1970s—loyal partisans were motivated by issues, the survey showed, while transient voters were influenced by factors such as leadership, personality and image. So the people who were attached to political parties were looking at elections as engaged, informed citizens. The floating voters, however, were more like consumers, open to the kind of pitches they were getting in the shopping world.

In the consumer sector, this new floating loyalty was damaging the big names that dominated the Canadian market in the immediate postwar years: the ones that had provided Goldfarb and other marketing consultants with lucrative cheques. At Ford, for instance, Goldfarb's market tests were showing that the brazen newcomers into the auto market, Honda and Toyota, were reaping greater customer satisfaction over the long term. Ford customers were generally happy over two years, but Honda and Toyota owners were satisfied with their cars as long as five years after purchasing them. The solution? Two-year leases for Ford cars. Goldfarb's idea was to get Ford patrons to keep renewing their customer happiness with their new vehicles, and thus, their attachment to the brand. If you couldn't count on long-term loyalty, why not constant-renewal loyalty? Car leasing, as a concept, began to catch on in a large way in the following years, as a direct response to North American consumers' desire for new things and their accompanying, fraying loyalty to old established brands. We would soon see that same kind of brand loyalty breaking down in Canadian politics, too.

The Rock-Star Pollster

Allan Gregg, born and raised in Edmonton, was a struggling graduate student at Carleton University when he discovered that his wife was expecting their first child. In need of some extra cash, he went looking for work on Parliament Hill and landed at the offices of the opposition Progressive Conservative party, just as Robert Stanfield was preparing to step down.

Gregg, in appearance alone, could hardly be described as "conservative." Just twenty-three years old, Gregg looked more like a rock star than a denizen of Parliament. His long hair trailed down to the middle of his back. He wore an earring. He didn't know how to knot a tie. But Bill Neville, the head of Conservative caucus research, decided to give Gregg a job interview, in the cafeteria of Confederation Building on Parliament Hill.

Gregg didn't talk like a Conservative, either. Bluntly, he told Neville he didn't really care about the fate of the Progressive Conservative party, or of any party, as a matter of fact. He was an academic—he wanted to teach. Gregg had been doing his Ph.D. thesis on voting behaviour, with heavy emphasis on statistics. Polling education was making its debut in academia, and he wasn't alone in his enthusiasm for the topic at Carleton University in the late 1970s. Also at the university in those years were some young students who would similarly go on to become nationally known pollsters: Frank Graves and Darrell Bricker, for instance.

Gregg was hired for the summer and he arrived at a fortuitous time. The Conservatives, like the Liberals before them, had been looking to the United States for its polling needs for the past decade, but this arrangement was wearing thin. At the time, Canada's PC party was using Robert Teeter of Market Opinion Research, who had also been doing all the polling for US presidents Richard Nixon and Gerald Ford. Teeter had been one of the pioneers in the use of focus-group polling in politics. His polls were expensive, though, and the Conservatives needed to save some money. And like the Liberals, Conservatives weren't exactly eager to publicize or extend their reliance on American pollsters. Martin Goldfarb had become the Liberals' home-grown pollster. Who would do the same for the Conservatives?

With all the naive confidence of youth, Gregg volunteered to help the Conservatives develop their own polling expertise north of the forty-ninth parallel. His working partners in this enterprise were two smart young aides named Ian Green and Stephen Probyn, who were also just in their twenties, also fresh from the halls of academe. They weren't entirely sure what they were doing, but they were having a good time, and amassing new skills and expertise for the party. "We basically cobbled together an in-house polling program," Gregg said. As a bonus, the new Conservative leader, Joe Clark, was impressed with their work, and he rewarded Gregg with promotions, titles and research junkets to the United States to build the party's polling expertise. Gregg became the national campaign secretary for the Conservatives, boldly and unabashedly enthusiastic for the potential of polls to be forces for good in politics. "Polls are our only empirical tie to the real world," Gregg told the *Toronto Star* in 1978.

Back in Canada, Gregg tried to find a Canadian pollster to handle the Conservatives' needs. He tried every available researcher in the marketing world, and none of them were suited to the task. For Gregg, political polling was a field in itself, with marked differences from the consumer world. So, for the moment anyway, the

Conservatives re-entered into their contract with the American poll-ster, Teeter. Gregg was put in charge at the Ottawa end of things. In those days before people had personal computers, Gregg had some-thing they called an online printer in his office, but it was really a mobile hookup with Teeter's computers—then, huge hulking beasts of machinery stored at Wayne State University in Michigan. Gregg's keyboard was about the size of a small electric piano, and like a virtuoso he would tap in the codes and the questions he wanted answered. With his long tresses, leather pants, trademark red shoes and earring, Gregg was seen as an eccentric young genius—anything but conservative, in fact. Older, more seasoned Conservatives were still suspicious of polling, seeing it as little more than voodoo.

Dalton Camp, the ad-guru pioneer for the Conservative party, told author Claire Hoy in his book about polling, *Margin of Error*, "When polling started, it wasn't taken all that seriously... It was something equivalent to doing an enumeration. Interesting, but not critical. The system was such that we took only one poll, before the election of course. It was too expensive to do more. I used to run the national [Conservative] office for $30,000 a month in the mid-1960s. A poll then would cost $20,000. That was big money to me."

Because computers and technology were alien to most Canadians in those days, it was Gregg's technical mastery—not to mention his wardrobe—that prompted much of the awe and/or suspicion. Journalist and author John Sawatsky dubbed him the "punk pollster." But Gregg's real aptitude at the time was in understanding what lay beneath the numbers, as well—their potential to be moved, given the proper cues.

Until Gregg came along, the standard Conservative polling ques-tions were blunt and revolved around voting intent: "Who are you going to vote for?" Polling was focused extensively on leadership. Gregg, through his research, started to plumb what it would take to change people's voting intent, and also what factors, beyond leader-ship, would influence their vote. As well, he was the first pollster in Canada to incorporate individual-riding data into the overall research, thus making his findings more microscopically accurate.

Zooming right down to the ground, Gregg came up with "typologies" of the electorate, slotting them into categories based on their likelihood to add to Conservative support. There were the "hard Tories," the people who would vote Conservative no matter what, and who had no real second choice at the ballot box. There were "soft Tories," people who were voting Conservative, but whose support could be swayed to their second choice. Then there were "soft others" and "hard others," sorted according to the strength of their allegiance to parties other than the Tories. The soft voters, the Canadians out shopping for political preference, were the most interesting to the Conservatives, and Gregg had managed to isolate the two dozen or so ridings where these newly malleable members of the electorate might turn the tide for the party.

Consumer marketers were looking for much the same thing in this era: people willing to put the vaunted value of choice over their old habits or loyalties. They were then still a rare breed in politics and the grocery stores. About three-quarters of the people who headed out to the stores in the 1970s already knew what brands they were going to buy. If they had come home with Tide detergent on the last grocery trip, they were pretty likely to buy it again. Brand loyalty could still generally be counted upon by purveyors of soap and politics, though as Goldfarb had noticed, Canadians were starting to wonder why they were sticking with the same old choices when they bought their cars and detergent. Politics wouldn't be far behind.

Certainly, loyalty to Pierre Trudeau's Liberals was wavering— enough that the Conservatives were able to eke out a minority-government win in 1979. Joe Clark, with Gregg's market research, focused his campaign on the grumpy consumer mood in the country. Conservatives kept asking the voters, "Do you want the next four years to be like the last eleven?" The answer, however briefly, was

"No." Then, just six months after gaining power in May 1979, Clark's government made a fateful decision that put them on the wrong side of Canadians and their wallets, delivering a budget that imposed an eighteen-cents-a-gallon increase in the price of gas. In the snap election that followed, Liberals managed to get on the right side of consumer-citizens again by promising to delay energy price increases and harsh budget cuts that would discourage spending. That was apparently what Canadians needed to hear, and it was enough to put the Liberals and Trudeau back in office.

As luck would have it, though, Clark's loss to Trudeau in 1980 actually helped Gregg build his home-grown polling machine for the Conservatives. It also freed him up to help out in some important provincial elections. When Gregg went down to Toronto to lend his services to the Big Blue Machine in the 1981 election, for instance, he chose twenty-five "volatile" ridings, province-wide, to poll every night. The findings were fed into direct-mail efforts to targeted regions and phone-bank campaigns to woo Conservatives to the Davis campaign.

Everything that the Conservatives were learning about modern campaigning in that provincial election was blazing a trail for Tory politicking on the big Canadian stage for the coming decades, and into the next century. On election night in 1981, Davis won a majority, and Gregg's twenty-five ridings were part of the bandwagon. Just six of those ridings had been Conservative before the election, and only six were *not* Conservative after the vote.

During that 1981 Ontario campaign, the polling costs alone were $1.5 million. Gregg had never spent that much before—and never would again, despite going on to run some impressive polling for the federal Conservatives and their provincial allies across the country over the next decade or so. Gregg and Goldfarb were early adopters, as we'd say today, in the application of polling to politics in this country. But their ascent was also fuelled by the fact that popular culture in Canada, as in most industrializing democracies around the world, had been swept up since the Second World War in the worship of science, evidence and psychology. Science and measurement were replies to a world that had felt far too unpredictable in the first half of the twentieth century.

Polling, in effect, was seen as an applied psychological science, whether the application was to benefit profit or politics. Early polls Davey commissioned for the Liberal party were called "motivational research" studies and used language such as the following in describing their methodology: "The depth interview is a psychological technique, similar to that used by psychiatrists and psychoanalysts in a clinical situation. Few direct questions are asked by the interviewer. The depth interview instead encourages the respondent to express his thoughts and feelings about the topic freely, at length, and in a conversational manner."

Goldfarb and Gregg stood out as pollsters for their respective parties because they brought new layers of science to their trade. Goldfarb merged anthropology with polling—his studies were as much ethnographies as they were research reports. He studied modern Canadian civilization in the same way that other anthropologists studied faraway cultures in remote countries. He understood material culture—how society could define itself around its belongings, including its consumer goods.

Goldfarb liked focus groups because they provided stories behind the numbers and gave him access to rare articulate voters. "You need to spend time listening to people, not just typical voters, but articulate people; people who can tell you how they feel, who can describe their inner feelings. Most people cannot. Most people have a rough time expressing affection overtly. They have a rough time expressing how they feel—why they feel hurt, why they are euphoric. And they don't like to talk about their financial circumstances." So on matters of emotion and money, two very important factors in consumer-citizenship, focus groups tended to give Goldfarb the deep psychological research he needed.

Gregg, on the other hand, was more of a numbers guy. He had come to polling via the statistical route, and he brought to the Conservatives a rigour and a dazzling understanding they hadn't seen before. He was immersed in what they called the "quantitative" side of things and cutting-edge ways of doing research surveys. It actually took Gregg a bit of time to figure out the value of qualitative research, as the focus groups were called. His real glimpse into the value of focus groups came when he worked with Nancy McLean, who had produced game shows and other early TV successes on top of her work with the Big Blue Machine. Innovative in her thinking about TV, McLean had been doing all the advertising and production work for the Ontario Conservatives, including those man-in-the-street interviews, and then had migrated to Ottawa to help out the new crowd around Clark for the 1979 election.

McLean and Gregg became inseparable as friends and colleagues. Gregg would do his quantitative polling and then, with McLean, the two would review consumer-like feedback to their efforts, through lots and lots of focus groups. McLean was instinctively adept at sifting through the feedback they were getting, knowing how to delve under the literal or off-the-cuff critiques of their efforts—and plumb what people were really saying about their gut reactions. Like Goldfarb, she understood that rare was the individual who could talk articulately about emotions and feelings. McLean was a big fan of clarity and simplicity in political communications, according to Gregg. "She was smart enough to know that sometimes being too creative can get in the way of things like comprehension and believability and trustworthiness and message."

In the 1979 election, for instance, the Progressive Conservatives were toying with the idea of negative TV ads against the Trudeau government. Gregg's numbers told him that people didn't like those ads in principle; that when poll respondents were asked whether they were a good idea, they almost universally said "No." But focus groups, watching rough cuts of the ads, told a different story. Canadians may have been telling the pollsters they didn't like negative campaigning, but they were open to the "We've had enough of Trudeau" message contained in the Tory ads.

The more that Gregg started to see how focus groups worked, the more he also realized they could serve another, unexpected purpose— as a reality check on politicians and the top campaign strategists. They were perfect ways to illustrate the distance between the abstract world of politics and the real lives of Canadian citizens. Gregg got in the habit of doing some focus-group sessions every Wednesday night in Toronto and inviting the senior Conservative strategists to watch. There, safe behind the one-way glass, they'd see some hard truths for themselves, right from the mouths of the citizens they were trying to lead. It often stunned them into changes of tactics.

In the 1979 campaign, the PCs had done up a TV ad featuring a hockey goalie in a net, fending off flying pucks. Every time a puck flew, the narrator would recite a line or snippet of a controversy from Trudeau's years in power. The hope was that Canadians would see themselves or the country as the goalie and the net. But the focus groups were confused. Were the Conservatives trying to say that Trudeau hated hockey? The ad campaign was abandoned. In this way, with research moving to the gut level of voters' reactions, Canadian politics was moving further along the path from advertising to true marketing.

THE BARGAINING

MARKET TESTED

Almost as soon as Canadian political players fully embraced polling and advertising in the 1970s, earnest voices began to be raised in buyers' regret. No question, people were having fun with all the new commercial tools for politicking, but what would they do to the higher calling of the profession? And so, for the next couple of decades, Canadian politicos seesawed between arguments over just how much our democratic system should be getting mixed up in the tools of the consumer marketplace. While that debate carried on, though, the country started to amass most of the raw ingredients of the all-out political marketing and consumer-citizenship that would dominate the twenty-first century. Resistance would prove futile.

In the midst of the 1979 election campaign, a clearly grumpy Geoffrey Stevens lamented in his much-read *Globe and Mail* column how politics was turning into the "Selling of the Canadian Politician," and in the process, untethering the voting public from the true, more civic-minded purpose of politics:

The 120-odd journalists who are travelling with Messrs. Trudeau, Clark and Broadbent today are less political reporters than they are stage props for the evening news. Dutifully, inanely, we follow Mr. Clark through the Syncrude project at Fort McMurray, Mr. Broadbent through a hospital in Regina, Mr. Trudeau through a boys' and girls' club in Saint John. Does Mr. Clark actually know anything more about the problems of small business than he did before he strode, rapidly, through a box company in Kitchener? Is Mr. Broadbent's understanding of the complexities of food pricing deepened because he was able to pose in front of the produce counter at a co-op in St. Boniface? Is Mr. Trudeau more sensitive to the diversity of the Canadian soul because he lit a string of firecrackers on a street in Chinatown in Vancouver?

Stevens complained that campaigns had become a physical endurance test rather than a challenge to inform and educate the citizenry. Somehow, he said, Canadian political journalists were helping to push the myth that if a politician could perform like an ad pitchman, he could also run a country: "What nonsense. What rubbish. All that's being established is that the three leaders, properly briefed, are able to make painstakingly stage-managed public appearances without falling into the orchestra pit. We are learning nothing about which man would make the best prime minister or how he would conduct himself if entrusted with that high office." Even the earnest New Democrats were embracing the slick new tools of the political trade, setting aside an unprecedented $1 million for advertising in the 1979 campaign with leader Ed Broadbent.

Terry O'Malley, ever upbeat, hauled out his Underwood typewriter and hammered out a defence of advertising's place in politics for the pages of the *Globe and Mail*: "For me, advertising is one of the real bases of democracy. It is the voice of reporting on one of the most important fundamentals in our society: the goods and services supplied to the marketplace." He also dropped an interesting bit of advertising-industry intelligence. Apparently, the most disliked form of ads were ones for household products such as soap and deodorant. However, O'Malley said, these were also the ads that proved to be most effective, simply because the soap and deodorant corporations had the money to saturate the airwaves.

There was a great bit of foreshadowing in O'Malley's column for the politics to come three decades down the road in Canada, when a federal Conservative party learned that you could make Canadians watch ads they didn't like and still persuade them to buy your product—as long as you had the resources to carry out a sustained PR effort. O'Malley, with the help of that handy soap metaphor again, was spelling out the formula for the unlikely success of attack ads. It was as simple as this: you may not like them, but they will get in your head anyway, thanks to rote, repeated exposure.

What the Canadian political media was witnessing going into the 1980s, in fact, was just the tip of the iceberg. Or, as Canadian band Bachman–Turner Overdrive sang in the 1970s, "You ain't seen nothin' yet." Advertising and marketing were not just shaping politics and election campaigns; their influence was being felt in government, too, in between elections. The ad gurus were starting to be consulted on what policies would be more attractive to the citizens and what measures would be more consumer-friendly. Need a program to fight inflation or hammer out a new constitutional deal? Don't call the political scientists. Call the ad guys. There were also political developments unfolding on the world stage at the time, particularly in Britain and the United States, which would prove to be crucial lessons for future generations of Canadian politicos.

Have It Your Way

A lawyer and a staunch capitalist, Margaret Thatcher, daughter of a greengrocer, had assumed the helm of the British Conservative Party in 1975. Although she had been educated as a scientist, she began her political career in the 1950s as a young MP for the riding of Dartford, a community in England that had been hard hit by the rationing and regulation fervour of postwar Britain. Further political experience, notably as health minister in the early 1970s, had put Thatcher on a constant collision course with unions and state-run enterprise. Tough, hard as nails, Thatcher believed business-minded people were best-placed to handle affairs of state—and political campaigning. Thatcher would seize every opportunity to link politics to shopping, charging through supermarkets with a grocery cart during election campaigns and urging voters to see government finances as a household budget. As she ascended to the prime minister's job in the late 1970s, pundits would call her "Margaret the Marketed" and her campaign "The Selling of Maggie."

The Thatcher-led merger of politics and marketing began with a fateful decision to bring advertising experts right into the inner circle of political decision making in the Conservative Party of Great Britain. Gordon Reece, a former television producer, had been working with Thatcher since 1970, coaching her on how to be more TV-friendly. Reece, almost immediately after his 1978 appointment as director of publicity for the new Conservative leader, sought out a high-flying British advertising firm, Saatchi & Saatchi, to do a total image makeover for the party. As Margaret Scammell wrote in her 1995 book *Designer Politics: How Elections Are Won*, the advertising firm was given a free hand to do for the party what it had done for its corporate clients:

> The Saatchi team went to work on their new account much as they would any other; its first task was to research consumers' emotional reaction to the "product" and then to reduce the client's objectives and most logical appeals to their simplest elements… Saatchi's stress on the general emotional appeal, rather than the particular policy aspects, led them to engage more heavily in qualitative, motivational research rather than quantitative surveys. Saatchi imported qualitative marketing research

direct from the commercial world: unlike quantitative research, it does not attempt to produce statistically measurable results. It relies on focus-group discussion and in-depth interviews with voters in target groups. In the commercial field it is used widely at the stage of product development to gain an early indication of consumer reactions. In advertising, it is used frequently to test copy before it is released.

By the standards of the twenty-first century this may seem like tame stuff, but it's impossible to overstate the significance of this development in political culture—probably the true moment when politics and politicians became products for consumer-citizens. This wasn't just salesmanship. Nor was it advertising. It meant, in fact, deliberately shaping the product to meet and anticipate voters' demands. That is what the professionals call marketing. And thanks to Scammell and others watching the Thatcher and Reagan method of politics, a whole new field of political science was born in this era, known as "political marketing."

Political people and politics watchers often treat the words "advertising" and "marketing" as synonyms. And indeed, it's true that advertising is a facet of marketing; the distinction is often described as a fuzzy one. But in terms of understanding how politics have been influenced by the consumer world and what defines political marketing, it's more useful to see them as stand-alone terms, chronologically. Advertising is what you do after you have a product to sell; marketing is what you do to come up with the product in the first place. If someone knits a sweater and puts it on a table at a bazaar, that's pure selling. If someone knits a sweater and then puts it on a mannequin, with a sign boasting of the sweater's warmth and comfort, that's advertising. If the knitter researches which sweaters have sold at the bazaar in previous years, then knits some to meet that demand, or even takes orders for custom-designed creations, that's marketing.

The Canadian ad business didn't exactly stampede to this notion of marketing when it first emerged. At a business conference in Montreal in April 1974 featuring advertising executives, corporate leaders and academics, the talk of "new marketing" fell on some skeptical ears. In the *Toronto Star*, reporter Robert Walker went so far as to say the idea sounded "kind of dumb" at first hearing. Business school professors were mainly the people behind the marketing push, Walker wrote, "by which they mean not merely advertising the product but also deciding in the first place what product to make, how and where to make it, how to get it to you and how much to charge." Some ad executives, Walker reported, detected something vaguely amiss with this approach, fearing it was an unhealthy manipulation of the market, maybe even undemocratic. One study of 156 Canadian corporations at the time showed that marketing managers were viewed dimly for "attempting to exercise control over their customers." But it was obviously a force that couldn't be resisted, for business or politicians. Who wouldn't want to get more control of their customers—or their citizens?

International political marketing expert Jennifer Lees-Marshment, who cut her teeth on this issue by studying Thatcher's approach to politics, has used the advertising-marketing distinction to come up with three types of political parties: the product-oriented party, the sales-oriented party and the marketing-oriented party. Or, if you prefer some rhyming acronyms, POPs, SOPs and MOPs. Product-oriented parties simply present themselves to voters and hope for the reward at the ballot box. That usually happens when they have a strong, singular position to present; in Canada, the Bloc Québécois or the early Green Party would be good examples. Sales-oriented parties, on the other hand, put a lot of effort into persuading voters to support them: putting popular policies in the front window, less popular or more complex ideas in the fine print.

Most parties in Canada, at one time or another, are sales-oriented. You want to sell politicians like soap? Be a SOP. Marketing-oriented parties, though, try to figure out in advance what the voters want and actually shape their policies, not just their public face, around voter demand. To do marketing in politics, you need to be willing to see your party as a malleable "product" that can be shaped and altered by consumer demand and market research. This means that you don't go to the pollsters and advertisers after you've decided on your policies and platform—you bring them in before, to help design what you're offering to the electorate. It's not the kind of politics that everyone likes. To this day, people in all parties can be as squeamish as those 1970s ad executives about shaping the political "product" to fit voter demand.

But marketing has been a powerfully profitable enterprise for the political parties that have put aside their reservations to do it. It has yielded those profits because it is answering to a market demand in the citizenry, according to Lees-Marshment. "We don't like to think of people, of politicians being a product, and we certainly don't like to think that they're designing what they say they believe in and they stand for," Lees-Marshment said in an interview. "The reason politicians treat voters as consumers is because voters act like consumers. Voters don't just vote according to how their parents voted or according to their party ideology… We change whom we vote for from one election to the next. We need persuading to support somebody. We also need the politician to offer us a product that we will like, just as we do in business—because we're consumers in every other aspect of our life. We also now act as consumers in politics."

It's probably not an accident that marketing-style politics were pioneered by market-friendly politicians dubbed the "neoliberals." Thatcher and Ronald Reagan both came to power in their countries in the late 1970s and early 1980s with promises to make government more businesslike and accommodating to the private sector. Famously, Thatcher told a newspaper interviewer during her long reign that "there was no such thing as society." Reagan, meanwhile, installed pollsters and market researchers within his inner circle, just as Thatcher had done with the Saatchi & Saatchi folks. They went beyond merely using ad people for political campaigns and relied on them to make governing decisions.

"Values Research"

By 1980, Americans were getting ready to vote Republican again in large numbers, for the first time since Richard Nixon's Watergate fiasco and resignation in 1974. The leading contender was former Hollywood actor and soap salesman Ronald Reagan. His run for the White House had begun in earnest during his stint as governor of California and gained fuel and credibility with the help of some pioneering pollsters.

Richard Wirthlin, Reagan's pollster, was a practitioner of something called "values research." The idea was to gauge not just what people thought or said they thought, but the underlying values that motivated them to make the decisions they did. Wirthlin would equip test audiences with dials, so they could register their emotional reactions to Reagan speeches. The results of this real-time testing would then be used to refine the speeches, so that Reagan could tailor his remarks to elicit maximum approval from his listeners. Wirthlin, a behavioural economist by training, borrowed this wisdom in large part from the commercial world, and he was honoured in 1981 with the prestigious "Ad Man of the Year" award—just to underline how much consumerist research had found its way into American politics. He was the first public opinion researcher to be so honoured, and the *Wall Street Journal* called him "the prince of pollsters."

Wirthlin is credited for figuring out that Americans didn't have to like everything a politician represented to vote for him; that the impression created was maybe more important than the nuts and bolts of platforms, beliefs or ideology. People would vote for Reagan even if they didn't exactly endorse his strong, pro-capitalist Republicanism. People would vote for Reagan even if they had been historically Democrats—hence the term "Reagan Democrats" was born. Reagan developed ways to talk to Americans as consumers on the emotional, gut level. He won the 1980 election against incumbent president Jimmy Carter, in fact, with this pointed question: "Are you better off today than you were four years ago?"

That slogan, not so coincidentally, was borrowed from Wirthlin's Canadian business partner, Allan Gregg, who had already tried a variation of it for Joe Clark in the 1979 election campaign, when Conservatives had asked Canadians to choose between the Trudeau record and the hope that a change of government would deliver. The two pollsters had met a few years earlier, when Gregg went on his polling-study junket to the United States to see what state-of-the-art practices might be imported to help Clark and the Progressive Conservatives. And when Gregg decided to set up his Decima polling firm in 1980—destined to become the same kind of powerhouse that Martin Goldfarb's firm was in the 1970s—he invited Wirthlin into a business partnership to expand his polling sights beyond the Canadian border. It was through Wirthlin that Gregg learned about what was called "values research." What was revolutionary about this approach, said Gregg, was that it recognized the complexity behind people's voting choices. Up until then, pollsters mainly believed that simple demographic statistics, based on class or socioeconomic data, predicted how people would vote. Or, as Gregg liked to put it, people were being simplistically sorted by "ageness or maleness or Italian-ness."

"His level of sophistication was so much more than anyone else's, by a long shot," Gregg said. "All the other pollsters at the time were basically ad men. They'd come more out of a communications background, but they didn't have really strong methodological skills." Gregg, with this kind of training and his background in statistics, would become part of the first generation of Canadian political pollsters to be strongly steeped in the methodology: sampling probability, standard deviation and all those other techniques relatively new to the business as it was evolving. But he was also learning the importance of consumer values in the political equation.

Throwaway Politics

Just as politics was getting into mass-marketing techniques, the private sector was rethinking those same approaches: Who was the mass, and where was the market? Here was the chief mass-marketing problem in the commercial world: once the market is saturated with your product, how do you create demand for more? "Planned obsolescence" was one way to get around the saturation issue. The president of General Motors, Frederic Donner, in a burst of candour, admitted in 1959 that his auto firm changed its models every year to artificially create demand for replacements. "If it had not been for the annual model change, the automobile as we know it today would not be produced in volume and would be priced so that relatively few could afford to own one," Donner told *Sales Management* magazine.

Disposable items also forced the mass market to keep replacing products they had already purchased once. In the 1970s and 1980s, people weren't thinking as much in terms of buying things for a lifetime. The new buzzword in manufacturing and marketing was "flexibility"—the businesses of tomorrow would be those that were nimble enough to adapt to the changing market trends. And "flexible specialization"—adapting your product to meet a niche of the market—would start to come into fashion. Just as radio had saved itself from obsolescence by bursting into niche markets in the 1950s and 1960s, other industries were learning the same lessons and dividing up the mass market to find particular bands of consumer loyalists. Two professors from the Massachusetts Institute of Technology, Michael J. Piore and Charles F. Sabel, were the leading voices at the head of this major shift in market thinking, ultimately laying out their case in a book called *The Second Industrial Divide*. Flexible specialization, they declared, would be a "a strategy of permanent innovation: accommodation to ceaseless change, rather than an effort to control it."

On top of all of this, some sober second thought was being expressed about the waste and credit carnage of North America's decades-long spending spree. In Alberta, for instance, the oil-fuelled economic boom had also seen record rises in personal debt. On average, each Albertan was carrying about $1,700 in debt in 1978, Statistics Canada reported—$379 more than the national average. Alberta's provincial government was so concerned that it began to launch programs for debt counselling and money management, as well as debt-warning TV ads—one featuring a young man up to his neck in mud.

Conrad Black, then head of the Argus Corporation, cast a disapproving eye over the rampant consumerism invading Canada during a McMaster University convocation address in June 1979. "Mass consumption installed selling, peddling, as the principal avocation of the Western world. Prodigality reigned until most governments, corporations and individuals were awash with debt. Credit sales, which had formerly offended the middle-class aversion to borrowing and had been chiefly identified with the poor, who made installment purchases because they couldn't afford cash on the barrelhead, flooded the economy. The idea of saving to buy something gave way to instant gratification."

But in the 1980s the political class, by and large, was still using most of the tactics of the mass-marketing school, looking for ways to appeal to as broad a section of the political marketplace as possible. That made sense. After all, civic life is all about the masses, isn't it? Yet the challenges of using mass-market style seemed to have limited application to the practice of politics. Obsolescence? Niche marketing? Disposable products? What place could these concepts have in a world where the institutions span centuries, and where democracy applies to all citizens, regardless of how much money they have to spend or where they live? If there is any field that should be concerned with the mass populace, never mind the market, it should be politics, right? "We all wanted a big-tent party," said Gregg. "We all wanted more voters. I remember the early days of the Conservatives, they would agonize over why they didn't have the ethnic vote. It bugged them. It bugged them terribly."

The people who didn't have much attachment to politics were increasing in ranks, and they were making their voting choices more on emotion, leadership and personality than they were on issues of policy or ideology. Fortunately for politicians, emotional pitches were exactly the kind of things that advertisers and marketing experts excel at creating. As voters were becoming more disengaged from politics, it was becoming more important to pay attention to the ad folks than the policy people. Complex, nuanced policy debates were for those who already had a view on politics, whose votes were already committed, for the most part. As Dalton Camp had discovered decades earlier, voters didn't want to be bored with reams of text; they wanted pictures and images and slogans. The more that political advertising resembled consumer advertising (as long as it wasn't too slick) the better. Politicians, whether in Canada or Britain or the United States, needed to grab the attention of the voters who merely shrugged at the affairs of state, who might determine their political preferences the same way they chose their soap.

Meet "Essex Man"

In Britain, Thatcher's political marketing team had distilled their target audience down to a disaffected constituency as well. Thatcher wanted former Labour voters who had checked out of British politics either because of cynicism or simple lack of interest or education. This type of voter would come to be known as "Essex Man."

Essex Man in Thatcher's Britain was an archetype for a new class of young men who lived in the suburbs, surrounded by consumerist trappings, right-leaning more by instinct than ideology—exactly the kind of people to whom Thatcher's hard-right conservatism would have appeal. The Essex Man was most vividly described in a 1990 piece in the *Sunday Telegraph* by Simon Heffer, himself a right-wing denizen of this suburban county sixty kilometres from London. Thatcher's Essex Man was a voter who was "young, industrious, mildly brutish and culturally barren." An Essex Man, Heffer wrote, was more attracted to democracy as a sport, with winners and losers. Or, as he put it, Essex Man "uses instinct and energy rather than contacts and education… He is unencumbered by any 'may the best man win' philosophy. He expects to win whether he's the best man or not."

With Reagan, meanwhile, the mass-marketing effort was all about reaching out beyond his party's political market share, appealing to disaffected Democrats—playing to their growing cynicism and disengagement with politics altogether to turn them into Republicans. Research and marketing in politics had become more sophisticated by the 1980s, and Reagan's advisers were able to shape their politician to appeal to this disgruntled, checked-out voter base, whose ranks were expanding across North America. They weren't just selling Reagan like soap; they were creating the product on offer to the citizens—marketing. They didn't need to make people feel good about Republicanism or its policies, just Reagan and his sunny disposition.

Reagan and Thatcher, along with their sophisticated political marketing teams, were the pioneers of politics for the apolitical—democracy for checked-out voters in the 1980s. The Essex Men and the Reagan Democrats, coincidentally, bore a remarkable resemblance to the hypothetical voters in that *Canadian Forum* series of the 1940s, more interested in the pedestrian realities of life than in lofty politics. The ad machines for the US Republicans and the British Conservatives designed their pitches around those concerns, to engage these voters not in debates of the head, but emotions of the gut, positive or negative. Each word of their ads was carefully market tested.

"Whatever else history may say about my candidacy, I hope it will be recorded that I appealed to our best hopes, not our worst fears. To our confidence, rather than our doubts. To the facts, not the fantasies. And these three—hope, confidence and facts—are at the heart of my vision of peace," Reagan said in a highly effective 1980 TV ad that was little more than a potpourri of "values" words, such as "strength," "restraint" and "inspired leadership." It worked daz-zlingly well through two elections in the United States in the 1980s. "It's Morning Again in America" was Reagan's sunny, value-saturated 1984 campaign slogan. Thatcher and her ad team were aiming their ad messages at the gut level, too. "Labour Isn't Working," blared the words on Thatcher's 1979 campaign posters, atop a picture of citizens lined up at the unemployment office.

Forget Shopping—We Have a Country to Save

Canadian politics was largely insulated, however, from the political marketing revolution taking place in the United States and Britain throughout the 1980s and 1990s. Canada had started to see a trickling decline in voter turnout, which slipped below 70 percent in the 1980 election. But Canadian politics was still caught up with loftier, more existential democratic questions in the 1980s, mainly revolving around the constitution and the Charter of Rights and Freedoms. The election of René Lévesque's separatist government in Quebec and the resulting 1980 sovereignty referendum had focused the collective political mind on keeping the country together. First with Trudeau's patriation of the constitution, and then with Brian Mulroney's efforts to recon-cile Quebec to the constitutional deal, Canadian politics through the 1980s was far more focused on the traditional stuff of politics: rights, powers and national unity. So Canadian politics wouldn't be making the full transition into the marketing realm for a while.

Advertising, though—that was becoming huge in Canadian politics in the 1980s. The government had caught the advertis-ing bug. Under Pierre Trudeau, government had increasingly seen advertising as the solution to all problems, a proclivity that would carry on for decades. Canada now had something called the Federal Identity Program, complete with an officially sanctioned brand label for the country: a "word mark" featuring the word Canada and a small flag over the final "a." The Liberals set up Information Canada to co-ordinate all public communications from government, which were often earnest efforts to get Canadians behaving better. (That office had arisen from a 1979 Task Force report, "To Know and Be Known," which urged the government to embrace the tools of modern public relations.) Participaction, for instance, was a nation-wide exhortation to fitness and good health, all conducted through advertising. By far, though, the grandest Trudeau-government advertising spending was the constitutional exercise, which earned its own special unit, the Canadian Unity Information Office, spending more than $32 million when all was said and done, to knit together the country and to fight Quebec separatism.

The big ad firms were recruited to the cause first of selling Canadians on the idea that we needed our own constitution, then on selling the deal that was hammered out by Ottawa and all the provinces except Quebec. In the fall of 1980, the Trudeau government unleashed a wave of TV ads produced by the MacLaren firm, featuring nature scenes, landscapes and flocks of Canadian geese. These were all about emotion and love of country. No one was going to try to draw Canadian consumer-citizens into complicated constitution-speak through these TV pitches. While a folksy version of "O Canada" played in the background in one, for instance, a narrator intoned, "Freedom is an important part of our heritage as Canadians. The right of each and every one of us [is] to strive, to rise, to be free, riding the winds of freedom, working together to make our hopes and dreams come true for all Canadians." These were appeals to citizens to get behind Trudeau's constitutional quest—advertising in the service of a national project. However high-minded the goal, the campaign looked more like Madison Avenue than Main Street. In some ads, the word "constitution" wasn't even mentioned. Moreover, this unprecedented ad splurge was raising eyebrows all over Canada, where people were objecting to their government—not just politicians—being sold to them like soap.

J.L. Foley, chairman of the Institute of Canadian Advertising, delivered a speech in Calgary lambasting the "unbelievable growth" in government advertising budgets—$29 million in 1979, making the government the largest single advertiser in Canada. Only a decade before, Foley said, the government had been the number-seventeen advertiser in the country. Foley condemned the Trudeau government's plan to create a central agency of record to handle all its advertising and the practice of granting accounts as partisan favours (which had been going on for decades). In his speech, he also cast all these advertising efforts as a way to bypass the people who should be communicating with the public—the members of Parliament. All this money being spent on advertising was "a further emasculation of Parliament and parliamentary democracy," he said.

When the Trudeau government tried to kick off a special debate in the Commons on the constitution in the fall of 1980, the opposition held up proceedings for two hours so they could hammer away at the explosion in advertising and polling costs. Here, too, the ads and polls were called an affront to parliamentary democracy. Toronto Conservative MP John Bosley wondered whether "we now have a new policy that public money will be used to tell people what they ought to think?" The NDP's finance critic, a fellow named Bob Rae, said, "I'll never look at a beaver or Canada goose in the same way again. I'll see them as Liberals in disguise."

Trudeau, for his part, had kicked off this raucous debate with a somewhat provocative insistence that he had nothing to do with polls. "I don't give a damn about polls. And I don't take polls." Of course the Liberals were indeed relying on polls, as Martin Goldfarb's increasing clout would attest. "Government by Goldfarb" was a real phenomenon. Allan Gregg was also on his way to becoming a national celebrity. Canadians were becoming altogether enamoured of polls, and everyone was getting into the act.

Newspapers and the media were commissioning their own polls—yet another innovation that came to Canada courtesy of

Goldfarb and the *Toronto Star*. Through research with *Toronto Star* readers, Goldfarb had learned that newspaper audiences wanted to read stories that were "exclusive"—stories they couldn't get in other media. They wanted to read about themselves, too, and their own lives, without a filter. Thus was born the regular *Star* poll, appearing four times a year or so, featuring raw survey results on matters deemed to be of interest to the paper's readers. Soon other newspapers joined in, commissioning expensive polls with questions designed by the editors of the paper and then duly reported on, at great length, often with multiple stories and charts, within the editorial pages.

"It made no difference what the subject may be, politics, censorship, health, spending, consumer behaviour or whatever, people wanted to hear and read and learn about themselves," Goldfarb wrote in his book *Affinity*. "This is what polling does. It allows people to find out whether they themselves are typical or atypical of the general public. They find out all of this by reading the results of polls."

Politicians of the 1980s may have wanted to continue to see their profession in high-minded, institutional terms—civics as akin to religion, education or even military service. But by the 1970s, thanks to a variety of factors, this more exalted view of politics had taken a bit of a battering. There was the Watergate scandal in the United States, for instance, which had led to the 1974 resignation of Richard Nixon. On top of Watergate's corrosive effect on the public view of politicians, it also paved the way for a more aggressive, oppositional form of political journalism, in which the media was more actively looking for scandal and corruption in the halls of power. That kind of coverage was confirming and fuelling public cynicism toward government—and the sense that business could probably handle things better.

Closer to home, high inflation and gas prices—and the government's seeming powerlessness to stop them—had put Canadian consumers in a surly mood. Furthermore, Canadians—and especially the baby-boom generation, who were in their adulthood—had been immersed in several decades of expanding freedom and choice, in the grocery aisles and in their public and private lives. Trudeau, who had helped bring in the legislation that made it easier for Canadians to divorce, appeared to be heading in that direction himself, with the very public deterioration of his marriage to Margaret. Television had bred a new familiarity with politicians that was also headed away from deference—and even into contempt.

Television and the mass media had democratized the public sphere, in ways that everyone was still trying to assess. Canadians had more access to information and news than ever, but they were also passive spectators. The political conversations they were seeing on their television screens and reading in the media were taking place before their eyes, but without their active participation. As US cultural critic Neil Postman would put it in his similarly named book, they were being "amused to death."

The voters liked entertainment. They liked business and shopping even better. Perhaps all that Cold War propaganda had seeped into the citizenry, with all the talk of how better shopping choices made for a more successful democracy. It may have been that people thought businesses were more responsive to their needs than their governments—given that they had far more transactions with the private sector, every day at the cash register. Allan Gregg told journalist Richard Gwyn in 1982 that his quarterly surveys at Decima were showing people losing faith in all the government-run industries, but rising confidence in the private sector—even advertising companies. "People don't trust businessmen and never have," Gregg said. "But they do give them high marks for effectiveness. I think what's happening is that people are starting to say, 'Let's give businessmen a try and see if they can't get us out of this mess.'"

This was the same year that the constitution was formally patriated and the year when CBC launched its flagship show *The Journal*, featuring host Barbara Frum and lengthy "double-ender" interviews with leading newsmakers of the day. Within months of its launch, *The Journal* was drawing 1.6 million viewers each night, almost double the audience that CBC had dared to imagine for it. The Commodore 64 computer, a forerunner to the modern PC, was making its debut in stores, while the number-one TV series in the US and Canada was *Dallas,* the saga of a wealthy Texas oil family.

In this atmosphere, as Trudeau's reign was winding down, and with the business-friendly Reagan installed in the White House, it probably wasn't a surprise that Canada's two main parties went looking for their own business types to take over the leadership. Eighteen months after that Gwyn article, the PCs chose Iron Ore Co. president Brian Mulroney to be their new leader, and a year later the Liberals plucked John Turner back from Bay Street and installed him as Trudeau's successor.

At the same time, politics was starting to attract more MPs with managerial backgrounds. In the 1950s and 1960s, for instance, there were roughly three times as many lawyers in the House as MPs whose career experience was in business or management. By the 1984 election, the numbers were roughly equal. Gregg's prediction was coming true: the 1980s would be a time when governments increasingly picked up on the language, practices and people of business. In so doing, the political class would encourage citizens to develop even more consumer-like expectations of their federal government.

Direct Marketing

For all their differences, there is one objective that political parties and businesses share—the need for cash flow. Staffers need salaries, advertising gobbles up money and party offices are expensive to run. So it is in the area of fundraising that political parties have had the most to learn from the marketplace.

By the 1980s, the Conservatives had mastered the ability to make direct contact with voters, thanks to US Republican know-how and the import of raw consumer-marketing techniques into politics. In the United States, an early pioneer of direct-mail methods was Robert Odell, a Republican, who kicked off the practice with mass-mailings of hand-typed, personalized form letters to potential donors in the 1960s. The real boost to his efforts came through fundraising appeals during political ad campaigns. As the flood of small donations poured in, so the mailing lists grew. By 1972, the Republicans had raised $8 million for Nixon's re-election campaign through direct-mail contributions. Throughout the fallout of the Watergate scandal, Odell solicited donations with long, carefully crafted letters that cast the potential donors as "friends" whose "help" was required.

Canadian Conservatives took note, and in 1973 when John Laschinger was the national director for the party, he took a trip to Columbus, Ohio, and learned the magic of the Ruby Red Grapefruit Company. Because this was an enterprise that operated by mail order, offering home delivery of Florida fruit, it had a valuable database of customers who trusted the mail and who had cash to spare, the kind of people that politicos need to fill party coffers. Laschinger learned that these private-sector lists were available for sale and managed to pry $50,000 out of the cash-strapped Conservative coffers to go "prospecting," as it's called. He purchased all the names of the Canadian clients on the Ruby Red Grapefruit mailing list as well as rafts of magazine subscription contacts and whatever other names and addresses he could lay his hands on in Canada. Laschinger bought the names of all the Canadian subscribers to *Playboy*, believe it or not (presumably the people who bought the magazine for the articles, as the old joke goes). He also sought out "list brokers"— people who purchased lists from the private sector and then sold them at a premium to charities or other groups who wanted to get into fundraising. The usual price was roughly one dollar a name. But if it yielded a fifty-dollar donation, that was an enormous profit. The Conservatives even enlisted Odell's help as a consultant to help design the direct-mail system.

The federal New Democratic Party was also exploring this new fundraising system, inspired by methods borrowed from the charitable sector. Stephen Thomas, a former geography and history teacher, was working at the Oxfam international aid organization when he started to see how the right kind of direct mail could yield a steady flow of donations. In the 1974 election, Thomas lent that wisdom to the NDP, directing a mass-mailing of letters that were signed by famous Canadians with an environmental or leftist bent: popular scientist David Suzuki and authors such as Farley Mowat and Margaret Laurence. Five years later, Thomas's work had netted the NDP enough money to wage its first truly national campaign, active in all parts of Canada. Thomas went on to found his own firm and become one of Canada's fundraising giants, honoured for the work he did to help the Red Cross, Amnesty International and Greenpeace, to name just a few organizations.

Slowly, steadily over the decade after discovering direct mail, the Conservatives built their list to eighty thousand names by the early 1980s and had raised $7 million in direct-mail donations for the election that brought Mulroney to power. That was a massive sum—the party spent only a little more than $6 million for the entire 1984 election campaign.

As Laschinger explained in his book *Leaders and Lesser Mortals*, the idea of reaching out to "members" was marketing psychology. "People like to belong to groups and they are flattered to be asked to join a cause. Credit-card companies, such as Diners Club and American Express (membership has its privileges) have long exploited the 'belonging' instinct," he wrote. "The card idea worked in political fundraising in the United States, so the Tories appropriated it and introduced a PC Canada Fund card." Although some were skeptical of the chances of success, it turned out that potential Conservative recruits were delighted with the cards, even if they were "meaningless and valueless piece[s] of pasteboard."

The Conservatives borrowed another American political marketing innovation, "exclusive" membership, to take this idea one step further. They created a "500 Club" for anyone who donated $1,000 or more a year. The lucky, well-heeled folks with this elite-level membership, which the credit-card companies were finding to be a boon, too, would get special invitations to receptions and increased access to people in power. In the 1988 election, the 500 Club was such a successful method of fundraising that it added $6 million on its own to the Conservative coffers. The Liberals, as usual, would pay the compliment of imitation, setting up a "Laurier Club," with the same donation threshold: $1,000 annually.

Direct-mail marketing, the Conservatives were finding in the 1980s, was an ideal way to attract money and also stay in touch with the base—making members feel special or influential. Laschinger and fellow Tories would constantly be surprised to see how partisans treasured their political memorabilia and souvenirs, whether it was a photo with a politician or a sticker they got in the mail.

Flexible and Angry

The 1984 election was a display of two other big forces that would shape the future decades of Canadian politics: a more volatile electorate and a more adversarial media. First, the volatility: the days of predictable loyalty to parties were over, and getting a pan-Canadian picture was much more difficult. The Canadian body politic had become more "flexible," in the marketing parlance of the time. Lawrence LeDuc, from the University of Toronto and one of Canada's leading political-behaviour experts, titled his study of the 1984 election "The Flexible Canadian Electorate." LeDuc's study painted a picture of a populace that was now wildly shifting its party preferences, often within the space of months or even weeks—"highly sensitive in their attitudes and behaviour to a variety of short-term forces." With the freedom to choose, it seemed, came the prerogative of changing one's mind, over and over again.

As Allan Gregg had been noting, too, Canada was moving well out of the days when 80 percent of the electorate could easily define their political allegiance. It was in Quebec, incidentally, where the pollsters first started to see political fealty unravelling in a large way—perhaps as a fallout of the Quiet Revolution of the 1960s, when the province also shrugged off its old religious underpinnings. By the mid-1980s, only about 40 percent of Quebecers were telling Gregg and other pollsters that they were loyal to one political brand or another. "That was the first time we saw the potential for the Conservatives to win [the next election] because people ceased to be anything," Gregg said.

And then there was the sharper edge to the media. It had become far more adversarial and personal—no doubt at least in part as a fallout of Watergate, too. Throughout the two months of the campaign, the media was in hot pursuit of gaffes, primarily by Turner and the Liberals. Bob Hepburn, the *Toronto Star*'s Ottawa bureau chief at the time, said in an analysis of the 1984 campaign, "With Turner, we always went after him as a group. We smelled blood and we attacked. With Mulroney, we attacked at the end, but at the end people had already made up their minds."

Mulroney became prime minister in September 1984, and within four months he flew to the New York Economic Club and declared before the blue-chip audience that Canada was now "open for business." Although the comment infuriated Canadian nationalists and the old Liberal establishment, Mulroney was unapologetically pro-American, especially when it came to promoting business and political ties between the two countries. He had a warm friendship with Ronald Reagan, famously illustrated at the so-called Shamrock Summit on St. Patrick's Day 1985 in Quebec City, when the two leaders sang "When Irish Eyes Are Smiling."

The volatile, personal and aggressive new state of politics would take a toll on Mulroney's early reign, especially in a chain of early cabinet resignations, over everything from strip club visits (Defence

Minister Robert Coates) to tainted tuna (Fisheries Minister John Fraser). Mulroney would be also dogged by more personal media coverage, whether it was renovations at 24 Sussex Drive or the patronage jobs he was handing out to friends.

Canada's consumer society continued to grow. Despite nascent hints of a growing environmentalism among the public and in politics—Mulroney used some of his goodwill capital with the United States to forge an acid rain treaty, for instance—Canadians were still spending increasing amounts of time shopping. It was during these Mulroney-government years that the courts started striking down all the laws against Sunday shopping—also an important, symbolic step on the path to creating a consumer-citizenry.

Throughout the latter half of the twentieth century, religion was steadily loosening its bonds on the Canadian population as a whole. Statistics Canada charted the decline in its census reports every decade. In 1941, fewer than twenty thousand people told the Canadian census-takers that they had no religion. In 1951, that number had nearly tripled. By 1971, almost one million Canadians were in the "no religion" category—a tenfold increase since 1961. Subsequent decades would see the numbers continuing to climb, so that by the dawn of the twenty-first century, in the 2001 census, people with "no religion" accounted for 16 percent of the Canadian population, or almost five million people.

Martin Goldfarb, with his anthropologist's eye, was learning through his research that the demand for Sunday shopping was a result of increasing numbers of working women and single-parent households in Canada. Their immediate concerns were logistical— where do we find the time to shop when we're finished working? But the denial of Sunday shopping spoke to their values, too: why was the law curtailing their freedom, or discriminating against them? Goldfarb's polling at this time repeatedly showed more than three-quarters of respondents heartily behind Sunday shopping. Canada's changing immigration patterns were multiplying the ways in which Canadians observed their religion. The old idea of every-body at a Christian church on Sundays simply wasn't reflecting many realities in the modern consumer nation. The populace didn't want to be in a dusty old institution on Sundays anymore; people wanted to go shopping.

The Supreme Court of Canada struck down the federal Lord's Day Act in 1985, effectively forcing provinces and municipalities to sort out their own laws on whether stores, bars, restaurants and malls should be open on Sundays. Sunday shopping, while hailed as a liberating, modernizing move, broke down another barrier between old pillars of society and modern consumerism. No longer was there a day put aside for non-shopping activities. Canadians were on their way to becoming 24-7 consumers.

During his two terms in office, despite the shift to a shopping culture, Mulroney would prove to be more of a provocateur than a panderer to Canadian consumers. His Conservative party may have been aggressively importing marketing know-how from the United States, but it was all in the service, for the most part, of "selling" conservatism to the mass market. Mulroney's party, in other words, was more about sales than marketing—more SOP than MOP. In government, while he was routinely accused of paying too much heed to the polls, Mulroney pursued policies that were decidedly at odds with mainstream opinion, and Gregg's market-research findings. He also wasn't totally in sync with his friends Reagan and Thatcher, who were having much more success tailoring their conservatism to market demand. Thatcher would often joke with Mulroney that he was too progressive; he would shoot back that Canada was a large and complicated country.

Free trade with the United States, for instance, sharply divided Canadian consumers when the negotiations started during Mulroney's first mandate. The Consumers' Association of Canada had historically supported the idea of free trade, but it was only a lukewarm sup-porter of the actual deal being hammered out between the Mulroney government and the United States. It pointedly refused on a number of occasions to endorse the Canada–US free-trade deal—reflecting a deep ambivalence within the membership. And once the election got under way—the famous free-trade election of 1988—the Consumers' Association remained mutely on the sidelines.

The External Affairs department, bracing for consumer worry, had in early 1988 pulled together a study loaded with reassurances about free trade's positive potential for consumers. According to the department, free trade would eventually bring about a 3 percent dip in the cost of living for low-income people, $800 in annual savings for middle- and high-income families, $85–$130 in annual savings in food spending and $8,000 in savings in the cost of setting up and furnishing a home. More competition would bring lower prices and more choice in the shopping aisles, External Affairs predicted.

But for all of free trade's potential to disrupt or improve the Canadian-consumer universe, the 1988 election wasn't really about consumerism or consumer-citizenship at all. In keeping with the larger, Canadian existential mood at the time, it was about sovereignty—not Quebec sovereignty, but the sovereignty of the entire Canadian nation in the face of the American giant to the south.

The 1988 campaign was another leap ahead in terms of snazzy machinery. Gregg's polling operation was at its apex. Decima was seen as the pre-eminent polling firm in the country. Gregg had understood that Canada was in the midst of a shift away from mass marketing, toward niche specialization. The culture shift would apply to politics, too. In an interview with the *Globe and Mail*, Gregg laid out the impressive capabilities of his polling research and its ability to micromanage the Canadian electorate: "We can target not just the possible swing ridings, but the swing polls within those ridings, and key voters within those polls. We can identify on a block-by-block basis their historical voting behaviour, their demographic profile, their inferred preference—and reach them, not by the old mass media techniques, but by telephone and direct mail."

And here's a not insignificant point: the pollsters and the party now had the machinery to do this better than individual MPs or local riding associations. The old party hands were no longer the experts. It was much like the tension on display in the 2011 movie *Moneyball*, when the baseball-stats whiz keeps confounding the veteran talent scouts with superior information about the pitching and batting records of potential recruits.

Gregg was using his stats to plan Mulroney's travel schedule, arranging to have the prime minister pay a call on the ridings more important to the party and its future electoral hopes. If his research picked up a softening of Conservative support in the British Columbia interior, the PMO would arrange to have Mulroney fly in for a visit to shake some hands and bolster spirits. Where once this intelligence had been gathered by long-time partisans on the ground, following their political noses, sophisticated market research such as Gregg's could show their information to be outdated, even irrelevant or wrong. The Liberals, with their calculations about "winnable" ridings and where to devote resources, had already been going down the same path.

"This line here. It's just getting in the way."

The 1988 election in Canada was notable for a sharper turn in the political advertising, with the Liberals unleashing a go-for-the-jugular attack on the Conservatives' attachment to the nation. Their big-guns ad was one in which Canadian and American free-trade negotiators were seated at a table featuring a map of North America. In the ad, the American says, "There's one line I'd like to change." The Canadian asks, "Which line is that?" And then a pencil eraser begins to erase the forty-ninth parallel. The American then says, "This line here. It's just getting in the way." The script was written by Terry O'Malley at Vickers and Benson, and it was written with his St. Catharines hometown in mind, where people feared what free trade might do to the thousands of jobs dependent on the huge General Motors operation in that city.

Gregg was conducting focus groups throughout the campaign. The first time he showed the Liberal ad to a group, they laughed. The second time, they went silent. Based in part on that reaction, the Conservatives decided to fight fire with fire. They quickly pulled together an ad showing the border being redrawn, with the tagline "This is where we draw the line." And then they released a wave of their own ads, mocking the Liberals' fitness to govern. Whether anyone liked it or not, Canadian politics had now embraced the utility of the attack ad.

In Gregg's view, attack ads only work when they confirm suspicions already lurking among the electorate. So in a big way, they are the offspring of market research—you have to plumb the depths of voters' emotions to find the vulnerable spots of your opponents. Attack ads are also the byproduct of the cynicism toward politicians that had started to surface in Canada in the 1980s. In all his polling and focus groups, Gregg kept seeing reasons to believe that "bombing the bridge," as it was called, would find a target with the voters. "It became very, very clear very early on that negative advertising was more comprehensive and comprehensible because people could understand it," he said. "But it was also more credible. It was way more credible to say your opponent was a crook than to establish your own bona fides as virtuous."

The "bridge" being bombed was also probably the last link to the older, simpler world in which political advertising could not stray into the baser arts of the consumer marketplace. Around this time, people also started to notice that marketing jargon had totally infiltrated the political backrooms. Journalist and author Graham Fraser, in his book on the 1988 election, *Playing for Keeps*, remarked on the phenomenon, "It is worth noting that the language of marketing, polling and product sales had sufficiently taken over the senior levels of all three parties [so] that all the strategists, regardless of the party affiliation, talked about the marketplace, market niche and moving numbers. It sounded as if the election process of choosing policies on the basis of their merits had been privatized."

Lorne Bozinoff, a thirty-something pollster with Gallup during the 1988 election, was also fusing marketing and politics when author-journalist Claire Hoy interviewed him for his book *Margin of Error*. "If you understand politics, you'll see marketing and politics are very similar. Not in a derogatory way, not the hard sell we associate with marketing," Bozinoff told Hoy. "Politics is looking at people's needs and how to meet those needs, selling ideas. Selling leaders is sort of like selling a product."

In fact, though, negative attacks and the hard sell would become easier to do in the public sector than it was in the private sector. Allister Grosart's long-ago warnings to 1953 Conservatives were being turned upside down. Now, you could be even more reckless selling politics than you could be vending soap or cigarettes (ads for the latter were well on the way to being banned altogether by the late 1980s). Thanks to the continued notion of politics as a higher calling—which was rapidly becoming antiquated—politics remained exempt from the Advertising Standards Canada code. That allowed political advertisers to slip under a lower bar. While a bank or a grocery store couldn't take out an ad to savage an opponent, for example, a political party could. If the floodgates opened to all-out attack ads in the private sector, the reasoning went, there was a real damage that everyone's profits would be hurt. Planting seeds of doubt about a competitor's wares could cultivate suspicion about the product altogether, for instance.

Obviously, a political parallel is possible. If politicians are running down each other's offerings, the citizens may sour on the whole civic "product." This was a large fear when attack ads first started in earnest on TV in the 1980s and remained a worry into the next century. Some partisans and political scientists have argued that negative ads, with their appeal to emotion, actually can wake up a sleepy electorate, rousing them to join or fight off the attacks. But other researchers have found that negative ads may simply suppress voter participation, sending people to check out from politics altogether.

The difference may lie in the target of the attack ad. If it's a policy or a principle or an ideal under assault, it may well be that a jolt of emotion will fire up people on both sides. But the nasty personal attacks may be of a different order. Because it's not something people see often in their ordinary lives or even in the commercial realm, negative advertising of the personal sort may simply convince citizens that they're seeing yet more evidence of politics' detachment from the real world. In the 1980s, however, the really harsh stuff hadn't yet got under way in earnest in Canada, and political ads ran only in official election periods. That too would change.

You Want Us to Pay What?

Engagement was high in the 1988 election, though—75 percent, reflecting a lively debate on the future of the country. Mulroney and the Conservatives received their second majority government and the free-trade deal was sealed by the end of the year. That left Mulroney free to pursue a plan that would definitely antagonize Canadian consumer-citizens. The collision would take place in the stores and at the cash register—and have far-reaching reverberations through the Canadian body politic. It was called the goods and services tax (GST). Its fate, in the years ahead, would be a revealing glimpse into how politicians increasingly had to see citizens as consumers, or, in the building lexicon of this era, "taxpayers."

Allan Gregg, plugged into the consumer and political market-place, was acutely aware that the GST was going to be a hard sell. But Prime Minister Mulroney, while a believer in polling, wasn't all that interested in any numbers except old-fashioned personal approval ratings for himself and his rivals. These were the only polling figures he regularly asked Gregg to provide. When it came to making decisions about government policy, Mulroney tended to go his own way.

Even before the 1988 campaign, Mulroney's government had announced its intention to wind down the tax on Canada's manufacturers and instead place a tax on goods and services, but the proposal didn't get a lot of attention amid the roar of the free-trade election. The shift of the tax from manufacturing to consumption reflected the shifting view of Canada's economic future at the time. Manufacturing was the boom driver of the immediate postwar years—consumption, or plain old spending, would be the future. This was the beginning of the Second Industrial Divide, after all, and consumer demand, not mass marketing, would shape the markets of the future.

Around the mid-1980s, Canadian manufacturers were starting to get into the consumption business, with direct-from-factory sales to shoppers. Already, the shopping universe was expanding for Canadian consumers, paving the way for the big-box-store revolution to come. A glance through the pages of any newspaper in those years would feature ads boasting "factory direct" sales from bedding manufacturers, or big discounts from the No Frills superstore: "Closest Thing to Wholesale." Everyone, it seems, was in the mood to cut out the middleman (or middlewoman)—the retailer with the provincial sales-tax burden. The giant Costco Wholesale chain had arrived in Canada, with its wildly successful retail formula of select membership lists and rock-bottom prices. For a minimal Costco membership fee, shoppers could feel elite and special even as they were saving money. Home-grown competitors would soon arrive. The Canadian Warehouse Club, a Costco imitator with more than ten thousand square metres of shopping space, opened in Vancouver in 1988 and attracted six thousand shoppers and $300,000 in sales each day of its opening weekend.

In that climate, with shoppers feeling simultaneously special but stingy, the idea of imposing a new federal tax on Canada's citizen-shoppers was going to provoke "a helluva political row," as Mulroney described it later in his memoirs. "Voters would never accept that this was just a simple replacement of the MST, a tax that they had never even heard of. Here was a tax on everything that moved, from your laundry bill to the doughnut you bought at the coffee shop." It was, in other words, a blow to Tim Hortons Canadians.

Mulroney was correct. His own Conservative caucus, taking soundings in their ridings at the Christmas break in 1987, reported back that constituents would not tolerate this new tax being imposed on food. The provinces also balked, resisting any initial suggestion about "harmonizing" the new tax with provincial sales-tax systems. This may have been the right thing to do, but who was going to explain that to Canadians, who were simply looking at their receipts and seeing more money leaving their wallets? Gregg, with his poll-ster's ear tuned to the electorate, also warned Mulroney that the GST was a perilous path, but the PM wouldn't be swayed. Friends would often joke to Gregg that he was working for a politician who was a slave to the polls. The mere suggestion made Gregg laugh. "Do you think I came to him and said this is what the consumer population really wants? They want to pay a bigger tax on everything they purchase?"

The GST, just like free trade and the constitution, simply made Gregg's job more difficult. As the Conservatives kept getting on the wrong side of surly consumer-citizens, Gregg was having a harder and harder time giving Mulroney the good news he sought when he was asking about popularity. And besides, the public wasn't in the mood to hear from the politicians anymore.

Meanwhile, in Alberta...

It is here in the story of political marketing's emergence that our gaze has to turn westward. Toronto may have been the birthplace for the influence of advertising and marketing in Canadian politics, but the future was starting to be written in Alberta in the late 1980s. A fledgling political movement called the Reform Party was tapping into many of the forces that would feed the power of political marketing for years to come. Reform's founder was Preston Manning, son of the long-reigning Social Credit premier Ernest Manning. The young Manning had tried and failed to go into the family business in the 1960s, with a losing run for a provincial seat, and had settled into life as a management consultant in Calgary. The dual experience gave him a chance to see politics as a business—and business as politics. Wearing his management-consultant's hat, he tended to deconstruct the established order of things. When he decided to make another political run in the 1980s, Manning resolved to deconstruct the federal Progressive Conservative party and Mulroney's grand governing coalition.

Manning got together with a couple of bright thinkers from the University of Calgary, two men by the names of Tom Flanagan and Stephen Harper, a professor and a graduate student, respectively, and began planning how to sever the Western base from the federal Tories—with a whole new political party. They were building a niche market in the midst of the old mass-market PC party. All of these Reform Party founders believed that the old Liberal–Conservative compact in Canada was disintegrating, and that "realignment" was coming. Manning had co-written a book with his father titled *Political Re-Alignment: A Challenge to Thoughtful Canadians*. They weren't actively planning for a future era of consumer politics, but they were laying important groundwork, especially in the arguments for Canada to be more sharply divided between right and left and for politics to rest on rugged individualism.

The consumer revolt over the GST was super-charged fuel for Manning and Reform. In 1989, Manning was one of the lead speakers at a giant "Axe the Tax" rally in Alberta, the first of many mass rallies against the hated tax. "The federal government should not be given additional tax revenues or levers like the GST unless and until it demonstrates the ability to control its spending," Manning told the crowd. About 1,500 angry Albertans had flooded into Edmonton's convention centre, vowing to use their consumer power to punish the Mulroney government.

Like all ambitious political parties in Canada before it, the Reform Party was also trying to see what it could learn from the United States. Virgil Anderson, one of Manning's chief strategists, had met a Republican political consultant, Frank Luntz, at a campaign management seminar in Washington and pulled him into the planning backrooms in 1991. Luntz was then just getting his start in the polling and political-advice business, and he'd worked with the legendary Richard Wirthlin, the man who had plied his polling magic for Reagan. Luntz had a Ph.D. in political science from Oxford, and he'd penned a well-received book called *Candidates, Consultants and Campaigns.* His real expertise, like that of Wirthlin, was in delving beneath the simple numbers to find underlying emotions and values in public opinion. In an $80,000-plus poll for Reform, Luntz had found strong support in the Canadian populace for no fewer than a dozen of the party's policies, especially the ones that played to the discontent also simmering in the consumer world, like those on reducing debt, balanced budgets and stronger guarantees from politicians.

Flanagan noted that Manning liked to talk in terms of "selling" policies, an approach the political scientist called "populism as methodology." He would criticize Mulroney's initiatives with a curt dismissal: "They'll never be able to sell that." By and large, though, Manning's politics weren't pitched at consumer-citizens. He preferred to tell his potential supporters that they were producers of democracy. If someone on a doorstep asked what he was selling, Manning was fond of turning the question back on the voter: "What are you going to contribute?" In this, though, Manning was tapping into the distemper of the times—the disgruntled, disengaged voters who believed that they could do a better job of running the country than the politicians had done. In just a decade, Canadians appeared to have gone through a staged process of withdrawal of faith in government. At the outset of the 1980s, they thought businesses were better suited to run things; by the end of the 1980s, it was the citizens themselves who thought they should be running the country.

But Manning's appeal to voters also vacillated on that age-old advertising question—the Barnum-versus-Powers conundrum—of whether the audience needed information or confirmation of their worst instincts. Manning borrowed a bit from both approaches. He said he wanted to generate a higher level of debate, but he also made dead-politician quips. (One of Manning's typical jokes on the circuit: "What's the difference between a dead skunk on the road and a dead politician on the road? There are skid marks in front of the skunk.") Manning's politics exhibited a mix of his religious, public-service upbringing and the modern world of marketing management. Like typical Canadian voters at the time, he was going back and forth between the fading model of politics as an institution and politics as just another shopping outlet.

There was also some tension within the fledgling Reform movement, notably between Manning and his young policy chief, Stephen Harper, which would play out in significant ways in the years ahead, with many implications for political marketing in Canada. In March 1989, Harper prepared a long strategy memo for Manning outlining what he saw as the weaknesses of populism as the core philosophy for the new Reform movement. Some of that memo first appeared in Tom Flanagan's 1995 book on the founding of the Reform Party, titled *Waiting for the Wave*.

Harper said the party should become "a modern version of the Thatcher–Reagan phenomenon." Essentially, without labelling them as such, Harper wanted Reform to go out and find the Canadian version of the Essex Men and the Reagan Democrats among working-class and urban-dwelling Canadians, giving them a "market-oriented" ideology. Reform, Harper wrote, should be concentrating on gaining "a sizeable chunk of the urban working class and rural sector 'swing' vote, without alienating its urban private-sector, middle-class 'core.' The key is to emphasize moderate, conservative social values, consistent with the traditional family, the market economy and patriotism."

A Fury in the Land

Mulroney was aware that the ground was shifting in Canada and that his government was the target of a free-floating antipathy to everything to do with politics. So he put former *Ottawa Citizen* editor Keith Spicer in charge of a commission called the "Citizen's Forum on National Unity." This too was an attempt to bridge the ambivalence that the political class was feeling about the old political institutions versus the modern consumer market. Spicer's commission was an old-style institutional inquiry into a contemporary sentiment at large in the nation. For a year, the Spicer panel went around the country taking the measure of public distemper toward the nation and its leaders—a giant focus group. Its findings showed a nation still very much attached to the idea of a collective Canadian identity in theory, but bitter and angry about how things were working in practice. Some of that "fury in the land," as Spicer called it, was consumerist in nature. "We are living beyond our means," one citizen in the Northwest Territories town of Hay River told the commission. "The one thing it [the GST] does do is remind me, every time I pay for an item or send out an invoice, how much I hate the government," an Alberta resident said in a letter to the Spicer forum.

As well, in the midst of this anger, a new protest organization had been born: the Canadian Taxpayers Federation, formed when the Association of Saskatchewan Taxpayers and the "Resolution One Association" of Alberta joined forces in 1990. The group gave voice to the increasingly popular idea that the relationship between citizens and government was solely one of customer and service provider. (The "taxpayers" label, incidentally, was also a US import. Kevin Avram, the founder of the Saskatchewan wing, had been at a conference in Austin, Texas, and came across someone from the Association of Concerned Texas Taxpayers. "As soon as I saw that name, I knew it was a sweetheart," Avram would recall later.)

The new Canadian taxpayers' group was non-partisan, but it had much in common with the raison d'être and methods of the nascent Reform Party. Its early tactics, like Reform's, were populist and rural-based—petitions and small donations from disgruntled citizens. And in a throwback to the Dalton Camp strategies of decades earlier in New Brunswick, it also supplied local papers with pre-written commentary pieces, which were often just cut and pasted into the editorial pages. "Let's Talk Taxes," these commentaries were called. Camp's slogan and advertising pen name, remember, had been "Let's Clean House."

The first targets for the Canadian Taxpayers Federation were, naturally, government spending and debt, but also lucrative political pensions and anything deemed to be waste in general. They were tapping into the larger, anti-elite, consumer-citizenry outrage in the Canadian populace. The head of the group's Alberta wing was particularly adept in putting the anger into consumer language. "We've all gotten used to Cadillac services from our governments," a young Jason Kenney, executive director of the federation's Alberta headquarters, said in a *Globe and Mail* interview. "But our Cadillacs are about to be taken back by the repo man."

Kenney himself, just in his early twenties when he was hired to be the public face for the taxpayers' group, learned a valuable lesson about political advertising in these years, which would serve him well as he climbed up the political ladder. At one point, the federation had conducted some major research about public-sector pensions and defined contributions. It was a complicated topic—and when the research paper was finally released, it yielded some minor news coverage and zero public attention. A week or so later, Kenney travelled to Ottawa to speak out against MPs who had opted into the gold-plated pension program. On a whim, Kenney went off to Canadian Tire and forked over $300 for a couple of hundred plastic-pig lawn ornaments, which he then planted on Parliament Hill to represent the "pension hogs" in the Commons. The media pounced. The Taxpayers Federation and Kenney were overwhelmed with requests for interviews for days and days afterward. "After the dozens of hours and thousands of dollars we'd spent on the policy paper, the three hundred bucks I'd spent on plastic pigs was a major news story," Kenney said.

Mulroney's reign in office ended with one last constitutional adventure: the Charlottetown Accord, which went down in flames of rejection for politicians in a national referendum. It would be the last time in the twentieth century, and for some time, that anyone tried to distract Canadian shopper-citizens with matters of nation building. Allan Gregg, at his focus-group sessions in Toronto, was all too aware of the rage building against the politicians involved and had plenty of early hints of what was in store for this deal. He'd done his usual thing, inviting senior political strategists to watch what ordinary folks were saying about the Charlottetown Accord, which had consumed so much of the Canadian political class's attention. Millions of dollars had been spent cobbling together the 1992 accord; millions more in the effort to sell it. (Vickers and Benson had been recruited for that advertising job, too, incidentally.) Behind the glass, again, Gregg and the strategists watched as all their focus-group participants were asked about the accord. None had heard of the deal; none could even say what was in it. One person did volunteer that he'd heard that Canada would have two senates: one for Quebec, one for the rest of the country (that was false).

But when these citizens were asked how they were going to vote, they had some very definite views. All were going to vote "no." Why? "Because those bastards [politicians] want it so badly, we're not going to give it to them," one focus-group participant said. There it was, in a nutshell—the citizens were starting to see Canadian politics as a simple transaction: voters give, politicians take. Citizens were becoming "taxpayers."

THE BRAND-WAGON

I f the future of Canadian politics would rest in a merger with shop-ping, Allan Gregg had a good head start. The *Decima Quarterly* reports produced by Gregg's firm, available for a $20,000 annual subscription, were a compendium of incredibly valuable informa-tion about the mood of the Canadian consumer. On behalf of his blue-chip corporate clients, Gregg was getting a chance to probe the Canadian psyche in depth about everything from the cost of living to attitudes toward immigration. Up to this point, most analyses of voter motivation had relied primarily on the solid, old statistics of the Canadian Election Study, carried out by political scientists and academics at each election from 1965 onward. Their inquiries into the mood of the citizenry were largely confined to the public mood about politics, from which the voters were increasingly disengaged. The Canadian Election Study didn't look into consumer preferences. The *Decima Quarterly* surveys, meanwhile, weren't strictly intended to help Gregg in his political advisory work, but they turned into a treasure trove of tips proving handy to politics as well. And that's because those worlds were moving closer and closer together in the 1990s: what people wanted as consumers, they tended to want as voters. This put Gregg at the nexus of the blurring distinction between consumers and citizens.

"Voter choice is really no different from consumer choice," Gregg would tell his political friends—a sentiment remarkably similar to what Martin Goldfarb had expressed in the 1970s about selling politicians like cans of tomatoes on a shelf. "It's no different to the extent that what you have is a relatively rational calculation between the intersection of self-interest and self-image." In people's capacity as voters or consumers, whether trying to pick a brand of soap or decide where to put their "X" on the ballot, Gregg said their choice would boil down to two crucial questions: "Are they like me and are they for me?" A good politician would position the "brand," Gregg said, "in such a way that your target voter is saying 'yes' to both questions."

The use of the word "brand" to describe a political party was still new in the 1990s, but it was quickly catching on in popularity and expanding as a concept. It was going viral, we might say today. Where once a brand was known as a product name or trademark, it was now seen as a set of ideas. US marketing guru Seth Godin would describe it this way: "A brand is the set of expectations, memories, stories and relationships that, taken together, account for a consumer's decision to choose one product or service over another."

Martin Goldfarb, equally entrenched in the consumer and political worlds in Canada, was seeing the same kind of trends at the end of the twentieth century. He was starting to realize the politicians' folly in believing they could sort the Canadian public according to their mere geography or political leanings. All through the 1980s, Goldfarb and his firm had been honing their skills in "psychographics," which the anthropologist/pollster saw as the bold new frontier in public opinion research. Psychographics were the result of polling people about their beliefs and value structures. Through these methods, Goldfarb had divided the Canadian consumer-citizen market into six basic groups by the dawn of the 1990s:

- Day-to-day watchers: Realistic, generally satisfied people, attentive to the world around them but content to be followers rather than leaders. About 24 percent of the Canadian population could be described this way in the 1990s, Goldfarb said.

- Old-fashioned puritans: People resistant to change, "conservative to the point of being defensive, traditional to the point of being inflexible, indifferent to the point of apathy." These people, who sounded a lot like Margaret Thatcher's Essex Men, represented 15 percent of the population.

- Responsible survivors: Cautious, risk-averse people who accept direction well, who accounted for 13 percent of the population.

- Disinterested self-indulgents: The 17 percent of the population who put their own wants and desires first.

- Joiner activists: The 19 percent of the population who were non-conformists, at the leading edge of opinion change.

- Aggressive achievers: These "confident, success-oriented people," Goldfarb said, were focused on success and accounted for about 12 percent of the Canadian populace.

Essentially, these too were "brands" of people, sorted by their values, not their politics. The 1990s would see a stampede toward these notions of people, politics and products as brands, and a rush by political and private marketers to set up niche markets to suit this fragmented population. Instead of sorting the Canadian map by political support, the strategists would learn to see people for what they wanted from their politics and their supermarkets.

Grocery List for Democracy

One marketing whiz in Canada seemed to have figured out the new Canadian psychographics, too: Loblaws president Dave Nichols. Although the supermarket chain had been floundering a decade earlier, Nichols had tapped into two apparently contradictory consumer trends and rebuilt the grocery empire. First, Nichols had introduced a whole line of generic, "no name" brands, to capitalize on Canadians' desire for value and rejection of the old, established brands. Then, he created his own niche market product line called President's Choice, which appealed to customer demand for more exotic, higher-quality consumables. With these two marketing innovations, Nichols turned around the Loblaws chain and also mapped the way toward methods that would be studied and imitated by the political class in obvious and not-so-obvious ways.

Actually, by the end of the 1980s, Nichols was arguably more of a success than any political party, and his presidency could legitimately claim more adherents than any other political leader of the time. One A.C. Nielsen survey found that Nichols's "Insider Report," a mini-magazine filled with anecdotes, recipes and product recommendations, was diligently read by 59 percent of the Canadian population. (It probably didn't hurt that Vickers and Benson was handling the Loblaws account, once again creating a mini-nation within the Canadian nation for its corporate client.)

Canadians seemed to like this top-down, heed-the-president approach when they were shopping, but they didn't seem to be in the mood for top-down government. All around, Gregg's polling was showing him that Canadians were no longer so keen to see government in charge of public businesses. "In the past, governments created airlines, broadcasting systems, oil companies. Experience has now persuaded Canadians that running businesses is a task better left to the private sector," Gregg wrote in his 1990 book, co-authored with Michael Posner, *The Big Picture*. That book, part state-of-the-nation, part soothsaying for the decade ahead, contained a generous mix of consumer and political wisdom, garnered through those Decima quarterlies:

> In the political realm, we may see a candidate for office who maintains that he or she doesn't believe in conventional politics, will not speak to partisan audiences and will declare all conflicts of interest. In the world of advertising, we may see commercials that do what they have seldom done—tell the truth about their products... In the past, leadership was a calculated balance between empathy and deference. Canadians needed to respect and revere their politicians, their clergymen and their captains of industry. But we also needed to have some sense of personal character—of what they'd be like to have to dinner. In the 1990s, deference will be obsolete... The only thing that will sell—apart from performance—is empathy.

Consumerism and politics were well enmeshed by the 1990s in the United States, too. Ralph Nader, an outspoken consumer advocate, was even starting to take some serious runs for the presidency. His 1992 campaign manifesto made specific reference to "citizen consumers" and the rights of all Americans to more control and information about their democracy. Nader believed in an educated, engaged consumer—not the disengaged, checked-out voters that Reagan and Thatcher had courted. And if Americans had believed Reagan to be a master marketer, they had yet to encounter Bill Clinton. The Clinton campaign represented a new milepost in marketing's merger with politics, as Bruce Newman would explain in his 1994 book *The Marketing of the President*:

The Clinton campaign organization resembled the best-run marketing organizations in this country, such as Proctor & Gamble, McDonald's, Quaker, and others. And as in these finely tuned marketing-driven organizations, Clinton's campaign organizers kept their finger on the pulse of the consumer, the voter. Just as McDonald's uses marketing research to decide where to open up new restaurant locations, Bill Clinton's pollsters used the same technology to determine which states to target with commercials. Just as Quaker uses focus groups to decide which new products to bring to the marketplace, Bill Clinton's researchers used focus groups to decide on how best to communicate their message of change about the economy to the American people.

One of the pollsters conducting those focus groups was Stanley Greenberg, the same man who had studied the Reagan Democrat phenomenon in the 1980s. Greenberg found that these people were coming back to the Democratic fold without much enthusiasm, but more out of disaffection with the status quo. Greenberg was starting to see the shape of the post-partisan world in North America. "They have not re-embraced the Democratic Party," Greenberg told the Associated Press in 1992, as Clinton was nearing his White House goal. "They switched then because they felt sold out by the Democratic Party and now they feel the same way about the Republicans."

In the foreword to *The Marketing of the President*, Jagdish Sheth laid out a series of conditions for marketing's true arrival in democratic politics in the 1990s. First, he said, was the triumph of capitalism in the Cold War and the subsequent elevation of democratic *choice* as the only option for governments. The second factor cited by Sheth was the end of elitism and any notions that people had to be educated or sophisticated about politics to vote. Technological innovation was the third factor—proper marketing requires databases allowing political parties to target individual voters, just as the private sector could turn its focus to individual customers. "This is similar to what other service industries have recently implemented; for example, mail-order catalogue stores (L.L.Bean), airlines (frequent flyer programs), long-distance telephone companies (MCI's 'Friends and Family' or AT&T's 'I' plan), and others." The fourth and most important factor for marketing to be merged with politics, Sheth wrote, was a prevailing mood of cynicism within the public—"to the extent that *caveat emptor* (buyer beware) is regarded as a safer approach to choosing parties and candidates than relying on the opinions of leaders, the press, party, or other institutions. In other words, the average public believes that they must personally take charge and even become vigilante voters."

Canada met all those conditions in the 1990s, as Mulroney and the Conservatives had been learning to their peril. Capitalism and choice were thriving in the consumer society. Anti-elitism was rampant, as the public rejection of the Meech Lake and Charlottetown constitutional accords had proven. Deals hammered out by "elite" politicians were toxic in Canada. Cynicism was also on the rise. Databases were starting to take shape, with the early work done on the "prospecting" front by the Conservatives and the imminent arrival of a national, digital voters list. So Canada was ripe for marketing-style politics.

With Sheth's conditions in mind, let's look at how the decade unfolded in political marketing terms for Canada. On some fronts, the 1990s presented some bold steps forward in the merger of consumerism and citizenship. Yet in other areas, Canada remained rooted to a more traditional, institutional form of politics.

Red Rebranded

The lead-up to the 1993 election and the campaign itself gave the country some marketing milestones. Allan Gregg accurately predicted that the Liberals, with their new leader Jean Chrétien, would probably benefit from the consumer-citizens' desire for authenticity, while his own Conservative party, with the smooth-talking Brian Mulroney, might not. With people souring on the whole idea of politics, Gregg was fond of saying that Canadians had stopped looking for great men and women and would settle for plain old good ones, even if they were a bit rough around the edges. Albertans had already proven this by electing Ralph Klein as their premier—a straight-shooting former mayor of Calgary who made no efforts to hide his fondness for smoking and downing a few beers at the bar. Chrétien, with his mangled English and slightly rumpled image, also appeared as a politician with those kind of everyman credentials. But it would take more than the right leader to win. The Liberals too were a major Canadian political brand at this point in their history, and this was to be a decade of "rebranding" in politics.

Chrétien was elected as Liberal leader at a June 1990 convention in Klein's hometown of Calgary. Literally at that same moment, the same day, the Meech Lake constitutional accord was collapsing in failure. Chrétien didn't have much of a honeymoon in the new job he'd fought so long to attain. Almost immediately, he was written off as out of touch with Quebec and the modern, fractious state of the Canadian nation. The Liberals would be sorry, critics predicted, for choosing a relic of the Trudeau years, a time synonymous with big government and out of touch with the more corporate style of governance in the modern era. Liberals would regret, the critics also predicted, their failure to choose the more business-friendly Paul Martin, former head of Canada Steamship Lines, who had supported Meech. For a while, the critics looked like they were going to be proven correct. Chrétien's early performance as a leader was shaky; he made some major gaffes, such as arguing that Canada should only engage in military action in the Gulf War until the shooting started. Even more recklessly, in a slip that would haunt him, Chrétien as opposition leader had promised that the GST would "disappear" if he took power, even though he had spent his entire leadership campaign being far cagier about his plans for the tax.

So the Liberals started applying some marketing lessons to their own beleaguered brand. The first efforts were less than successful, to put it mildly. Chrétien started using a teleprompter, which made him look even more unsure of himself, and wooden. "What happened to the old Jean Chrétien?" was the headline on a story by Southam News reporter Joan Bryden in November 1990: "Accustomed to taking oratorical flight without aids, Chrétien's delivery rarely gets off the ground when he's anchored by a text. And the teleprompter, used for all his major speeches now, can't disguise the fact that Chrétien is being scripted. The passion, the humour, the endearing fractured English—all the trademarks that have for years made Chrétien one of the country's most colourful and popular speakers—are missing." The lesson? There's smart marketing and dumb marketing.

In 1991 Chrétien's office got a shakeup with a new chief of staff—former Quebec City mayor Jean Pelletier, who brought an elegant form of discipline to the operation. As well, Chrétien found a new communications director named Peter Donolo, who had been working for Toronto mayor Art Eggleton and had attracted favourable notice for his speechwriting skills. Smart, funny and an astute observer of cultural and political trends, Donolo was also young— just thirty years old: young enough to have grown up in a political age saturated with television, commercials and consumerism.

The efforts to make Chrétien into a new product reminded Donolo of the "new Coke" fiasco—a reference to Coca-Cola's disastrous effort to update its iconic product in the mid-1980s. Facing a steadily declining lead against Pepsi over fifteen years, Coke's executives decided a bold move was needed. So it whipped up a new recipe, did taste tests against the old one with thousands of cola consumers and unveiled the testers' favourite as the "new Coke." The public backlash was large and immediate. What Coke had not appreciated was the emotional bond with the product. It was a powerful marketing lesson: it's the *idea* of the product, not just the material object itself. People felt that their old memories and attachment to Coke were being tossed aside, as well as the old formula. Coca-Cola was forced into retreat, reissuing its old product as "Coca-Cola Classic."

There was indeed a direct connection here to the political realm. A politician, maybe even more than a mere cola drink or product, carries the freight of people's emotions and memories, too. He (or she) is a "brand." And when the Liberals tried to cook up a new recipe for Chrétien as leader, citizens—especially Liberals—started to wonder what happened to all they'd invested in and expected of the old Chrétien, the man they thought they knew. It was as Gregg had predicted—emotion and authenticity were becoming crucial to Canada's consumer-citizens.

The solution? "Chrétien classic." Under Donolo's suggestion, Chrétien was outfitted in an ordinary guy's denim shirt, and the portrait was plastered on posters and pins to play up his "little guy from Shawinigan" reputation. Or, as Donolo would put it, "to make a virtue out of his rough-hewedness." To demonstrate that Chrétien was not "yesterday's man," that he was vibrant and fit, Donolo arranged for a camera to capture a picture of Chrétien water-skiing at his cottage.

The Liberals also decided at this point to amicably part with Martin Goldfarb as their pollster and went shopping for another one. In strode Michael Marzolini, a far more subdued character than the larger-than-life Goldfarb. Marzolini earned Chrétien's seal of approval by promising blunt candour in private and a low profile in public. Marzolini had taught himself computer programming at night while working at a Toronto technology firm. Like Gregg, he made forays to the United States to study the methods of Reagan's pollster, Richard Wirthlin. Goldfarb was a hero to Marzolini, but while the former pollster liked anthropology, the new pollster was more of a military aficionado, preferring to pepper his presentations with talk of "carpet-bombing" polls. Marzolini did believe, however, that you could learn a lot through anthropological observation. He once embedded himself for a week in the low-income community of Regent Park in Toronto because he didn't believe he was learning enough about that demographic slice of Canada through telephone polling. He also did a lot of his thinking and reflecting while smoking cigars on the sundeck of his upscale Yorkville office, watching the shoppers below on the sidewalk. Marzolini, taking over from Goldfarb, knew that he would be giving very different advice. Canadians had lost their appetite for grand visions or promises and were far more disposed to politicians who would promise to save their money, get on with the job of governing and leave them alone.

It was at a big conference the Liberals held in November 1991, just across the river from Ottawa in Aylmer, Quebec, that the Liberals would actually recast their policy and focus. The lead-up to the Aylmer Conference was pitched by the media as a tussle between the traditional left and the new right. Somehow, the party had to shake off the impression, certainly sealed in the 1988 election, that the Liberals were anti-trade and anti-modernization. The Liberals invited Lester Thurow of the Massachusetts Institute of Technology to lecture the Grits on economic matters such as innovation, technology and globalization. Each pole in the Liberal party had its champion at Aylmer. On the left was Lloyd Axworthy, former cabinet minister and brother of Tom Axworthy, Trudeau's principal secretary, while Roy MacLaren, founder of *Canadian Business* magazine, was the leading voice for the people who wanted to shift the party in a more rightward direction. By the end of the Aylmer conference, the Liberals left little doubt about where they were tacking their sails. Chrétien called protectionism "passé" and globalization "a fact of life." Roy MacLaren was gleeful, summing up the Aylmer gathering as a victory over the old left wing: "Eat your heart out, Lloyd Axworthy." That quote, more than anything else, was broadly circulated as the result of this rebranding conference.

Chrétien put Paul Martin, the businessmen's businessman, in charge of the platform leading up to the 1993 election. His co-author was former Ontario cabinet minister Chaviva Hosek, who hailed from the leftward end of the Liberal spectrum and who had been working as an adviser to Chrétien since shortly after the David Peterson government defeat in 1990. Hosek and Martin were tasked with the job of creating a credible, comprehensive platform that could bridge the big-government Liberalism of old and the new, more business-friendly politics of Canada in the 1990s. In format, it would be similar to Clinton's 1992 campaign document *Putting People First: How We Can All Change America*. But the Liberal document would be even more specific: it would list all the promises, properly costed out over four years. No other political party had tried this before in Canada, but the party had to prove its credibility in an era of damaged political brands. The Liberals were changing the product in response to the market—much more than advertising or mere selling.

The result was the famous Red Book of Liberal promises, titled "Creating Opportunity." The labelling was a political synonym for "new and improved"—the political equivalent of a product upgrade. No longer would the Liberals be known as the advocates for big-government programs. In fact, a lot of their promises revolved around what Liberals would *not* do: buy more helicopters and add to the national debt, for instance. Chrétien liked to say he had three promises: "Jobs, jobs, jobs." The days of building governments were over and the days of enhancing individuals' lives had arrived. Deliberately, the Liberals had chosen to make the Red Book look like a corporation's annual report—another nod to critics who said the party was out of touch with the corporatism of 1990s Canada.

The Red Book also functioned as a political-product guarantee. Consumer-citizens were delighted with guarantees in the commercial sector. In the 1990s, the marketing world in Canada and beyond was embracing the importance of "customer relationship management" and "after-sales service." The proliferating big-box stores on the Canadian landscape, as well as the expansion of goods available through freer trade, meant that sellers in the Canadian marketplace were vying for intangibles such as loyalty and reputation. The same was true in the political sector. Marzolini, in his week living among the low-income people in Regent Park, had listened closely one evening when chatting to a woman who said that politicians should arrive in power with a checklist of tasks and be kicked out of office if they failed to deliver. The platform became that checklist, which Chrétien brandished as a talisman—literally waving it in the face of doubting citizens or skeptical journalists.

"It's all written here," Chrétien said at the Ottawa campaign launch of the Red Book in mid-September 1993. "You can come with this book in front of me every week after I'm the prime minister and say, 'Where are you with your promises, Mr. Chrétien?' And we are going to check—I'm telling you everything that is written there I intend to implement."

This election campaign was launched in a very different world than any previous one in Canadian history. Canada now had an all-news network, CBC Newsworld, which promised to greatly accelerate the speed of exchanges between the rival parties. Where once a political party could count on a whole day to "get out the message" to the public, the rapidly changing headlines in the all-news universe meant that rivals could pounce within the hour. The daily airwaves carried fast-changing, back-and-forth squabbles among the parties. It was all more noise for average citizens to digest—or tune out.

The 1993 election was a great leap forward in the world of digital political marketing, too. Thanks to a couple of by-elections and then the 1992 referendum on the Charlottetown Accord, Elections Canada had been experimenting with putting voters lists in computer-friendly format. By 1993, the agency was able to come up with a national list, rather awkwardly named the Elections Canada Automated Production of Lists of Electors, or ECAPLE for short. It meant that for the first time Canadian political parties had access to a digital database, filled with precious names and addresses of supporters and would-be supporters. This was a goldmine for politicos—a wealth of information far more vast than any Ruby Red Grapefruit Co. list or private-sector mailing list, such as the type "prospected" by John Laschinger in the 1980s.

With advances in technology, too, parties could begin to adapt this basic list to develop their own, more specialized databases. The Liberals, for instance, enlisted the services of a company called ProMark Software to manipulate the voters list into user-friendly lists for campaigning and get-out-the-vote (GOTV) efforts in the 1993 election. They also sought out the help of Compusearch Market and Social Research, a new "geo-demographic" data service, to map out ridings according to voters' incomes and lifestyles. Custom maps for local campaigns were provided to local Liberal ridings for a nominal cost. In this way, information that used to be gathered by local volunteers and politicians was now professionalized, digitalized and centralized—another step in taking politics further away from art and more toward science, just as polling had done.

The Reform Party, seriously in contention in a federal election for the first time in 1993, had feared that as outsiders from the West they would see an onslaught of negative attacks through this campaign. Still relying on advice from Frank Luntz, Reform attempted to "inoculate" the media against any negative campaigning, sending out a letter to journalists in the weeks before the writ dropped. "We hope in the interests of fair play, you refuse to be co-opted by any negative advertising campaign… whether directed against the Reform Party or anyone else," said the letter, which was signed by Reform spokesman Allan McGirr and accompanied by a small book by Luntz. Reform, for its part, served notice that its campaign would be the opposite of slick—no leader's plane, no fancy bells and whistles, and advertising filled with so-called ordinary Canadians.

"It's the same kind of war that's going on with soft drinks. The generic brands are cheaper and they taste just as good," McGirr told one reporter. So while the Liberals were going with "Chrétien classic," the Reform Party upstarts were going generic. Interesting strategy—using ad culture to fight against the creep of advertising into our higher, civic life.

Reform's worries about negative campaigning did come to pass in the 1993 campaign, just not in the way the party had anticipated. As a Liberal victory seemed increasingly imminent and the Conservative campaign grew increasingly desperate, the election airwaves were suddenly punctuated with a hard-hitting assault—on Chrétien's face. His lopsided countenance, the product of an unknown childhood affliction, was put front and centre in a wave of Conservative ads with the tagline "Is this a prime minister?" In the ad, ordinary voters attested to their discomfort with Chrétien: "I personally would be very embarrassed if he were to become prime minister of Canada." Reaction was swift and furious, prompting the Conservatives to quickly pull the ads. Telephone lines at Tory headquarters were jammed with calls, and even Conservative candidates went public with their fury. "Distasteful," said one in Vancouver.

Election night in October 1993 smashed the old political order in Canada, leaving just one mass-market "brand" party on the landscape—the Liberals. Turnout had dipped below 70 percent for the first time since the 1950s, marking the beginning of a decline that would grow even worse within ten years. The new, separatist Bloc Québécois represented the majority in Quebec; the Reform Party represented a large swath in the West. Neither the New Democrats nor the Conservatives won official party status; they were reduced to rump status in the Commons. In this new, regionally "specialized" Canadian political marketplace, the governing Liberals were left to try to tap into the mass mood of Canadian consumer-citizens.

Immediately upon taking office, the Liberals borrowed a little bit of inspiration from Loblaws' Dave Nichols and pitched themselves as the "no-frills" party, all about value for the dollar. Chrétien dispensed with the Mulroney limousines and the special prime-ministerial aircraft, which the Liberals dubbed the "flying Taj Mahal." The new Liberal government issued its first budget in plain, generic packaging—a simple white cover, with no fancy graphics or extravagant type. "This is a Chevrolet government, not a Cadillac government," Chrétien liked to remind people after he took power.

The fixation on brands and labels in Canadian politics, up to this point, mostly was at the sales end of things. Although the Liberals had slightly modified their product at the Aylmer conference, adjusting the party's philosophy and outlook to be more business-friendly, their branding efforts could not really be called "marketing" in the true sense of the word. Once entrenched in power, where they would remain for the next twelve years, Liberals would flirt with a lot of modern marketing concepts and tactics—branding, focus groups and, of course, the now-ubiquitous advertising. But all those efforts were more about selling than changing their "product" to suit Canadian consumers or citizens.

Perhaps because of their long history in government in the twentieth century, the Liberals were still reasonably old-fashioned about the idea of government as something separate from the consumer marketplace. Chrétien, very much in keeping with the managerial, administrative style of Liberal rule in the 1950s, with the "systems men," exhorted his ministers to rely on their public servants and their departments. The old Consumer Affairs Ministry, incidentally, was wound down when Chrétien took power and absorbed into the larger Department of Industry, which was envisioned as a kind of super-ministry to oversee the entirety of private-sector interests.

Soon after coming to office, Chrétien asked Marzolini to test the public's appetite for limits in government spending—a bitter pill the Liberals were going to have to swallow, to fight the out-of-control federal debt, at more than $40 billion and climbing in 1993. Marzolini told Chrétien that cuts to spending would be incredibly risky. Partly because Canadians had been so focused on the constitution for the previous decade, the populace had some knowledge of how the country worked, but economic literacy was woefully low.

Only 25 percent of Canadians knew the difference between a deficit and a debt and only 40 percent knew how many millions were in a billion. Nor could Marzolini detect any useful ways to improve this situation in his polling data—Canadians were busy with their own lives and not all that receptive to getting economic lectures from politicians or even the so-called experts. When Marzolini asked a thousand Canadians how they would get federal finances back into the black, a full 20 percent of respondents believed that the massive drain on the federal budget could be resolved by getting rid of free haircuts and subsidized meals for MPs—a drop in the bucket, expense-wise, for the federal treasury. These responses also signalled that Canadians saw government as more of a problem than a solution in the early 1990s.

The GST loomed large as a problem, too, its fates tied to the emerging forces of political marketing and consumer-citizenship. Canadians believed that the Liberals were going to scrap it, and Chrétien had only himself to blame for this perception. Although he had in fact been careful during his leadership and 1993 election campaigns, saying the $18 billion in annual GST revenues would have to be retained, Chrétien was haunted by his reckless 1990 vow to make the tax "disappear." Canadians weren't interested in the fine print of this promise—the business about replacing the tax revenues, for instance. Citizens were reminded of their resentment toward the tax, and by extension, the government, every time they went to the cash register.

Some were so angry that they were avoiding the tax altogether, through the so-called underground economy that emerged in the 1990s, which was basically a shoppers' revolt against the GST. These people were conducting their transactions away from the eye of the taxman, exchanging goods and services under the table. In essence, they were revolting against the idea of government. "The underground economy is not all smugglers. It is hundreds of thousands of otherwise honest people who have withdrawn their consent to be governed, who have lost faith in government," Paul Martin said weeks after he was made finance minister in the Chrétien government. Actually, what Martin may well have been describing was simply the modern consumer-citizen—the kind of person who put his or her consumer needs ahead of a willingness to be taxed. A "taxpayer" more than a citizen, in other words.

For a couple of years, the Chrétien Liberals would wrestle with how to handle the hot potato of the GST. The dilemma perfectly captured the ambivalence of the times, between the rigours of governing and succumbing to the demands of the angry consumer-citizens. Privately, the government polled on the wisdom of reducing the GST by a couple of points. Polling of course showed that the measure would be hugely popular, but the nation's fragile financial recovery couldn't handle the loss of revenues. Martin tried a public apology of sorts: "We made a mistake," Martin said at a 1996 news conference where he unveiled the details of the "harmonized" tax deal with the Atlantic provinces, yet another bid to calm the troubled waters. One minister, Sheila Copps, went so far as to resign (then quickly run again, successfully being re-elected) to show her regret over promising to axe the GST during the 1993 election campaign.

Somehow, however, the Liberals were able to ride out the GST controversy relatively unscathed. Yet cynicism and anti-elitism— necessary conditions for marketing in politics—were alive and well in 1990s Canada. The Reform Party, under leader Preston Manning, was using its new bully pulpit in the Commons to slam government as too large and too wasteful. Reform had some powerful advocacy organizations amplifying its voice, the Canadian Taxpayers Federation and the National Citizens Coalition. The way in which these protest groups eventually moved to the pinnacle of power in Canada, like the story of the GST, teaches us a lot about how the forces of marketing and consumer-citizenship took over Canadian politics in the years ahead.

Protest Power

Throughout the 1990s, the NCC and the Canadian Taxpayers Federation became ever more vocal, making vigorous use of advertising and publicity stunts to protest against what they saw as spending waste and excess in government. Even after Chrétien's government had brought in its historic 1995 budget, with its drastic cuts to health and social transfers to the provinces, and with Canada's fiscal circumstances headed back into the black (helped by that revenue from the GST), the Taxpayers Federation and the NCC kept up their steady drumbeat against government spending.

The NCC spent $150,000 in one ad wave alone in 1996, for instance, to tell Canadians what they called "tales from the tax trough," protesting money spent on a canoe museum and financing for social-science research on obscure subjects. A full $105,000 of government money had gone to a study comparing hockey coaches and symphony conductors, according to the "trough" tales. The Canadian Taxpayers Federation showed a similar fondness for alliteration in its regular news releases. Spending at the Department of Industry, then headed by minister John Manley, was assailed with a 1996 news release titled "Taxpayers Tricked by Manley's Treats." How were their campaigns working? There was no question that the groups were attracting more members and more media attention; they had gone from being fringe elements to being commentators on the federal scene—reflecting a harder edge within the citizenry as a whole.

The increasing allegiance between the Reform Party and these groups was apparently sealed when Stephen Harper, the co-founder of the Reform Party and by far the biggest star of the caucus, announced before his first term as an MP was up that he was leaving politics to head up the National Citizens Coalition. It seemed like an odd match. Harper wasn't much of a populist and had seemed hugely uncomfortable with some of the Reform Party's over-the-top, anti-government stunts in the early years, such as trying to sell Manning's limousine or threatening to turn the opposition leader's residence into a bowling alley. No one could really picture Harper buying a bunch of plastic pigs and planting them on Parliament Hill. It was widely expected that this thoughtful, policy-wonk politician would tone down the NCC, making it more of a think-tank than an advocacy organization. He would make it more institution-friendly, in other words, and less attached to the consumerist revolt that had driven it to date. At around the same time, the Canadian Taxpayers Federation's Jason Kenney decided to leap into elected politics.

Dalton Camp, the man who had helped lead Canadian politics into the advertising age, wasn't at all delighted with how that allegiance had turned out. By now, after some time in Mulroney's backrooms, not to mention a heart transplant and some health crises, Camp had situated himself safely in the spectators' stands. On top of his weekly job as a panellist on Peter Gzowski's *Morningside* show, Camp also penned a regular column in the *Toronto Star*.

In a 1994 column, Camp complained that political advertising was indeed, as British ad man David Ogilvy described it, "the most dishonest in the world." Camp blamed television: "The truth seems to be no medium is better suited for the propagation of untruths than television; there is no medium so effective as television not only for dissembling and distortion but for inventing reality." The source of Camp's vexation was mainly US political advertising, especially the ads he had been watching about gun control and health care south of the border. "Only television can use obfuscating charm and sleaze to such powerful effect. A well-packaged lie can penetrate the thickest skull, given enough frequency, a modicum of cleverness and the money avarice can command." In tone, it was harder-hitting than the defence of advertising that fellow ad man Terry O'Malley had penned in 1978, but it rang a familiar alarm. Camp and O'Malley, the pioneers of political advertising in the modern age, were serving a warning that in the wrong hands, TV ads could take our civic life into dark places. The problem, though, was that the citizenry was already headed to that dim view.

All over Canada, not just in Ontario, the mid-1990s saw pockets of citizen discontent with the old line of politics. In British Columbia, the provincial government set up legislation that would allow citizens to "recall" their MPs if they could accumulate enough signatures on a petition. In essence, it was the equivalent of a money-back guarantee in the stores. Unhappy with your political product? Send it back and get a full refund—no stamped, self-addressed envelope necessary. The BC government also made it possible in the 1990s for citizens to initiate referenda on issues of their choosing.

One columnist in the *Vancouver Province*, Alan Twigg, saw the recall legislation as a symptom of cranky consumer-citizens, bringing their "culture of complaint" in the stores to the political realm. "Trouble is, nearly everyone is a complainer these days; almost everyone is a victim. If you read the papers, you'd think society has been transformed into a pack of wounded banshees," Twigg wrote. "Sometimes we have to take our medicine. If the nurse or doctor dispenses medicine to us that doesn't taste good, should we throw a tantrum and ask the hospital to remove the nurse or physician from the hospital staff? The recall legislation allows our push-button culture of complaint to seek immediate redress for any bad-tasting medicine."

But by tapping into this vein of grievance and consumerist demands on the state, Canadian conservatives were seeing the shape of politics to come. In the meantime, a man named Tony Blair in Britain set about a rebranding exercise on the left that would be much studied and imitated by the left and the right in Canada for years to come. Blair proved that any kind of politics could be framed as marketing-friendly.

Labour, New and Improved

Britain's Labour Party, like Canada's Liberals, had suffered from reputation malaise during its time in opposition in the 1980s and 1990s. Confronting the real prospect of two decades of Conservative hegemony in Britain, Neil Kinnock, then leader of the Labour Party, cast about looking for ways to revitalize the party in the run-up to the 1994 election. Like Thatcher, he was not afraid to reach into the commercial realm for some political lessons. Philip Gould, a former ad executive, was recruited by Labour to take the pulse of modern British citizens, not just to test their politics but their deeper hopes and fears, just like a market researcher would. He went out to the middle-class suburbs and sought out former Labour voters who had become converts to Thatcher-style politics—the people Labour was going to need if it ever hoped to reclaim power in Britain. This was an exercise primarily in emotions, not ideology, and as such, it was closer to the consumer model of market research, where Gould's real experience lay. Perhaps not surprisingly, given that context, the British focus-group participants framed much of their talk about hopes and needs in terms of what they wanted to buy. Here's how the BBC documentary *Century of the Self* summed up the findings of Gould's focus groups: "They no longer saw themselves as part of any group, but as individuals, who could demand things from politicians in return for paying taxes, just as business had taught them to do, as consumers."

Gould called these people "aspirational" Britons, who could be lured to vote Labour if they were assured it wouldn't cost them or damage their upwardly mobile lifestyle. Despite Gould's advice, however, Kinnock and the Labour Party went into the 1994 campaign with a promise to increase taxes—and were battered at the polls. That defeat, and the lessons contained in it, paved the way for the ascension of leader Tony Blair and his ambitious effort to overhaul the old party into a "New Labour" movement. In that effort, Blair would be guided by Gould and his ongoing focus groups.

"I found that the people had become consumers," Gould said in an interview with the *Century of the Self* documentary makers. "People now wanted to have politics and life on their own terms. Not just in politics but in all aspects of life, too. People see themselves, as they are, as autonomous, powerful individuals who are entitled to be respected, who are entitled to have the best, not just in going to Tescos or wherever, but the best in terms of health and education, too."

Thatcher, recall, had dubbed these folks "Essex Men" and in Blair's time, they would come to be named "Basildon Men," a more geographically precise descriptor. Basildon is the capital of Essex county, and an epitome of the "aspirational" suburban culture in Britain. And then, thanks to a speech by Blair himself in 1996, yet another even more consumer-friendly name would emerge: "Sierra Man" or "Mondeo Man," after the type of car these Brit voters typically drove. Blair had told a convention of Labour Party faithful an anecdote about an encounter with a self-employed electrician in his Sedgefield constituency who had chatted with him while polishing his Ford Sierra: "His dad voted Labour, he said. He used to vote Labour, too. But he'd bought his own house now. He'd set up his own business. He was doing very nicely. 'So I've become a Tory,' he said. In that moment, he crystallized for me the basis of our failure… His instincts were to get on in life. And he thought our instincts were to stop him. But that was never our history or our purpose."

Labour's goal, Blair said, was to prove that it no longer stood for the kind of government that would interfere with consumerist hopes and dreams. So the New Labour formula for success was to focus on the high aspirations of these consumer-citizens, while simultaneously preaching low ambitions for government. It was neither right nor left, but the "Third Way." Blair went into the 1997 election campaign with five modest promises, framed as a "pledge card" to wary citizens. Those pledges included vows to cut class sizes, fast-track punishment for young offenders, cut waiting lists for national health care, get under-twenty-five-year-olds off the jobless lists and the solemn promise not to raise income taxes and to keep heating taxes and inflation low. These were all replies to the concerns that Gould had heard in his suburban focus groups, designed to touch the "aspirational" Britons where they lived.

Blair's ascent to power in 1997 relied heavily on the political marketing successes of the previous decades, notably his supposed political rivals on the right-hand side of the spectrum. Not only did he copy Thatcher's pitch to the suburbanites, he also took his inspiration from Clinton and yes, even Canada; Blair's pledge to voters was also inspired by the success of the Liberals' Red Book. Political-product guarantees were still very much in fashion. And political marketing, pegged as it is to people checked out of politics, continued to prove that it could leap partisan divides.

So by the late 1990s, a progressive left-wing trio dominated the Canada-US-Britain triangle of democracies, as surely as Thatcher, Reagan and Mulroney had presided over the 1980s. And just as the Republicans and the British and Canadian Conservatives had lent each other political marketing tips and examples, the same was true of the Clinton-Blair-Chrétien triumvirate. In both decades, though, the Canadian efforts would be somewhat less intense than those of either the Brits or the Americans. The puzzling question: Why?

One simple word may explain Canada's laggardly pace in political marketing and toward consumer-citizenship: "sovereignty." Throughout the 1980s and 1990s, Canada was preoccupied with successive Quebec referenda, constitutional crises and existential debates about the future of a united Canadian nation. The free-trade election had also churned up angst-ridden discussion about Canadian sovereignty with respect to the United States. While the political pros in the backrooms were playing with the increasingly sophisticated tools of political marketing, the governments themselves were, well, governing. Moreover, as we've seen with the Liberals' GST troubles, total brand overhauls and true marketing—adjusting the product to consumer demand—are far more difficult to do when a political party is in power.

But the Chrétien government did embrace sales language and sales techniques in its time in power—especially advertising. Nowhere was this more evident than in the response to the near

144

loss of the federalist side in the 1995 Quebec referendum, which set in motion the events that would crush the Liberals. Chrétien and the Liberals had been unprepared for the closeness of the struggle, believing that a low-key, managerial reply to the separatists would be the best strategy. It was the wrong approach; Quebec's separatists came within less than 1 percent of winning a mandate to break away from Canada on the night of October 30, 1995. In the aftermath, Chrétien and his cabinet built a recovery plan that was based partly on reason—a Supreme Court of Canada reference on the terms of separation in future, for instance—and partly on emotion. To win a place for Canada in Quebecers' hearts, the Chrétien government scrambled to amass every single advertising tool they could muster. They wanted props: Canadian flags and the Canadian symbol inserted wherever possible in Quebec. Heritage Minister Sheila Copps launched a massive giveaway campaign of hundreds of thousands of Canadian flags. And fatefully, the federal Public Works Department was put on notice to saturate Quebec with advertising for the federal cause. In one of many testimonies that he would give about this effort, Charles (Chuck) Guité, the civil servant in charge of the advertising and sponsorship program, said, "We were basically at war trying to save the country."

This war would produce many casualties in the end, not the least of which was the Liberal rule over Canada. Through increasing revelations of how federal money was spent and squandered by Liberal-friendly ad firms, Canadians would come to see this whole program as crime and scandal. Much of that scandal was exposed in agonizing detail in the media and then through Justice John Gomery's painstaking commission of inquiry through 2004–05. But Chrétien and his advisers, even after the fact, determinedly stood by the fundamental principle: the sovereignty of Canada had to be defended in the political marketplace, with the tools of consumerism. It's worth a somewhat lengthy look at Chrétien's testimony to the Gomery Commission for a blunt, no-apologies explanation of why the government of Canada felt it had to get into the advertising business to fight Quebec secession:

> The visibility in Quebec of the Government of Canada had been significantly reduced from the mid-1980s until I became prime minister. The visible face of the government of Canada had even been removed from postboxes, from the airport in Montreal and even from immigration court. There was a vacuum and the vacuum was being filled by the Quebec government with constant, subliminal messaging... We were going to restore the visibility of the government of Canada in Quebec. Whatever Quebec's Parti Québécois government was doing which, in our view, directly or indirectly promoted separation, we, as the Government of Canada, would at least match to promote a united Canada.
>
> If they were putting up billboards, and they did, the Government of Canada would put up billboards, and we did. If they were advertising on the radio and television, and they did, the Government of Canada would advertise on the radio and television, and we did. If they were sponsoring community events, and they did, the Government of Canada would sponsor community events, and we did.
>
> Sponsorship is much more than just billboards, flags and word marks. It is involvement with organizers of community events, people who are often opinion leaders in their communities, letting them know that there is also a Government of Canada that relates directly to citizens, that the Government of Canada does more than just collect taxes while the Québec government delivers programs. This type of federal presence amongst community leaders was part and parcel of our overall strategy. That is why we committed to spending a significant amount of money every year to be part of community events.

And we did not restrict the program to Québec because the Government of Canada should be present in communities across the country.

Note in Chrétien's explanation how much advertising is seen as the solution to government's most serious problems, and how citizens are seen as passive consumers on issues as important as sovereignty and the future of the country. As the old saying goes, when all you have is a hammer, every problem becomes a nail. If government is primarily in the business of communicating, or advertising its services, then every problem becomes a publicity concern. And attention to image and communications was making itself felt within Chrétien's government in a number of ways after the deficit was wrestled down in the late 1990s, not just in Quebec. Between 2001 and 2003, public service jobs in communications grew by a whopping 28 percent. It was entirely in keeping with the ever-increasing trend to see the citizens as consumers of their own government.

Throughout Chrétien's tenure as well, the civil service exploded with talk of citizens as government "clients," and increasingly it looked like the sole job of the state was to supply services to its taxpaying citizens. All the bureaucratic buzzwords revolved around "client-centred service" and value for the tax dollars of consumer-citizens. Take a look at this federal Treasury Board publication from the early 2000s, boasting of a new "Service Improvement Initiative":

The essence of the Service Improvement Initiative is that the continuous and measurable improvement of client satisfaction is the most reliable indicator of improvement in service quality and service performance: it is what quality and continuous improvement should now mean, and how they should be primarily, though not exclusively, measured. Leading-edge service organizations in the public sector, like their counterparts in the private sector, now use a results-based approach to the continuous improvement of client satisfaction, integrated with the annual business planning cycle.

What had happened to the idea of the federal government as a generator of ideas or bold national projects? It may have been the bruising constitutional dramas. It may have been the recessions of the 1980s, the big deficits and debt, and the resulting belt tightening in the 1990s. Perhaps it was the rise of think-tanks and the voice of business in the 1980s and 1990s, arguing that the best ideas for running Canada came from outside government. Or maybe it was just the aging of Canadian society and the baby boomer demographic moving from its idealistic youth into practical, stolid middle age. Whatever the reason, and it was probably a combination of all these things, the federal government adopted a posture of service-first in the 1990s, less prone to pushing big ideas on the Canadian public and concentrating instead on government as a "service provider." If nothing else, that would serve as an ad slogan.

Reg Whitaker, a research professor emeritus at York University, watched the Liberal government very closely, in all its ups and downs. Writing in 2001 in *Policy Options*, Whitaker lamented the descent of politics into market practices, seeing the language of business creeping into every corner in the corridors of power:

> Parties are no longer about commitment, in the sense of principles, loyalty and tradition. Long ago, partisans rallied to Sir John A. Macdonald's Tories under the slogan "the Old Man, the Old Flag, the Old Policy." No more. A party is not a collective project. It is a "mutual fund." Commitment has become investment, and investment demands appropriate returns. If "wasted," it should be pulled out and put "elsewhere." The party's name and symbols are no longer marks of allegiance, but are merely a "brand." Brands are corporate marketing devices for products.

Brand identification is intended to promote sales. If sales falter, re-branding may be required.

Whitaker was right about the branding business. Suddenly, as the twenty-first century was getting under way, everyone across the Canadian government seemed to be swept up in the idea of "branding."

Brand Canada

It was Tony Blair, once again, who gave a lot of countries ideas about rebranding nationhood, with what came to be known as the "Cool Britannia" campaign. "Cool Britannia," the name, actually came from a Ben and Jerry's ice cream flavour (vanilla with shortbread), launched in the United States several years before Blair came to power. Blair's branding campaign came from a marketing agency, Demos, and two of its sharpest thinkers, Geoff Mulgan and Mark Leonard.

Leonard published a report called "Britain™: Renewing Our Identity," in which he argued for the country to position itself as more than the sum of its history or institutions. The bold proposition was that Britain would be shedding its stodgy old image to become a modern, vital presence on the world stage. Other countries had attempted similar efforts: Spain had a new logo and tourism campaign; Ireland was in the midst of becoming a "Celtic Tiger." Leonard described the new British "brand" for Blair in his report:

> The most important lesson is that the task of renewing identity goes well beyond flags and logos. The key priority is to define a shared ethos, and shared stories, to reflect the best of what Britain has become in the late 1990s. I suggest what some of these stories might be, emphasizing Britain's place as a hub, an importer and exporter of ideas, goods and services, people and cultures; Britain's history as a hybrid nation; our traditions of creativity and non-conformism; our role as a silent revolutionary

creating new models of organization; our readiness to do business; and the ethos of fair play and voluntary commitment. These stories should be our trademarks. Together they add up to a new vision of Britain as a global island, uniquely well placed to thrive in the more interconnected world of the next century.

There was nothing new about governments using ad companies to promote tourism in the country. Dalton Camp had been benefiting from that kind of political–private crossover for decades in Canada. But here's where that marketing distinction comes in handy again. Branding the nation, in the new context, was about moulding the country itself to suit the market, not just selling its virtues. Blair, just forty-three when he took office, with a young family, was in a good marketing position, too, to preside over this branding update. After all, he had turned the stodgy old Labour Party into "New Labour." Why couldn't he do the same for "New Britain"? He established a rebranding advisory group called Panel 2000, studded with leading private-sector celebrities such as Stella McCartney, and held a reception in 1997 at Downing Street for all of Britain's "glitterati." But when all was said and done, the Cool Britannia campaign receded to the background as Blair's time in office went on, and it was remembered primarily as a failed experiment, even a "fiasco," by some. His branding of a left-wing movement, however, would linger as an example for many Canadian politicos.

In Canada, nation-branding was initially seen as a way to tackle some old debates with modern tools of the market—but also to improve Canada's image abroad and self-image at home. Identity discussions had been part of the Canadian fabric virtually since the country was born in the nineteenth century, and right up to the sovereignty debates of the latter half of the twentieth century. It was almost an industry in itself: What is a Canadian? How do we separate the Canadian identity from that of the Americans, our British colonial masters or even the separatists in Quebec?

The Chrétien government got caught up in the idea of branding itself around 2000, when Brian Tobin, a man with a flair for marketing and politics, was minister of industry. The former broadcaster, who had been part of the Liberal "Rat Pack" in the 1980s, had left federal politics to become Newfoundland premier in the 1990s. But he had returned to federal politics after a brand makeover of his own. He had transformed into a more business-friendly style of Liberal politician, with his eyes on being prime minister someday. Under Tobin's watch, the federal government launched a "Brand Canada" initiative. It was in part an advertising campaign to raise awareness of Canada outside the borders, but a side benefit would be to get Canadians thinking in more modern fashion about their country, too—that we were more than rocks and trees and water, as the old Arrogant Worms song said. High-profile Canadian expatriates, mainly businesspeople, would be tasked as "brand ambassadors" for Canada in their travels abroad, particularly in the United States and Europe. Their job would be to talk up Canada as a site of potential investment, as well as tourism.

"There are some things we can learn from the Americans... In the United States, you're never confused about what somebody wants," Tobin said in an interview with Canadian Press in 2001. "We Canadians—we're subtle, we're more discreet, we're more reserved, we're less likely to pound the table and to sing our own song of celebration... Maybe we have to be a little less reserved and a little more forward, a little more in-your-face." It was a plan that fit neatly with the belief that while the government shouldn't be running businesses, perhaps it should be using the tools of business to do its governing. Where once Canada used teaching or preaching to get citizens thinking more patriotically about the country, now we were talking of "branding" and labelling.

Another big proponent of the Brand Canada idea was a real, honest-to-goodness expert in branding and marketing—Paul Lavoie of the wildly successful Canadian ad firm Taxi. Lavoie saw branding as a way to unite the country, an updated constitutional discussion, if you will, free from the tedium of first ministers' conferences or complex power struggles. "We have not managed our brand carefully, or with a shared purpose," Lavoie told *Marketing* magazine. "We've allowed our diversity to define us in broken fragments according to short-term tactics, not long-term goals."

Officially, the Brand Canada program may have started out as a big marketing idea for the country, but in its implementation, it fizzled into a mere funding program for international trade shows. There were several reasons it became sidelined. First, and most important, were the terrorist strikes in the United States on September 11, 2001. As Tobin and others were fond of observing in the aftermath, this was a time when people felt they needed their governments. Polls in the United States showed a massive increase in people's trust in government, to levels that hadn't been seen since the 1960s. If only briefly, it seemed that Americans—and Canadians—were shaken back to some older ideas, about government being a force for good in people's lives.

Tobin, in the days and weeks after the attacks, would repeatedly urge Canadians to keep shopping, just as President George W. Bush was telling Americans to keep the economy rolling. "What we're seeing now is a very important part of the economy in retreat and that's consumers," Tobin said in a speech in Strathroy, Ontario, about a month after the 9/11 attacks. "Two-thirds of Canada's economy is driven by consumption... what can stop us [our economy] is a response and reaction by citizens, while understandable initially, to fright, to cocooning, to huddling away."

Then Tobin himself stood down from federal politics, bowing out of his candidacy for the Liberal leadership at the same time. Any energy or enthusiasm he contributed to the Brand Canada campaign left with him. The program was officially terminated in 2005. It would seem that Canada, like Britain, would realize that branding had its limits as a tool of government. Private-sector companies were having better luck with branding—right into the realms of patriotism and nationhood. Some brands, such as Tim Hortons, would have a lot more success turning into nations of their own.

6

AND NOW, A WORD FROM OUR SPONSORS

I t is here in the story of consumer-citizenship that we have to pause
and take a step out of politics and into the radically altered landscape of the Canadian consumer nation in the fifty years since the
end of the Second World War. When we see just how much shopping changed in half a century, we may be able to better understand
how our politics, influenced by the marketing world, was changing,
too. While Canadian parties were wrapping their minds around marketing at the dawn of the twenty-first century, the market itself was
in the midst of several tectonic shifts. Put simply, consumers weren't
the same people they were when Keith Davey was telling his radio
station to pursue the buying power of "young marrieds."

In the first place, being young and married was no longer a
typical condition in Canada. Starting with the 1991 census, that old
scenario of an Ozzie-and-Harriet-type family—two parents at home,
with children under age twenty-four also under the same roof—was
true for fewer than half of Canadian families. By the time the 2001
census rolled around, only 44 percent of Canadian families fit that
description. And just as Canadians were living their lives differently,

they were also buying things differently. The changes in just twenty years, in fact, had been staggering.

Big-box stores had arrived in Canada, and with them, the decline of traditional department stores and independent retailers. Eaton's closed its doors in 1999 amid much commentary on the death of a Canadian institution. Big bookstore chains were imperilling local independents—a US trend that formed the plotline for the hit romantic comedy *You've Got Mail*. The same thing was happening with Canadian grocery stores and drugstores, which had increasingly become concentrated within the hands of a few large supermarket players such as Loblaws, Sobey's and A&P.

What's more, the free-trade agreements sweeping the globe had opened up the Canadian market to a lot more imports. Canadians who wanted to buy shoes in 1989, for instance, would find that about half the footwear for sale was foreign-made. In 1995, imports represented 70 percent of the footwear market. Imports had flooded the pharmaceutical industry, too—from 18 percent of the market in 1983 to 76 percent in 2000. Along with all these changes came the birth of the "connected" consumer—with access to shopping all the time through the internet and their banks—whose transactions mostly revolved around pushing buttons and swiping plastic with magnetic strips through machines.

And lastly, but most significantly, came the arrival of a lot more choice for services such as telephone and cable and even energy, which had once been more or less monopolies in Canada because of heavy regulation. Now, instead of just calling up Ma Bell or the gas and cable company and asking to be hooked up, Canadian consumers had the luxury, and the burden, of figuring out which service to choose. Freedom and choice, those tenets of the postwar consumer boom, were alive and well in the Canadian commercial world. Now people weren't just spending their hard-earned money on stuff, but also on mysterious, invisible things they couldn't touch, such as cell service and broadband space.

In what would prove to be a significant shift for political parties, too, the economy was in the midst of eliminating the middleman (or middlewoman). Where Canadians once went to travel agents to book their trips, for example, they could now use their own online booking systems. Travel agents were quickly becoming extinct, and the same fate seemed to be awaiting brokers in other career realms, whether real estate, banking or the stock market, and even in education, publishing and journalism. In a world where anyone could publish on the internet through blogs or ebooks, would we soon need newspapers or book publishers to serve as gatekeepers? The fancy term for this trend was "disintermediation"—popularized in Don Tapscott's 1995 book *Growing Up Digital*. All of these developments collided to create a world in which Canadians were busy—pumping their own gas, doing their own travel arrangements and reading up on which telephone or cable service to get, or how best to spend or invest their money.

The sheer pace at which new electronics were arriving in the market was staggering. Between the 1970s and the early 2000s, most Canadian music listeners had replaced their old records with eight-track tapes, then cassette tapes, then compact discs, then MP3 files. Their television sets and telephones were becoming obsolete every couple of years with new advances in screen and satellite technology. And the voluminous instruction manuals for their new gadgets would leave people feeling they needed an engineering degree. It left Canadians precious little time to read up on politics, let alone volunteer or attend a political meeting. Thanks to the incredible complexity of their commercial world, citizens didn't have a chance to be anything but consumers. Who could blame them for checking out of political discussions that seemed increasingly remote from their day-to-day concerns? Who had time to figure out what those politicians were arguing about in Ottawa, when you couldn't even figure out how to program your home entertainment system?

In 2002, the federal government wanted to get a picture of this new consumer. It commissioned focus-group testing (naturally), which was carried out over several fall evenings in Halifax, Calgary and Montreal. While observers sat behind glass, these Canadian citizens told their interviewers about their all-consuming job of consuming. No matter which city or which group, participants were virtually unanimous—they believed that they were now consumers twenty-four hours a day, seven days a week. Even when they weren't actively buying stuff, they felt they were shopping. Merely researching a product purchase made a person into a consumer, the participants told the interviewers. Perhaps most significantly, these Canadians also told interviewers they were consumers when it came to government:

> A number of participants also pointed to examples when they were a consumer of government products. Examples included taxes, labour laws and unemployment. One respondent in Montreal mentioned the health-care system as an example of consuming government services, while education—particularly post-secondary education—was a popular example in the four English groups.

The ostensible purpose of this focus-group research was to find out how citizens would be served by a new government internet "gateway" to help handle their consumer concerns. But the larger finding was a significant cultural marker for a new century: Canadians were now having trouble seeing where their lives as consumers stopped and their existence as citizens started. They were one and the same. As the report put it:

> Consumption, for these participants, is about much more than buying products and services. Canadians are faced with endless situations in which they are consumers—from shopping and

comparing before they buy, to transacting with retailers and service providers and dealing with the same organizations after the transaction (perhaps to complain or call upon a warranty). Participants also told us that being a consumer extends far beyond traditional products and services to include utilities, education and government services… Even when they are not actively engaged in a purchase or post-purchase activity, they must cope with the impulse to buy and the unceasing flow of advertising and other commercial messages. In this increasingly complex environment, they find themselves needing more consumer information than ever.

The consumer overload didn't end there, though. Something interesting happened in the shape of Canadians' household finances as they became 24-7 consumers at the dawn of the twenty-first century. Up until this point in the country's history, Canadians spent less than their disposable income each year, meaning that some of it was put aside for saving or investment. However, from 1996 onward, they spent almost all of their earnings, leaving very little for saving. It followed, then, that personal debt, reliance on credit, was increasing. From 1992 to 2002, consumer debt grew by 10 percent each year on average for each Canadian. Between 1980 and 2005, per capita consumption expenditure in Canada more than tripled—from $6,870 to $23,560.

Canadians were spending much less of their household budgets on needs, and more on what they wanted. In 1961, clothing and footwear costs amounted to 9 percent of Canadian consumer spending, while food, beverages and tobacco accounted for 19 percent. Nearly fifty years later, these percentages were cut in half—just 4 percent of total consumer spending was devoted to clothing and footwear and only 10 percent went toward food, beverages and tobacco. (Some of that latter decline is probably partly explained by declining rates in smoking, too, which was once lumped in with spending on other basic "need" items.) As always, Canadians were still spending a lot of their budgets on their homes, in rent or mortgages and furnishings.

While politicians were being eviscerated for out-of-control spending and inattention to debt, Canadians were in a buying and debt spree of their own. Clearly, these were "do as we say, not as we do" times in terms of the fiscal disconnect between Canada's citizens and their politicians. But it's not as if the politicians could bark back—in a consumer nation, as we know, the customer is always right. One uproar in the late 1990s illustrated the simmering anger in the consumer-citizenry—over "negative-option billing," the practice of automatically adding charges for extra services to customers' monthly bills without asking for approval. It was up to subscribers to be alert to the additional charges and decline them; otherwise, the companies would simply assume everyone wanted them. Seven new cable channels had been rolled out on January 1, 1995, and added to the services of 7.5 million customers in Canada. Within three weeks, the Canadian Radio-Telecommunications Commission had received over nine thousand complaints from angry citizens.

The issue captured the distemper of the times for Canadian consumers, who felt overwhelmed by new charges for things they used to get for free, and by a mind-numbing array of choices. But it also poked at national unity issues—some of these new cable channels were French-language services. If you gave Canadians the choice simply to tune out French, what did that say about the still-fragile efforts to build bridges between the two solitudes in this country? The taxpayers, not the citizens, were asking, "What, we have to pay to keep the country together?" In short, if Canadians were simply consumers, unconcerned about larger unity matters, would they want French-language TV channels?

By 1999, Parliament did manage to pass a law making it illegal for companies to bill with the negative-option tactic, but the result was simply more paperwork. Service agreements became even more laden with fine print to obtain customers' consent for extra charges. One survey by Visa Canada, carried out many years after the legislation on negative-option billing came into place, found that only one in four web shoppers read all the online text and 27 percent said they read nothing at all.

Just Hang Up

Canadians were also getting annoyed with advertising. One study of the time, by the Leger and Scholz marketing firm, showed that Canadian consumers were pummelled with an estimated four thousand "promotional stimuli" each day, and TV was only part of the problem. Billions of flyers were being stuffed into mailboxes, and ads were appearing on public transit and in washrooms. On top of all that, there had been an explosion in "telemarketing"—sales calls to people's homes, often using predictive-dialling technology. In 2001, one survey showed that 61 percent of Canadians would prefer not to receive any such calls in their home. The United States had introduced a do-not-call list to rein in this practice, and Canada decided to follow suit.

In late 2004, Paul Martin's Liberal government introduced Bill C-37, called rather vaguely "An Act to Amend the Telecommunications Act." The existing Canadian Radio-Telecommunications Act already required individual companies to keep their own lists of people who asked not to be called. The do-not-call list was an attempt to give consumers one-stop shopping, so to speak, in opting out of annoying calls at home. Here again, things got interesting on the political front. Political parties were not expected to be covered when Advertising Standards Canada brought in its code of conduct in previous decades, the idea being, as we'll remember, that no one wanted to interfere with their freedom of expression. When the government introduced its own legislation for a do-not-call list in Canada, however, there was initially no mention of keeping political parties outside the law.

This sent a chill through the collective political class in Canada, regardless of party stripe. All the political parties relied on tele-marketing: for fundraising, for building memberships and for get-out-the-vote efforts during election campaigns. John Laschinger, with his Ruby Red Grapefruit and *Playboy* subscriber lists, had set that ball in motion. The very things that were bugging Canadians in the private sector, advertising and unsolicited phone calls, were now vital tools of the political trade. Charities in Canada had also become reliant on telemarketing for finding donations, and newspaper outlets had been rounding up subscribers with phone-call campaigns. What did charities, news media and political parties have in common? They all claimed to be more than mere commercial interests—they played a public-service role, too. And so, after some intense lobbying from these groups, formally and informally, the do-not-call legislation suddenly landed before the Commons Industry Committee in May 2005 with a series of amendments, granting some wide exemptions to the registry. In fact, in a rare show of consensus among rivals, the Liberal government and the Conservative opposition were in hearty agreement that it would be wrong to limit political parties' ability to place phone calls to Canadian households.

"In terms of political parties in Canada, we think it's a serious omission by the government not to include that. The reality is, we all operate during campaigns—we phone, we do get-out-the-vote campaigns," Conservative MP James Rajotte stated when he pro-posed amendments to the bill to the committee. Even the Bloc Québécois was on side. "We have to find a way to protect parties at both levels," Paul Crete, a member of Parliament for the Bloc, said at this same hearing.

The tension, in short, was playing itself out in the early part of the twenty-first century. Was politics a business, or a public service? Political parties wanted to use the tools of business—advertising, telemarketing, polling—to reach the citizens. But they still saw their profession as something separate from the private sector. And what about those busy Canadian consumers? Did they see the distinction? Increasingly, when Canadians needed a fix of patriotism they weren't looking to their governments, but to the places where they were shopping and consuming.

Doughnut Democracy

In 1997, Toronto's local CBC radio station featured a discussion with a marketing director for Country Style doughnuts—not Tim Hortons—to talk about the emerging cultural importance of her product. Cathy Mauro made the bold suggestion that doughnut shops were to Canada what pubs were to Britain. "I find that if you really want to be where it's happening at ten or eleven o'clock at night, you go to a doughnut shop," Mauro said.

How did doughnuts so quickly become Canadiana? This was a remarkable bit of revisionist history, because doughnuts were seen in the 1950s as primarily an American product. Steven Penfold, a Canadian historian at the University of Toronto, devoted an entire book to the doughnut's place in this country's culture. Penfold unearthed a June 1950 ad in the *Canadian Hotel Review and Restaurant* trade magazine. "Your AMERICAN Guests want DOUGHNUTS," said the ad, the text of which was wrapped around a picture of a dozen solid, plain doughnuts sitting on a lace-doilied plate.

Nothing about the founding or early days of Tim Hortons would seem to point toward its destiny as a Canadian political symbol. Tim Horton the hockey player had apparently become hooked on doughnuts while living in Pittsburgh from 1949 to 1952 and playing for the Hornets, a farm team for the Leafs. When he returned to Toronto, he became a regular patron of a little place called Your Do-nut Shop, right beside the barber who gave him his regular brush cut in Scarborough's Colony Plaza. He decided to get into the coffee-shop business with the help of some business partners, notably Ron Joyce, who built the empire after Horton's tragic death in a car accident in 1974.

It was a consumers' empire built out of strict attention to quality and convenience and, maybe most important of all, predictability, reliability and same-ness. All Tim Hortons coffee had to taste the same. That apple fritter you bought in Thunder Bay had to taste exactly like the one you scarfed down in Vancouver. The logos, the packaging and the decor of all Tim Hortons franchise locations were carefully chosen to ensure ease of use for car owners, with drive-through windows and ample parking. It's important to note what was happening. While other businesses in Canada were getting into niche marketing, Tim's was keeping itself firmly planted in the mass-marketing mindset of the 1950s school of consumerism—the Fordist economy, as it was called. You might even say that Tim's was a paragon of Fordism in the modern age.

Certainly, the doughnut shop was linked to the mass-production society of the car manufacturers who helped change the landscape and the political culture of the country in the 1950s. Tim Hortons' head office is in Oakville, Ontario, in the shadow of the giant Ford Motor Company of Canada plant and surrounded by the affluent suburbs that arose in the postwar boom. Its product and even its employees and owners are created in assembly-line fashion, through the "Doughnut University" training centre for franchise owners. Cars have almost always figured largely in Tim Hortons' choice of locations, too. A large part of the success of Tim Hortons was linked to car culture and the willingness of the company to make its retail outlets car-friendly, with drive-in windows and lots of parking.

But the real genius behind Tim Hortons is modern marketing wisdom, leaps and bounds ahead of the era in which its nostalgic appeal lies. Tim Hortons is an idea, not just a product. It trades in images. Cleverly, Tim's managed to align its brand with the same kind of citizens who had built the consumer nation in the 1950s—the commuters and the suburbanites, the canny shoppers looking for value and mass-produced reliability. These were exactly the kind of people who were proving useful to the political class, too—older voters or people disenchanted with politics, in search of simplicity in a complex consumer world. The alliance was sealed with some highly emotive advertising.

In 1997, Tim Hortons launched its "True Stories" ad campaign, to show the place of the doughnut shop in the lives of ordinary Canadians. It was this campaign—salt-of-the-earth citizens mixed with the sweetness of doughnuts and double-doubles—that vaulted Tim's from being a mere doughnut chain to being a patriotic icon in the Canadian imagination. The ads were a result, no surprise, of market research, which showed that Tim Hortons represented more than a product to its patrons. In 1996, Tim Hortons' marketing chief, Ron Buist, conducted focus-group testing on what people liked best about the restaurants. To Buist's surprise, it was neither the dough-nuts nor the coffee, but the daily ritual that Tim Hortons represented in Canadians' lives and its place in their immediate communities—their familiar piece of home in a busy, unpredictable world.

The first "True Story" featured an elderly woman named Lillian who made a daily pilgrimage with a cane up a hill in Lunenburg, Nova Scotia, to get her cup of coffee. The second ad showed Sammi the dog picking up coffee for his owner at a drive-through Tim Hortons. Subsequent ads, all inspired by real-life tales, would play up the familiarity of Tim's in people's lives. One of the most power-ful, tear-jerking commercials, called "Proud Fathers," told the story of how a Chinese immigrant had discouraged his son from playing hockey, only to reveal years later that he'd been watching and quietly cheering him on all along. Many of the commercials featured hockey. None included politicians, of course. Yet Tim Hortons' "True Stories" were giving Canadian politicians a glimpse into the lives of people whose votes were precious in a consumer age. These ads were also giving political strategists, Conservative ones especially, some ideas about how to present politicians to consumer-citizens.

Patricia Cormack, a sociologist with St. Francis Xavier University in Nova Scotia, extensively probed the connection between those

Tim Hortons ads and the rise of the doughnut shop to a national treasure and has written several scholarly works on the links between Tim's and civic culture. In 2013 Cormack released a book, *Desiring Canada*, in which she and co-author James Cosgrave took a close look at the ways in which the Canadian identity was being shaped by pleasurable pursuits—eating doughnuts being one of them. In effect, Cormack argued, while politicians and governments were busy turning citizens into consumers, Tim Hortons was turning consumers into citizens. For Cormack, the Tim's marketing campaign provided citizens with a virtual town square and a shared narrative—something that politics has always aspired to provide. "Banal nationalism," a phrase coined by social-psychologist Michael Billig to describe the pride of citizens in their everyday existence, was the main patriotism on display in "True Stories."

Cormack writes, "While some of the themes taken up by Tim Hortons—ruggedness, endurance, civility—do piggyback on clichéd versions of Canadianness, it is how and where these characteristics arise that shifts the ground of national identity to Tim Hortons itself. It is on this ground that the local, small, sensual and ambiguous articulation of national identity can thrive. It is also on this ground that Tim Hortons authorizes itself as the site and source of Canadianness." Moreover, in a country whose national symbols up to now had all been rural or historic—landscapes, the Rockies, the shores, the beaver, the forests—Tim Hortons landed as the first urban symbol. Or, more properly, the first *suburban* symbol, situated in the great mass-market middle that politicians coveted.

Label This

The very first months of the twenty-first century saw a vivid display of ambivalence about the branding mania that had invaded the political and consumer culture in previous decades. Canadian author and activist Naomi Klein, not even out of her twenties, in 1999 published her blockbuster book *No Logo*, which asked people to resist the corporate takeover of public space. Klein warned that branding was unravelling the old order, turning the market into a competition for consumers' minds, not just their money:

> The old paradigm had it that all marketing was selling a product. In the new model, however, the product always takes a back seat to the real product, the brand, and the selling of the brand acquired an extra component that can only be described as spiritual. Advertising is about hawking product. Branding, in its truest and most advanced incarnations, is about corporate transcendence. It may sound flaky, but that's precisely the point... The brand builders conquered and a new consensus was born: the products that will flourish in the future will be the ones presented not as "commodities" but as concepts: the brand as experience, as lifestyle.

Klein didn't invent this notion of consumer products turning into symbols. Cultural theorists such as Roland Barthes and Jean Baudrillard had been writing on the same themes for some time. "Governing today means giving acceptable signs of credibility. It is like advertising and it is the same effect that is achieved—commitment to a scenario, whether it be a political or an advertising scenario," Baudrillard wrote in his book *America*, a study of the culture of the United States in Reagan's time. The marketing world had also been talking about the quest for customer "mind-share" and "mental real estate" since the 1970s. But Klein took these ideas into the realm of activism and the anti-corporate resistance emerging in North America as the old century ended and a new one began. *No Logo* became an immediate international bestseller, described by the *New York Times* as a "bible" for the anti-globalization movement, and it was summarized this way by the *Village Voice*: "Nothing short of a complete, user-friendly handbook on the negative effects that nineties überbrand marketing has had on culture, work and consumer choice... *No Logo* may itself be one of the anti-corporate movement's best hopes yet."

Even as Klein's book was still flying off the shelves, Canadians were finding yet another brand to rally them to new heights of patriotism. No, not in doughnuts, but beer. Beer already was a point of Canadian pride and history. The two big beer giants, Molson and Labatt, could boast corporate origins dating back to pre-Confederation times. John Molson started brewing beer in the late 1700s in Quebec, and the Molson descendants had their hands in every major business of Canada's founding—railroads, hotels, even banks. Labatt was founded in 1847 by John Kinder, beginning its brewing history in London, Ontario, that petri dish for consumerism through much of the 1900s. Labatt's pilsner lager, Blue, borrowed its name from the Winnipeg Blue Bombers, and Labatt's 50 ale was so dubbed to mark the midpoint of the century that shaped Canada.

Beer drinking and the great Canadian sport of hockey also went hand in hand, thanks largely to the brewers' historic sponsorship of hockey teams and TV's *Hockey Night in Canada*. Beer consumption in Canada and the brewers' profits were tied to the NHL season. Endless commercials for Molson and Labatt played on the hockey theme, featuring strapping young Canadian lads knocking back some beer after a pickup hockey game or enjoying some brew while they watched the pros play.

With their provenance so tied up in Canadian history and culture, it's probably not an accident that the fates of beer also ran parallel to political and consumer trends in Canada. When the country was preoccupied with American influence, Canadians would toast the differences between their superior beer and the inferior American brands. In 1985, for instance, the *Washington Post* reported on how Canadians had been forced to swallow their disdain for US beer during a brief brewers' strike in Ontario, when bar owners were forced to stock their shelves with what patrons complained were more "watery" brands. "Nobody really likes it, but when there's nothing else around, it's okay," Shelley Whitteker, manager of Toronto's Black Bull Tavern, told the *Post*. In 1993, after Mulroney's free-trade deal paved the way for American beer to pour into Canada, *Montreal Gazette* columnist Jack Todd vented, "American beer is watery, sugary near-beer. It's what you drink when you're out of beer. It's what you'd get if you poured yourself a half-glass of Labatt's finest and then topped your glass off with Tang."

When Canadians started turning against the big established brands in the commercial and political world in the 1980s, the beer industry replied with an explosion of new brands and micro-brews. And as wine consumption was steadily climbing in North America over the decades after the Second World War—Canadians drank five times more wine in the 2000s than they did in the 1960s, according to StatsCan—drinking beer was a way to proclaim common roots. Politicians loved to be photographed hoisting a brew with blue-collar folks on the campaign trail.

"I've been working all my life," Chrétien boasted for the cameras in 1993, as he helped load a case of beer into a truck. In the US, the class divide within the Democratic Party was dubbed the "wine track" versus the "beer track." Beer drinkers, like Tim Hortons customers, didn't want fancy, foreign names for their beverages. Beer drinkers could even be a country unto themselves, as ad man Terry O'Malley learned way back in the 1960s when he dreamed up the anthem and thumbs-up salute for "Red Cap Nation."

In 1980, *Second City TV* comedians Rick Moranis and Dave Thomas introduced the hoser characters Bob and Doug McKenzie to their audiences—beer-swilling boors, clad in toques and lumber-jack plaid, who delivered wisdom from the "Great White North" on a couch surrounded by Molson Canadian beer cases. Their characters were an instant hit, north and south of the border. A comedy album of their routines sold 350,000 copies in Canada in 1982 and a whopping 3.5 million in the United States. A *People* magazine article from that year said that the show's Canadiana catchphrases—"g'day," "eh?" and "take off"—were "on adolescent lips from Halifax to Victoria."

No beer company has performed the task of nation-building better than Molson Canadian and what came to be simply known as "the rant." In April 2000 Molson unveiled the now-famous ad during the annual broadcast of the Academy Awards. In the one-minute spot, Joe Canadian, clad in a plaid shirt and jeans, stands in a movie theatre against a flickering backdrop of national images, telling Americans what Canadians are, and what we aren't:

> I am not a lumberjack or a fur trader, and I don't live in an igloo or eat blubber or own a dog sled. And I don't know Jimmy, Sally or Suzie from Canada although I'm certain they're really, really nice. Uh, I have a prime minister, not a president. I speak English and French, not American. And I pronounce it *about*, not *a boot*. I can proudly sew my country's flag on my backpack. I believe in peacekeeping not policing, diversity not assimilation, and that the beaver is a truly proud and noble animal! A toque is a hat. A chesterfield is a couch. And it is pronounced *zed*! Not *zee*, *zed*! Canada is the second-largest land mass, the first nation of hockey, and the best part of North America. My name is Joe, and I am Canadian!

Molson had some hints in advance that this ad would go over well with Canadians. Its ad firm, Bensimon Byrne, had done extensive research in its bid to cement the Molson brand as the paragon of patriotism. During test runs in movie theatres, audiences had actually stood up and cheered. Bensimon Byrne, in later analysis, would acknowledge that this was an "audacious" escalation in the long-running beer war between Molson and Labatt. In focus-group testing, ad executives learned of an interesting culture shift that was under way in the country: Canadians were not so willing anymore to be reserved about their attachment to the country. "Younger

Canadians want to shout it from the rooftops. Many of us regard flag-waving patriotism as distinctly American. Younger Canadians told us, and showed us, that this is simply not the case for them," the ad firm wrote in a 2001 piece for "Canadian Advertising Success Stories," a regular news bulletin issued by the Canadian Congress of Advertisers. Molson and Bensimon Byrne estimated that the sheer news coverage had generated the equivalent of nearly $9 million in free advertising for the product. But more than help sell beer, it also helped "sell" the idea of Canada—to Canadians.

There was a somewhat amusing irony here. Ever since the near-victory of separatism in the 1995 Quebec referendum, the federal government had been trying to come up with ways to talk up Canadian patriotism. Heritage Minister Sheila Copps had been handing out flags and the Chrétien Liberals were spending millions of dollars on government advertising and sponsorship, including a flood of "Heritage Minutes" TV ads, intended to enlighten citizens about their shared history. But a simple beer commercial found a much swifter route into the hearts and minds of Canadian consumer-citizens.

In the pages of *This Magazine* in late 1996, Nicole Nolan flatly declared that Copps should pass the patriotism-building torch to the beer companies—that they were doing a better job of inspiring love of Canada, especially among young people. "Copps and her flags seem trapped in an agonizingly archaic dance, recycling dusty notions in a desperate attempt to fuel national spirit," Nolan wrote. "Witty, cosmopolitan, simultaneously proud and self-deprecating, the Molson and Labatt ads are the only blips on the radar that are even attempting to rethink what 'Canadian' means in the late twentieth century." Faced with a choice between the Canada in the beer ads and the country depicted in the "gruesome" Heritage Minutes, Nolan said it was no contest. "The government's heritage moments, promoting such Canadian high points as the Underground Railroad and the first female MP, are so smarmy and sugar-coated that they've been parodied by both *Saturday Night* magazine and *Frank*."

Nolan's cheeky reproach spoke volumes about how commercial companies—beer, but also Tim Hortons—were doing a better job of speaking to Canadians than politicians were. Certainly, the advertising was superior. There were several reasons for this mismatch between political and commercial advertising, some of them similar to the warnings about the differences that Allister Grosart underlined in his 1953 memo to the Conservatives. Fifty years later, some of those rules still held true. Private companies had more money, naturally. They could take risks, without fear that one wrong move could spell ignominy and doom with the Canadian public. Commercial advertising also had the luxury of time to build a product into a much-vaunted brand. As Terry O'Malley had found in the 1970s and 1980s, the deadlines, urgency and "finish line" of election day meant that the pace of political advertising was more rushed and ad hoc. Political ads ran on TV only during elections for the latter half of the twentieth century. Tim Hortons could spend months, even years, unfolding its "True Stories" to Canadian viewers. Beer companies could take decades to come up with the ads that Nolan found so Canada-friendly. Political parties, however, had just sixty days, and then, when election campaigns shortened in the 1990s, just thirty-six days to establish their "brand." In that shortened time frame, political-ad makers seemed to agree, one couldn't afford to be subtle, creative or even funny. Humour is notoriously difficult to pull off in politics.

Politicians couldn't even be funny about beer. Jean Chrétien, in 1994, had joked that beer and joblessness went hand in hand. Explaining why he'd rather see the government pay people to work than leave them unemployed, Chrétien inelegantly put it this way: "It's better to have them at 50-percent productivity than to be sitting home drinking beer at zero-percent productivity." Chrétien was forced to apologize. And then, more infamously, there was the "beer-and-popcorn" remark during the 2005–06 election campaign, which helped convince Canadians that the Liberals really were out of touch with the average voter. Prime Minister Paul Martin's communications chief Scott Reid was on TV, arguing that it was better to have a national child-care program than the Conservatives' $100-a-month child benefit. But then he brought beer into the discussion. "Don't give people $25 a day to blow on beer and popcorn," Reid said. "Give them child-care spaces that work." In the ensuing days, Conservatives refused to let the issue drop, pronouncing themselves saddened by the Liberal "insult" to Canadian parents.

The only innovation in political advertising from the 1950s, it seemed, was the negative ad—attacks on competitors that wouldn't be tolerated in the commercial world. Did Tim Hortons go on TV to attack the patriotism of Starbucks, erasing the borders between Canada and the United States? Did the beer companies make fun of the facial features of rival beer drinkers? In 2000, the *Toronto Star* assembled some ad experts to judge the advertising on offer during the federal election campaign. For the most part, they turned up their noses. Politicians just didn't get it, they said. One of the people judging the ads was Jack Bensimon, whose firm created the Molson rant. "Political strategists aren't comfortable in working the way we work," Bensimon told the *Star*. "They find a bigger comfort zone working in the area they're most familiar with, negative advertising, and that's rational and issue-orientated."

So when Canadians wanted to find ads that connected to their emotional, patriotic selves, they were looking to the TV pitches for beer and doughnuts. An unlikely diet for a healthy nation, perhaps, but a potent mix for a politics that could be built on the same images that made Canadians feel so warm about those products. The shape of Canadian politics to come in Canada would turn on these questions, which amounted to a dare for any political party bold enough to complete the bridge between consumers and citizens; between politics and marketing: What if you could learn the lessons of the beer-and-doughnut marketing success and turn it into a political force? What if you could snatch political power from the same forces that made Canadians so proud to be consumers of beer and Tim Hortons products? What if you could pull all this off with a leader who didn't drink beer or coffee?

SEALING THE DEAL

MARKET LEADER

Before Canada's political marketing tale plunges into the twenty-first century, a quick recap of the story so far may be in order. This shopping expedition through Canada's political history has taken us from the heart of Toronto in the 1950s and back and forth to Ottawa through the following decades, with a quick stop or two in Alberta. Winding through the first few decades after the Second World War, we saw the political class getting swept up in all the fun of the advertising and polling worlds. But by the 1980s and 1990s, Canadian politics was being rocked by the same forces that were rippling through the consumer world: niche markets and the rejection or rebranding of old, established labels. Citizens were not clear whether business or government could do the best job of running the country.

Someone else was on a parallel journey all those years: a man named Stephen Harper, whose biography closely tracks the progress of Canada into the era of political marketing. Born on April 30, 1959, Harper was raised in Leaside and Etobicoke, middle-class enclaves of Toronto, where advertising, polling and television first gained their major foothold in Canadian political culture. At the age of nineteen, in 1978, a disillusioned Harper dropped out of the University of Toronto and headed to Alberta, where the grassroots foment against old, established politics was simmering.

Through the 1980s and 1990s, Harper shuffled between big-brand and niche parties, much in the same way that Canadians were switching their loyalties to car companies or detergent labels. He had arrived in Alberta as a Liberal. "When Stephen first came to Edmonton, he was a Trudeau Liberal. He thought Trudeau was god," Frank Glenfield, Harper's first boss at Imperial Oil when he moved west, recalled in an interview with the *Edmonton Journal*. But soon after Harper's immersion into economics at the University of Calgary, he shrugged off his Liberalism and became a Progressive Conservative. That didn't last long, though. He worked on Parliament Hill as an assistant to Calgary Progressive Conservative MP Jim Hawkes for a while in the 1980s, then he went back to Alberta and got involved with the fledgling Reform Party. He rose quickly in those ranks, becoming a leading Reform MP in the 1990s, but Harper eventually walked away from that brand, too, choosing to take up a job with the National Citizens Coalition as the twentieth century was drawing to a close. This ambivalence about his ambitions closely matched Canadians' shifting feelings about politics, it seemed, through these decades of waning attachment to parties and declining turnout at the polls.

Fatefully, though, Harper would return to politics in 2002, first to lead the Canadian Alliance and then, in 2004, a brand-new Conservative party created by the merger of the Alliance and the Progressive Conservatives. Although he would see this as his signature achievement, it wasn't the only merger Harper achieved. On his route to the top political job in Canada, this avid student of the marketing age would merge consumer and civic culture in a way that no politician had achieved to date in Canada.

Tim Hortons Canadians: The 10 Percent

In the fall of 2005, Harper and some of his top communications aides descended on Toronto to film some TV commercials, in preparation for an election that could come anytime under Paul Martin's fragile minority government. Although Martin had seized power from Jean Chrétien in 2003 with huge hopes of revitalizing the Liberal "brand"—putting a new and improved label on a party that had enjoyed twelve years in power—the scandals over the waste and corruption of Chrétien's advertising and sponsorship program had taken their toll. It was a fitting coda in this consumer-citizenship age: a political brand destroyed by a bad advertising campaign.

The Harper team had commandeered some vacant commercial space on Queen Street West—at the very trendy heart of the Liberals' Toronto stronghold—to do the filming. While they were there, the man in charge of Conservative marketing, Patrick Muttart, was presenting the team with an arresting, visual slide show. Like many political strategists before him, Muttart had studied demographics, particularly the statistical profiles being provided by the party's pollster, Dimitri Pantazopoulos, which allowed him to sort citizens into likely or unlikely supporters of the Conservatives.

Allan Gregg had done the same thing with his "typologies" back in the 1980s. Here, though, is where Muttart's marketing knowledge came in handy. Unlike other strategists, who would present findings such as this with charts, statistics and graphs, Muttart had found a colourful way to explain to fellow Conservative operatives how he was "segmenting" Canadian voters: he created fictional archetypes out of the demographic data and gave these archetypes names and lives. "Dougie" was a single guy in his late twenties who worked at Canadian Tire, and who could be lured to the Conservative cause if they could get him to shed his political apathy and vote. He agreed with Conservative policies on crime and welfare abuse, but he was more interested in hunting and fishing than politics. Up on the screen, Muttart flashed pictures of a typical "Dougie," along with his house, his car and the Canadian Tire where he worked. Then there were "Rick and Brenda," a common-law couple with working-class jobs, who could also probably be persuaded to swing to the Conservatives if the party pushed the right buttons with their bread-and-butter concerns about taxes or the costs of keeping up their home. Up on the screen shone the faces of this couple, their suburban home and their minivan.

Conservatives had to go looking for their potential supporters where they lived, Muttart said. "That means going to Tim Hortons, not to Starbucks," he said. "That means going to Canadian Tire instead of Holt Renfrew." Of course, some voters were not worth chasing. "Fiona and Marcus," for instance, were a high-income, childless couple who lived in an expensive condominium, who didn't mind paying high taxes and would probably always vote Liberal. And in that same vein, Muttart's little slide show finally landed on "Zoe," a single, urban female, fond of yoga and organic food, living in a highrise in Toronto, who was probably a lost cause—nothing was likely to lure her away from the Liberals or New Democrats. Forget about Zoe, Muttart said.

Harper and the team watched the slide show with nods of approval and the occasional chuckle. This was an eminently clear way of seeing Canada's political map, perfect for people like Harper, a baby boomer who had grown up with television images and characters. These weren't just numbers; they were stories, or commercials. With Zoe's face still up on the screen, lunch arrived for the group: plates of sandwiches—fussy, fancy sandwiches. The group burst out laughing when they saw who had supplied their lunch: Zoe's catering company. Muttart had put a Canadian twist on Margaret Thatcher's "Essex Man" or Tony Blair's "Basildon Man." Or, if you want to cast further back, you could say that Muttart had located Canada's version of Reagan Democrats, or those marketing-susceptible voters who were sketched out in *Canadian Forum* articles by the mysterious Philip Spencer in the 1940s.

Muttart believed that a Canadian conservative coalition could be built by appealing to multiple segments of the population, some with little to no interest in politics—the squeezed working class who saw themselves reflected in those Tim Hortons "True Stories" ads, for instance. Other segments were generally apathetic to politics but might rouse themselves to vote if they heard something they liked about their consumerist concerns. This smart-marketing politico was figuring out how to turn Canadians' shaky attitudes toward politics into an asset for his party. In advance of the 2005 campaign, Muttart had spent a lot of time travelling and reading and divining the lessons of other successful political marketing campaigns to woo the middle class. He was politically ecumenical in his studies, finding things to learn from Tony Blair's New Labour as well as from Margaret Thatcher and the Republicans under Richard Nixon and Ronald Reagan.

Muttart had pored over past Canadian election campaigns, too, taking careful note of everything from the "visuals" to the personal dynamics. But it was in Australia, under Coalition Prime Minister John Howard, where he found some of his largest inspiration. Howard had also built a base of appeal around the working class— the "battlers," as they were called Down Under. In a 2004 radio interview, Howard described this demographic slice of Australia in terms of their aspirations: "The battler is somebody who finds in life that they have to work hard for everything they get... somebody who's not earning a huge income but somebody who is trying to better themselves."

Whether you wanted to call these people battlers or Essex Men or Tim Hortons voters, Muttart knew that the most distinguishing characteristic of this constituency was its lack of attachment to politics. Unlike the voters of earlier times in Canada, they didn't base their ballot choice on any brand loyalty—if they voted at all. They were neither right nor left on the spectrum; indeed, they might have right-wing views on one issue, left-wing views on another. They were not the kind of people who gathered around the TV every night at ten o'clock to watch CBC TV's *The National* or political-panel discussions on any of the networks. That mass-media market, and the fuzzy, familiar middle-political mindset, had exploded into a five-hundred-channel universe. Tim Hortons voters were more likely to catch a snippet of the news from supper-hour broadcasts, which had more of a local focus—if they watched the news at all. If they were feeling stirred to patriotism, that was probably the result of an ad for doughnuts or beer.

Muttart and Pantazopoulos had done some digging into media-consumption habits in Canada, and by their estimates, only half of the Canadian voting public paid any attention to news at all, either in newspapers or on TV. The strategists also calculated that people who follow the political news usually have a point of view on which party they support; these news consumers often knew, even before election campaigns began, how they were going to cast their ballots on election day. That meant that 50 percent of the electorate was unlikely to be swayed by campaign twists and turns. What about the other half, though? A hard truth: most of them didn't vote at all; turnout rates were hovering at about 60 percent in Canada in these modern times. But by Muttart's rudimentary calculation, that still left about 10 percent of the population who would vote, even though they hadn't been following the news regularly. In a close election, this floating, politically disengaged part of the electorate could be crucial—and they wouldn't be getting their information through the media. For these people, you needed other ways, sometimes "brutally simple" ways, to get their support, Muttart believed.

And that's where the marketing knowledge was important— which Muttart happened to have in spades. "The only way to reach these people is through television advertising or direct-mail post-cards," Muttart explained in a 2012 interview, rattling off some more numbers. "With television advertising, you've got a thirty-second spot... which roughly equals eighty-two words." In more direct marketing, the type in which political material is delivered to homeowners through the mail slot, Muttart said that there's a "three-second rule." Three seconds is the time it takes for someone to decide either to read the postcard or toss it in the trash. Whether it's three seconds or thirty seconds, neither of these methods of communication lend themselves to subtlety, Muttart contended: "Academics usually criticize people like me for this type of communication, but what are you supposed to do, when you're down to the final weeks of the campaign and you're competing for the attention of the least informed, the least engaged and the least intense voters, who are going to decide the outcome of an election campaign? This is why political marketers have to be so blunt and so direct."

The Marketing Department

Many marketing and advertising people have lent their expertise to Canadian political parties over the years, but none had ever really had a figure like Patrick Muttart, so pivotal to the inner circle. André Turcotte, who did polling and a bit of market research for the old Reform Party in its early days, describes Muttart as essentially the vice-president of marketing for Harper's Conservative party.

"The most important change that Conservative strategists made after the 2004 election was to bring all market intelligence in-house," Turcotte, now a communications professor, wrote in an analysis of the Conservatives' political marketing success. "They broke away from the usual practice of relying on a pollster-of-record and took internal control of the market intelligence process." Not only did Muttart watch the polls, but he actually was the author of the overall "campaign narrative"—a combination of polling intelligence, policy, image and advertising, all in one linked package. And now that Canada seemed to be entering a period of minority government, the campaign didn't start or stop with elections. A big part of Muttart's job was to consider everything the Conservatives did in terms of potential gains or losses in future elections, twenty-four hours a day, seven days a week, similar to how Canadians were consuming their products and services.

Muttart's talents stood out largely because they were unusual in the Conservative party, as it was constituted circa 2005. Bright, young, in his early thirties when he came to work in Harper's office, he had honed his marketing skills working for the Delta Hotels chain and also in the Navigator public relations firm in Toronto.

"There are not a lot of Conservatives or people on the political right who have an interest in design, in the visual presentation of political ideas," Muttart said. This was especially true among the ranks of conservative-minded politicos in Canada, who tended to be "policy wonks" or people attracted to issues of procedure or ideology. Conservatives drew a lot of their supporters from business, military and engineering backgrounds, for instance, where you'd find people primarily concerned with political "mechanics" or systems. "Advertising, marketing, design, staging—you don't tend to find a lot of people on the Conservative side of politics or the political right who tend to go into those disciplines," Muttart said.

How did he come by these skills? Even Muttart himself is not sure. For all his appreciation of creativity when he sees it, Muttart doesn't paint, draw or play a musical instrument. He grew up in a working-class family in Woodstock, Ontario, and first became interested in politics while delivering the *Woodstock Sentinel-Review* after school in the early 1980s. Walking between his customers' homes, he'd start reading the paper. In 1984, when he was twelve, the Liberal leadership race was under way, and young Patrick was fascinated by the battle between John Turner and Jean Chrétien. He liked the looks of Turner and was intrigued by the way he was pitching himself as the candidate with winning credentials. Muttart was also fascinated with the parties' signs and logos, especially the way the Turner team had fashioned the Liberal logo to incorporate the candidate's name into the design. He was delighted when Turner won, and volunteered to help the local Liberal candidate in the 1984 election: a fellow named Alfred Apps, a former student council president of the University of Western Ontario. Muttart would go on to be a volunteer for Apps in a couple of subsequent provincial campaigns, but by the time the 1988 election rolled around, when he was eligible to vote, Muttart had migrated to the Conservatives. (Apps, meanwhile, would end up as president of the Liberal party from 2009 to 2012.)

In previous decades, the marketing and advertising people had to navigate around politicians who felt decidedly ambivalent about borrowing sales techniques from the commercial sector—bristling at being sold like soap or tomatoes. But Muttart didn't face any such obstacles in the Conservative inner circle. "Never once was there a debate about the importance of marketing or the need to use marketing strategies to deliver political messages to Canadians," he said.

First and most importantly, Stephen Harper saw the wisdom of marketing. Contrary to what one might have expected from this serious, dry student of economics, Harper also paid vivid attention to political packaging. When he had been running as a Reform MP in the 1993 campaign, he had parted ways with the uniform, centrally approved brand and put up his own style of signs. And when he took over the Conservative leadership, once the Canadian Alliance had merged with the old Progressive Conservatives, one of the first items on his to-do list was redesigning the party logo.

There were robust discussions over type styles and colours. Harper himself had been sketching out ideas in his spare time. It would be mainly blue, of course, since Conservatives of all stripes in Canada had been embracing that colour for a century. "Stephen thought blue was a good strong colour," Tom Flanagan said. But what should the accent shades be? The old Reformers had wanted to include some green, to evoke the links to the grassroots. Meanwhile, the traditional PC logo, to the consternation of some in the Alliance/Reform wing, had included a red flag. Red was seen as the Liberals' particular hue, and the presence of it pointed to a certain lefty leaning among the

PCs. Inside the fourth-floor boardroom of the opposition offices in Parliament's Centre Block, a lively debate ensued over whether to mix green or red into the new Conservative label. Harper finally weighed in, choosing a red maple leaf to hover beside a big blue "C." He told his caucus that this new Conservative party could not keep allowing the Liberals to wrap themselves in the red-and-white flag of Canada—that Tories would have to take back the colour red from their rivals.

Harper had also been struck by an old story about Ronald Reagan and his understanding of how images worked in politics. Back in the 1980s, CBS correspondent Lesley Stahl had gone back through Reagan's public appearances, posing with disabled athletes or at a nursing home, and shown viewers how the pictures were direct contradictions of the president's deeds, particularly cuts in funding to these very constituencies. It was a tough piece, and Stahl expected the White House to be furious with her. But they were not. In fact, Reagan's staff was delighted. "Nobody heard what you said," Stahl was told. The pictures were all that the viewers remembered. Harper took that lesson to heart, and his staff would learn to pay as much attention to the staging of his announcements as to the substance within them. He found himself a makeup artist to keep on staff. And even though his tastes didn't run to beer or coffee, Harper would market himself as the kind of guy who would be happy to linger over a double-double at Tim Hortons or knock back a few ales after a hockey game. If everything else in the Conservative camp was getting a marketing makeover to suit the consumers, so would the leader. People would only remember the pictures anyway.

"Stephen Harper was probably the first true, modern communications prime minister. He was born in the TV era. He grew up in the 1960s, the 1970s, the 1980s. He spent a lot of time following politics," Muttart said. Harper had also dabbled in some marketing himself. His stint with the National Citizens Coalition from 1997 to 2001 had taught Harper a thing or two about how to lob political ideas into the marketplace. From its humble beginnings as Colin Brown's protest against government spending in the 1970s, the NCC had grown to be a powerful grassroots ally to conservative politicians in Canada. The NCC and the Taxpayers Federation had been wildly successful at driving home to Canadians the idea that they were consumers of government services, and cranky ones at that.

"Throughout my time with him he would personally reference [NCC] campaigns that he ran," Muttart said. "He ran an organization that was in the business of erecting billboards, running direct-mail campaigns. So I don't think we've ever had a prime minister who had direct, personal experience being a marketer." This, Muttart said, was the crucial difference between Harper and any of his predecessors in the job—he was Canada's first marketing prime minister.

Much of his marketing knowledge came from on-the-job training. When he first arrived at the NCC offices, Harper had wanted to tone down some of the hard-sales tactics of the coalition, to make it more of a think-tank and less like an advocacy group. That tug of war, or the bargaining between institutional and consumer politics, was still going on in his mind, in other words. He changed the name of the NCC's newsletter from "The Bulldog" to "Freedom Watch." Harper didn't like personal attacks on politicians and he wasn't fond of NCC's "pigs at the trough" campaign against MP pensions. Gerry Nicholls, who worked at the NCC as Harper's vice-president, tried to persuade Harper that the high road often went right over people's heads—or at least the people the NCC was trying to reach. At one point, Harper turned his own hand to writing a radio ad, which went on for over two minutes and included a scattergun of attacks on Liberal corruption and election laws that limited third-party advertising. "It was a mess," Nicholls said in an interview. Harper was eventually persuaded to keep the NCC radio ads to thirty seconds and one main idea. He had learned, in other words, what Muttart knew about the eighty-two-word limit for television and the three-second rule for direct mail.

Gradually, Harper also started to come around to hard-sell marketing, Nicholls said, especially when it came to attacking the Wheat Board and Elections Canada. In August 2001, he sent out a "personal letter" (actually drafted by Nicholls) that started, "The jackasses at Elections Canada are out of control. Please excuse my language, but when I learned Elections Canada's bureaucrats have pressed charges against a Canadian citizen, I just blew my cool. That is the exact language I used." The letter was a protest against a citizen who was facing fines of up to $25,000 for prematurely posting election results on his website. "And no, it wasn't part of a criminal conspiracy, or luring children toward violent pornography. It was actually something government officials seem to believe is a lot more dangerous—information."

Nicholls was a fan of the communications school of Arthur Finkelstein, a Republican strategist famed for attack ads in the United States that featured a lot of repetition, demonization of opponents and name-calling. "Punchy, short on substance and long on emotion"—that's the formula for a good ad campaign, Nicholls believed. And Harper, by the end of his tenure at the NCC, was getting more comfortable with the hard, blunt and simple method of communicating. In the 2001 provincial election in Alberta, the NCC ran radio ads against the Liberals that starkly stated, "You have a simple choice in this election. You can either vote for the Liberals or you can vote for Alberta."

So by the time Harper came to leading the Conservative party into the 2005 election campaign, he'd been well seasoned in the art of the political attack—on the receiving end, more than the giving end, however. In the 2004 election campaign, the Liberals had pulled together a whole series of ads organized around the idea that Harper and his Conservatives were scary. The advertising came from the Bensimon Byrne agency, the firm responsible for the Molson rant.

The most powerful Liberal attack ad featured a female narrator, her words set against a background of ominous music, intoning about all the frightening things that would happen to Canada if Harper were the prime minister: troops in Iraq, US-style health care, a rollback of abortion rights. As the camera zoomed in on a picture of the Canadian flag, the narrator said, "Stephen Harper says that when he's through with Canada we won't recognize it." And then, as the flag began to burn, came the final thrust: "You know what? He's right." Jack Bensimon was later quoted as saying never "in all my marketing experience [had I] witnessed as powerful an impact for a single ad." Not long after the ad was launched, the Liberals began to rally from a downward spiral in the polls and in the end eked out a minority victory over the Conservatives. Even among some Conservatives, negative impressions of Harper lingered. The always fearless John Crosbie, formerly a top minister in Brian Mulroney's cabinet in the 1980s, told the *National Post* in 2005, "Among our friends, the women think he's scary." One of Muttart's main objectives going into the 2005 election, then, was to somehow erase this "scary" label that had been successfully affixed to Harper.

Muttart also had a staunch ally in Doug Finley, the gruff, Scots-born campaign chief for the Conservatives. Like Muttart, Finley had dallied with the Liberals in his past—as well as with Scottish nationalists in his native land. When Finley was nineteen, he helped in the campaign that elected the first Scottish National Party MP to Westminster. Finley moved to Canada in 1968, just in time to see Pierre Trudeau elected prime minister. With his degree in business administration, he got a job with Rolls-Royce, moving up to director of corporate planning and business development. In his spare time, he volunteered on Liberal campaigns in Quebec, including the 1974 election. He then moved on to Winnipeg with his second wife, Diane, and stayed out of politics for a while. It was only after he moved to southern Ontario in the late 1990s that he drifted toward active Conservative politics, first at the provincial level, then with the Canadian Alliance. Finley obviously impressed Harper when he was running the Perth–Middlesex by-election campaign for the

Conservatives in 2003, because when Harper ran for leader of the newly merged Conservative party in 2003, Finley was his campaign manager. And when Tom Flanagan stepped back from his role as campaign chief overall—after the unsuccessful Conservative campaign in 2004—the reins were passed to Finley.

Finley was notoriously fond of organization and technology, and campaigns he had run included lots of high-tech bells and whistles. This was largely a product of his business and sales background, according to Muttart. "His business life was spent in sales and marketing for large corporations, so he actually had experience with client contact-management systems. He had experience with marketing collateral. He had experience making sales presentations," Muttart said.

Pantazopoulos, the pollster, also had a keen eye for marketing techniques. After his early years working with the Reform Party, he had gone to the United States to work first with Frank Luntz and then with a company called Market Strategies Inc., where renowned consultants Fred Steeper and Alex Gage became his mentors. Gage would turn out to be a highly influential force in the Republicans' early efforts to turn consumer data into political intelligence and the resulting transformation of American campaign methods in the twenty-first century. Pantazopoulos, meanwhile, also liked to use consumer analogies when he was framing political situations, which was probably in part a product of his bachelor's degree in commerce from Carleton University. He had read carefully and absorbed the sales wisdom contained in Robert Jolles's book *Customer Centered Selling*, especially the insights about "decision cycles." Over thirty years selling computers for Xerox, Jolles had come up with an eight-stage system to anticipate and eventually meet consumer needs, over and over again. Pantazopoulos saw how this approach could be transferred to the political world, if the strategists could present a political platform or politician as the answer to voters' needs and problems. It would be Pantazopoulos's job, then, to identify those needs and problems through extensive on-the-ground surveys. It would be Harper's job to present himself as the reply to consumer-citizens' demand.

Another person who would end up doing a lot of marketing for Harper was Dimitri Soudas, who also had found his entree into politics through the Liberal party. Part of the Greek community in Montreal, the son of a single mother, Soudas had started dabbling in politics when he was fourteen years old, as one of a young band of volunteers working for local Liberal MP Eleni Bakopanos. He fell out with the Liberals when he applied to do an internship on Parliament Hill and learned that the positions went to relatives of high-ranking party members. Stung by the rejection, Soudas went looking for a new political party to support. His best friend Leo Housakos had been involved with the Progressive Conservatives in Quebec but had migrated to the Canadian Alliance, running as a candidate in 2000. Although Housakos didn't make it to Ottawa after that campaign, his friend did. Soudas moved to Ottawa in 2002, not long after Harper had come back into politics as leader and when the Canadian Alliance was in strong need of bilingual, Quebec talent.

Soudas and Finley weren't the only former Liberals in Stephen Harper's circle, either. Mark Cameron, who had worked in the office of Stéphane Dion, had slowly migrated over to the Conservatives during the Canadian Alliance years. Cameron and Muttart had penned a devastating memo to Harper and Flanagan after the 2004 election, dissecting the anatomy of the campaign failures, especially in the domain of communications. They believed the Conservatives had to get far more serious about political marketing, paying attention to market research and strict message discipline.

Harper was impressed enough with the memo to put Muttart in charge of upping the Conservatives' marketing game for the next election. Jason Kenney, who had left the Taxpayers Federation in the late 1990s to enter elected politics, said that when Muttart started to make his marketing presentations to staffers, "you could hear a pin drop" in the room. Kenney, like Harper, had been well schooled in the arts of grassroots politicking and direct marketing through his work with an advocacy organization. He had learned that hundreds of plastic pigs on the lawn of Parliament would garner more attention than hundreds of pages of text. And Kenney had also migrated to the Conservatives from the Liberals—he had even worked in the 1980s in the office of Saskatchewan Liberal leader Ralph Goodale.

The presence of former Liberals around Harper, not to mention his own early dalliances with other parties, would not be an insignificant factor in the Conservatives' marketing approach to politics. These were people who knew a thing or two about the floating-loyalty phenomenon that was now a crucial factor in a "flexible" Canadian electorate. All of these allegiance shifters had watched what the Liberals had done right (and wrong) in the marketing realm and were ready to take some of those lessons to another level.

The Conservatives' decision to forget about Zoe, for instance, was actually another leap forward using an old strategy of political marketing efficiency. Patrick Muttart, by deciding where election-campaign efforts should be directed, was merely following in a straight line from the strategic wisdom that Keith Davey, the ad guys and Martin Goldfarb brought to the Liberals back in the 1960s, and then Allan Gregg, with his "typology" demographics and ridings, brought to the Conservatives in the 1980s. Where the previous marketing-savvy politicos advised that resources be directed to winnable geographic regions, however, Muttart was simply focusing more precisely: to winnable *individuals*. With the benefit of far more refined polling techniques, and thanks to improvements in technology over the decades, the Conservatives could "hypersegment" the Canadian electorate beyond vague regions, into pockets of individual Canadians, organized largely around lifestyle and neighbourhood. It didn't hurt either that the Conservatives had a pollster, Pantazopoulos, who had been working in the United States with some of the pioneers in analyzing consumer and political data in micro-segments. This approach was arriving in Canada as "politics by postal code"—something the consumer-marketing world had learned many years earlier.

Muttart's analysis of the Canadian electorate, in fact, was so precise that Conservatives knew which 500,000 voters they needed—swing voters in swing ridings. So while the media and the pundits were transfixed by the big horse-race numbers of national polls, the Conservatives paid them little heed. They didn't even bother with national polls after 2005, choosing instead to do nightly tracking polls among the small, micro-targeted constituencies they needed, as well as regular focus-group sessions that helped the party continually shape itself around what they were hearing from voters on the intangible plane of emotions and values.

More to the point, this micro-targeting also showed the Conservatives what votes they did not need to seek: supporters of Liberals, New Democrats and Greens who would cancel out the others' votes if the Conservatives' opposition remained scattered among a number of party alternatives. Conservatives, using micro-targeting, could also concentrate their pitches on people who were more likely to cast a vote on election day. The early Reform Party had taken this approach, too, to some extent, eschewing mass-market, pan-Canadian ambitions to focus on pockets of strength in the country (mainly in the West). Allan Gregg, watching this innovation in political polling, was struck by how far this took the new Conservative party away from the old "big-tent" approach of politics past.

"Every party that I've worked for wanted to be more popular. They always wanted more votes," Gregg said. "And these guys are saying we don't need more votes. We just need to make sure that the other guys are sharing a pool collectively... When I created the target-voter typology, the inherent assumption was that all voters aren't created equal. But this is a whole new generation of thinking in that regard: 'If my voters are twice as likely to turn out as yours, they're worth two times as much.'"

The Five Habits of Successful Political Marketers

Now that the Conservatives had become more sophisticated about political marketing, it was time to overhaul the platform, too. The 2004 Conservative platform had been far too complicated, too abstract to the concerns of Tim Hortons Canadians. If the Conservatives were serious about reaching these voters, they needed to make their party more accessible to people. This platform-overhaul effort was textbook political marketing—changing the product to line it up with the market research. The Conservatives, according to Jennifer Lees-Marshment's categories, were leaping from being a sales-oriented party to being a marketing-oriented party—from SOP to MOP.

The overhaul was carried out mainly by chief of staff Ian Brodie, relying heavily on Patrick Muttart's advice about reaching swing voters. The biggest change was to the Conservatives' tax policy. Their old promises had involved complicated changes to tax brackets and personal-income exemptions. But who among their target audience would care about this kind of nuanced change? Fixing the dreaded GST, though—that would get some notice. They wouldn't make reckless promises to make it "disappear," as Chrétien had, or try to mince words about its continued existence, as Paul Martin had. The Conservatives' new, marketing-approved platform made a bold, easy-to-understand vow—if the Conservatives won power, they would reduce the GST by 1 percent immediately, then by another one percent by the end of their first mandate. It would cost them $12 billion to $14 billion a year in revenue, not to mention a wave of criticism from economists, but the payoff would be power. And that, in politics, is like a major windfall in profits.

That GST promise showed just how far politicians had now travelled to accommodate consumer-citizenship. The GST, all on its own, had become a story about the evolution of political marketing. Brian Mulroney had been able to risk a "helluva row" in the Canadian public to introduce the GST, though it probably helped hasten the collapse of the old Progressive Conservative brand. Jean

Chrétien had been able to withstand the furor over his fuzzy promise to eliminate the GST. And though Liberals did internal polling on reducing the tax, they had decided that the treasury couldn't take the hit, and the public seemed to go along with this decision, if grudgingly. But the Conservatives, tailoring their politics to the realities of marketing, recognized that this tax "product" had to be shaped around market demand. The GST had moved through all those stages that Jennifer Lees-Marshment outlined, with her POPs, SOPs and MOPs. Under Mulroney, the GST was a take-it-or-leave-it product. Under Chrétien, it was something that needed to be sold or massaged to the electorate. Under Harper, it was a commodity that needed to be modified to answer consumer demand. The GST, like the politicians, had come into the marketing age.

On health care, meanwhile, the Conservatives also applied some marketing wisdom to their platform. Canadians felt like consumers when it came to using health-care services, and one of citizens' main complaints was to do with the waiting times they faced for medical attention. So the Conservatives threw out their more technical campaign promises from 2004, revolving around better ways to finance health care, and kept it simple again—with a "Patient Wait Times Guarantee." Consumers, as we've seen, love product guarantees.

On child care, the Conservatives would deliver another consumer-friendly promise, with a heavy dose of nostalgia in it, as a bonus—a baby bonus if you like. Rather than make grand promises to create a national child-care program, the Conservatives would instead give Canadian parents one hundred dollars a month for every child. It was indeed like the old baby-bonus program, which had evolved over the years into a far more complicated affair, targeted to families most in need. The Conservatives promised to make it all simple again, and called it the "Choice in Child Care Allowance." There was that old word from the 1950s explosion of consumerism again: choice. Consumer-citizens love choice—in the grocery aisles and in their government services.

The other two big promises revolved around "accountability" and law and order. The Conservatives were promising to clean up government, the justice system and the streets—an echo of Dalton Camp's "Let's Clean House" slogans of another era, but also a reflection of the more modern collapse of confidence in the legal and democratic systems. Those problems were actually complex and cultural, but political marketing usually demands simplicity. So these promises were summed up sparsely in the priority list as "clean up government" and "crack down on crime."

Like Blair's New Labour campaign, the Conservatives had distilled their platform down to five points or "priorities," as they were called. But although Muttart spent a lot of time studying Blair's brand of political marketing in the lead-up to the 2005 campaign, there was another, far more pedestrian reason for the Conservatives' five-promise platform: it would get them from Monday to Friday on the first week of the election campaign. Commercial sector marketers actually prefer the number seven when they're making lists, according to Muttart: "Seven Habits of Highly Successful People," and so on. But the Conservatives, in 2005, were looking for a way to make one announcement a day through the regular business week.

The reaction to the five priorities was swift and mostly enthusiastic, even if the seasoned pundits saw through the marketing strategy, especially on the GST cut. Don Martin wrote in his column for the CanWest media chain, "The GST cut is a shameless stunt to win votes, they'll argue. Well… DUH. This IS an election campaign, after all, where politics becomes the art of buying mass appeal. And promising to cut the GST just as Christmas consumerism peaks is an idea that registers with every cash receipt. Vote Conservative and in five years you'll save two bucks on every one-hundred-dollar purchase. Simple."

James Wallace wrote in the *Sarnia Observer* that while official Ottawa might be bickering over who was to blame for the GST and how to fix it, the cut would be noticed by "Joe and Jane Canuck who will trudge to the mall this holiday weekend, with the short end of their paycheck in hand (income taxes and assorted deductions having consumed a sinful portion) and be forced to shell out another seven percent in tax on every dollar they spend on Christmas presents, shovels for the coming snow and nearly everything else they buy."

The Conservatives also designed an advertising campaign to match their marketing strategy, aimed as it was at Tim Hortons voters, or to use Wallace's words, "Joe and Jane Canuck." Back in the spring of 2005, the Conservatives had prepared a series of "brand ads" that were intended to take the harsh edge off Harper's image—and to show him as a leader of a team, much as Chrétien had done in the early 1990s when his leadership had been perceived as a potential liability. In the Conservative ads of 2005, Harper was filmed in a campaign office holding policy conversations with young, attractive members of his caucus: former Progressive Conservative leader Peter MacKay and Alberta MP Rona Ambrose. The TV ads ran in selected Ontario ridings in late August and September that year.

Muttart took a hard marketing look at the ads and found them too "Zoe" for the audience the Conservatives were trying to reach in the election campaign. Ironically, perhaps, the very people designing the ad strategy for the Conservatives, not to mention all those young aides around the Hill, were more like Fiona and Marcus than Rick and Brenda. So it was back to the drawing board. The ads filmed for the election were considerably less artsy, or as Tom Flanagan described them in his book *Harper's Team*, "artfully middle-brow." They were designed to resemble a five o'clock newscast—a medium, as Muttart knew, quite familiar to the disengaged Canadian voters.

In the accountability ad, for instance, Harper sits on a low-budget stage set with an actress playing a TV interviewer, who is modestly dressed in a rumpled brown blazer, with her hair pulled back in a ponytail. "How is it that hundreds of millions of dollars goes missing and no one goes to jail?" the interviewer asks. Harper then launches into his pitch to clean up government before wheeling around to field a question from an ordinary Canadian voter on the background screen. The spots all ended with a grainy shot of a portable marquee, the kind often used by small-town merchants, with the words spelled out: "Stand Up for Canada." The initial reaction from the ad community was not positive. In the *National Post*, the Conservative advertising was described as "contrived" and Harper's performance as "wooden." Ad experts preferred the Liberals' high-production spots, which featured crowd scenes of diverse people and positive newspaper headlines, just like the testimonials that Dalton Camp used to feature in his advertising decades earlier.

But the Conservatives weren't aiming for the experts. The ads were designed for non-political Canadians, who knew that all advertising, to some extent, is contrivance. As Tom Flanagan would put it in his book, "Although many observers said they were hokey, they were well conceived for the job they had to do—to communicate the essence of our policy to middle-aged or older, family-oriented, middle-income people without high levels of formal education. These were our swing voters, the people who would bring us victory if we could bring them on side."

Yaroslav Baran, then working in the war room for the Conservatives, said Muttart's fictional characters made it easier to keep communications aides' eyes on the target audience. He told his fellow war-room staffers that they weren't designing their message for press gallery reporters. Every piece of communications, Baran advised, whether it was a press release or an ad, should be imagined as letters to Dougie, or Rick and Brenda. It was good practice for marketing communications in government, too, which is all about speaking over the heads of traditional media and straight to consumer-citizens.

Warren Kinsella, a Liberal blogger and author of books on hardball politics, was sitting in the spectators' stands in this election—figuratively and literally. No great fan of Prime Minister Paul Martin and his loyalists, Kinsella was not playing any active role for his party. Early in the campaign, he was sitting in an arena in Leaside, where

Harper had grown up, coincidentally, when suddenly he was struck by the idea of the campaign as a class struggle at the coffee shop. Kinsella tapped out a little blog post with his BlackBerry, saying that the election was about Tim Hortons voters versus Starbucks voters. Soon after his post went online, he received two messages: one from Muttart, another from Conservative policy chief Ken Boessenkool. The blog post, they said, was dead on. Conservatives were looking for their voters at the doughnut chain.

That was quite the turnaround from 1957, when Camp's Madison Avenue wizardry, complete with customer testimonials and image-heavy ads, defeated the Liberals. A half-century later, that kind of sophistication was out of fashion. Not even advertising could help the Liberals, now that the world had shifted to the sharper arts of marketing. As with the sponsorship program, they had overplayed their hand on the bid to prove that Harper was scary. Sometimes, repetition works in advertising. At other times, as in the 2005–06 campaign, constant repetition merely makes consumers suspicious of the source. This was certainly the case when reports emerged of a new wave of Liberal attack ads. Implying that a Conservative government would militarize Canada, the ads were accompanied by a menacing drumbeat. "Stephen Harper actually announced he wants to increase military presence in our cities. Canadian cities. Soldiers with guns. In our cities. In Canada. We did not make this up," the ad warned. Reaction to the ad, even in the early hours, could be summed up as, "Seriously?"

Facing an immediate backlash, the Liberals pulled the ad before it could get into circulation. Their fates were already on a downward trajectory anyway, defeat almost certainly sealed when news broke in late December that the RCMP was investigating possible leaks from Finance Minister Ralph Goodale's office, related to a decision on how to tax income trusts (Goodale's office was later cleared of all suspicion). That blockbuster of a news story gave fuel to the Conservatives' constant campaign refrain about the "corrupt"

Liberals. The off-the-cuff remarks about "beer and popcorn" by Martin's communications director Scott Reid made the Liberals seem even more distant from the Tim Hortons constituency that Conservatives were courting. You make jokes about beer at your peril among Canadian brand-patriots.

It actually helped the Conservatives, too, that the 2005–06 election campaign took place over the Christmas and New Year's holidays, even if they hadn't initially planned for such a long campaign. Their consumer-citizen pitch was aimed at a huge section of the electorate that was busy with shopping, with little appetite for complicated platform statements or dissections of the subtle differences between the political rivals. The Conservatives, with their shopping-friendly, easy-to-understand five priorities, had given Canadians just enough to chat about over the holidays while they relaxed over their new gift purchases. Pollster Nik Nanos explained it to the *Toronto Star*: "Having a holiday in the middle of a campaign provides the unique chance for family and friends to gather and talk about what is happening politically. Corporate research shows that word-of-mouth opinions have a great impact on consumer behaviour. I don't think one can underestimate the impact of friends, parents, siblings and neighbours on voting behaviour."

An election that featured a shopping break entirely suited a party that had organized its appeal around shoppers and consumer-friendliness. On January 23, 2006, Canada handed a minority government to Stephen Harper and his Conservatives. The country, or at least a crucial part of it, had rejected a sales-oriented Liberal party, hobbled by its own obsession with advertising, in favour of a party that knew how to do marketing. The challenge now for the Conservatives was to see whether they could apply the lessons of successful marketing campaigns to governance. Could they keep shopping for votes while they were running the country?

RETAIL RULES

There was a great scene in the old *Seinfeld* TV sitcom in which Jerry Seinfeld gets into an argument with a rental car agent. He had arrived to find that the car he reserved wasn't available, and he would have to make do with another model.

Seinfeld: "But the reservation keeps the car here. That's why you have the reservation."

Agent: "I know why we have reservations."

Seinfeld: "I don't think you do. If you did, I'd have a car. See, you know how to take the reservation. You just don't know how to *hold* the reservation. And that's really the most important part of the reservation: the *holding*."

The same is true of campaign promises. Anyone can make promises, but it's the keeping of them that counts. This is even more important for politicians with a marketing bent. Politics has always treated people harshly for breaking their promises. But when the voters see themselves as consumers of democracy, they place a high premium on customer satisfaction. "The maturing consumer wants a lot," Martin Goldfarb wrote in his book about branding.

"We expect guarantees for our products. We want answers from politicians. We want loyalty from our friends. We want the powerful
to be humbled."

Paul Martin had tried to throw a wrench into the Conservatives'
tightly scheduled plans for the election in 2005 when he announced
a campaign that would last much longer than the minimum thirty-
six days, stretching from November to January, over the Christmas
holidays. While that shopping break had played well to their marketing strategy, it had also presented a logistical problem for the
Conservative campaigners. They had to adjust their timetable accord-
ingly and figure out a way to relaunch their campaign after the break.
So on January 2, Harper announced that if he won the election his
government would move "aggressively" on the five key priorities: the
GST cut, $100 monthly cheques for parents, wait-time guarantees
for health care, a crackdown on crime and, of course, "cleaning up"
Ottawa. The very first piece of legislation in a Conservative government, Harper promised, would be an accountability act, to enforce
tighter controls over how lobbyists and pollsters deal with government. That to-do list, an act of campaign improvisation, would
immediately become a formal agenda—a prewritten Throne Speech,
more or less, when Harper assumed power on February 6, 2006.
Conventional wisdom says it is easier to do political marketing when
parties are out of power. But Harper and his Conservatives would set
out to turn that wisdom on its head.

Words that Work

Exactly four months after the Conservatives came to power,
Republican strategist Frank Luntz paid a visit to Ottawa, in part
to celebrate this victory for the right in Canada, in part to offer a
bit of advice for this welcome new Conservative government. Luntz
had been more of a spectator than a participant in the Conservative
victory in Canada. First of all, the Tories had their own marketing
geniuses now, Patrick Muttart in particular. And Luntz had been

otherwise occupied. In the fifteen years since Luntz had worked as a young pollster for the fledgling Reform Party, his fame and fortunes had soared. He had been named one of *Time* magazine's fifty most promising leaders under forty and he had earned an Emmy for his voter-research spots on MSNBC/CNBC in the 2000 US election. Along the way, Luntz had worked with corporate giants such as Disney and General Electric, on top of his Republican market research. He was about to release a book, *Words That Work*, and on this visit to Ottawa, he would give his Canadian friends a sneak peek at some of the wisdom he intended to share.

Luntz's main purpose for the visit was to speak to a Conservative organization known as Civitas, which billed itself as non-partisan: a "premier venue in Canada where people interested in conservative, classical liberal and libertarian ideas can not only exchange ideas, but meet others who share an interest in these rich intellectual traditions." Meeting at the Brookstreet Hotel in Kanata, a good distance from Parliament Hill, Civitas' audience was dotted with stars of the Canadian conservative movement—despite its non-partisan billing—including some of the new prime minister's old bosses, mentors and current staff. Preston Manning was there; so was Tom Flanagan, as well as Harper's new chief of staff, Ian Brodie—all people very interested in what they could do to keep the power they'd newly gained.

Journalist Elizabeth Thompson, then with the *Montreal Gazette*, parked herself outside the door of the Civitas meeting and recorded Luntz's remarks to his Canadian friends. What she heard was basically a manual on mixing marketing with governance—a how-to guide on talking to citizens as consumers. And as such, it was also an eerie portent of what was to come from the Conservatives in their subsequent years in power, even if Luntz was not in Harper's inner circle of advisers. Luntz's speech, thanks to Thompson and her tape recorder, would be a useful way to understand the strategy of governance that Canadians were about to see: power marketing. "You have a gentleman who could well be the smartest leader, intellectually," Luntz told the crowd. "Now that's half the battle." But being smart, he warned, was not as important as having an ear for average Canadians, who had better things to do than translate political jargon.

Luntz said Harper would have to talk about taxes, for instance, in terms of people's everyday existence—that world in which Canadians were consumers, twenty-four hours a day, seven days a week. "If he wants to talk about reducing taxes he's got to relate it on a day-to-day basis, on a personal basis to every Canadian. When you wake up in the morning and take your first cup of coffee, you pay a sales tax. You go out to your garage, you pay an automobile tax. When you drive to work, you pay a gas tax. At work, you pay an income tax. You turn on the lights, you pay an electricity tax. You flush the toilet, you pay a water tax. You stayed the night at this hotel, you paid a hotel-occupancy tax. You fly home to wherever you're from, you pay an airport tax. You get home at night, you pay a property tax. You turn on your TV, you pay a cable tax. You call the family, you pay a telephone tax. People in the United States have taxes. You're taxed from the moment you wake up in the morning to the moment you go to sleep at night. You're taxed from your cradle to your grave."

Luntz reminded the Conservatives that in today's post-partisan times, people don't vote as much for policy as they do for emotions and intangible personality traits—trust, consistency, stability. "We would rather vote for someone who we completely trust than someone who agrees with us on the ten issues that we care about the most," Luntz said. "We now vote for people in terms of who they are as people rather than just their intellectual capability and so [being] a straight shooter is so important... The key here is consistency. The key here is stability."

Luntz urged the Conservatives to find some national symbol and firmly tie Conservatives to that imagery. "What is the symbol of Canada that matters more than anything? Is there one? Other than the Canadian flag, is there one?" he wanted to know.

"Health care?" came a voice from the audience. Silence. Someone in the room suggested a beaver, an idea that was greeted with some laughter.

But Luntz had a better idea: hockey. "If there were some way to make hockey [part of what] you all do... do it. Because it's not political. It's not partisan." Not only that, he said, but hockey would give the Conservatives some real marketing tools to reach the citizenry: "That's what the public [needs]—some kind of symbol and pictures. And visuals matter more than anything else." This wasn't new to Tim Hortons and the beer companies—very Canadian corporations, in the public's eye, that had framed many of their ads around hockey rinks and players. If these patriotic corporations had learned the benefits of pairing their products to hockey, why shouldn't it work for a political party, with the same kind of "customers" in mind?

Conservatives should go looking for people who weren't part of the voting public up to this point, Luntz said. In the States, this was called *exurbia*, he explained, and such voters were a type of blank slate. "We have these areas that are outside the suburbs where people are moving further and further from the city, where they're prepared to commute for an hour or more because they just don't like what suburbia's become," he said. "No one knows that they're there. They're brand-new communities. They've been built within the last five years. They're not targeted. They don't get all that crappy direct mail because it's brand new so they're not on anybody's list. Find those areas. Those are the areas of opportunity for you because they're not traditional." Luntz advised the Conservatives, above all, to keep things simple and consistent. "You need a lexicon that is... crisp and clear and repeated and common." He need not have worried about the Conservatives' ability to pull this off.

New and Improved

It was immediately apparent that the newly minted Harper government was indeed very attached to slogans. In press releases, it repeatedly referred to itself as "Canada's New Government," selling itself like detergent, new and improved. Bureaucrats were ordered to insert the phrase into government communications at all opportunities. One scientist at the Geological Survey of Canada, Andrew Okulitch, balked at the directive in the fall of 2006 and was sacked (though subsequently reinstated). In his email to his bosses, which was made public, Okulitch protested the infiltration of marketing buzzwords into the official, institutional business of government. "Why do newly elected officials think everything begins with them taking office? They are merely stewards for as long as the public allows. They are there to foster good policies even if (horrors) they were set up by another party," Okulitch wrote. "While this ridiculous and embarrassing policy is in effect, I shall use Geological Survey of Canada... as opposed to idiotic buzzwords coined by political hacks."

Everyone appeared to realize that this was a government doing marketing. Journalists sought out experts from the commercial sphere to explain or comment on the "new government" labelling exercise. "From a purely marketing perspective, keeping the same identification once it's established and has some value is good," Adam Finn, a University of Alberta marketing professor, told the *National Post*. "You only get rid of it when it's so old and tired people have moved on." Stan Sutter, an associate publisher at *Marketing* magazine, said in the same story, "Every government wants to keep that kind of new-car, fresh smell as long as you can."

At least one cabinet minister, in a rare show of candour, admitted he was finding the label tiresome after fifteen months in office. Newfoundland's minister in cabinet, Loyola Hearn, admitted to reporters that he was puzzled by the way the phrase had lingered. "I asked that question actually some time ago: Why do we still call ourselves the new government? If it happens to be written in the script... I skip it, and if I'm doing my own stuff, I don't use it," Hearn said. Still, regardless of how obvious its tactics, or the backlash from critics, the Conservatives stuck faithfully to the "new government" label. It was a rule of thumb within the Harper communications shop: if the journalists were complaining about hearing the same words too much, that meant that the phrase was just starting to seep into the public consciousness. And so the "Canada's New Government" slogan was still appearing in press releases a couple of years into Harper's first term in office. Message to Canadians: we're fresh and clean, and we may even smell a bit like soap, or a new car.

On March 24, 2006, Harper's new communications director, Sandra Buckler, sat down with the executive of the Canadian Parliamentary Press Gallery. Buckler had a considerable pedigree in Conservative politics, federally and in Ontario, but she had also worked as a lobbyist with some big corporate players in Canada, including Bombardier, Coca-Cola and De Beers. One of Buckler's goals in sitting down with the press gallery, it appeared, was to spell out the ways in which the government would be adhering to marketing principles in its dealings with Parliament Hill journalists. "We're a different kind of government and we place a heavy value on communications and we like the visuals," Buckler said. "This is a government that places a high emphasis on communicating directly to people and finding the best opportunity on how to do that."

The media had already noticed. Harper was holding occasional press conferences, but in the Commons foyer, where he was flanked by flags and a podium—visual reminders of his power. His office, primarily through Buckler and press secretary Dimitri Soudas, was insisting that reporters put their names on a list to ask questions, a request that stirred outrage in the press gallery because of fears it would lead to the Conservatives picking the questions, and the questioners, that would be most friendly to the government. At one testy encounter with journalists in April 2006, Harper pointedly refused to take a question from CBC TV reporter Julie Van Dusen because she wasn't on the PMO-approved list. "Why are you ignoring the lineup? We're in a lineup, and I'm next," Van Dusen snapped at the PM.

PMO–press relations were rapidly deteriorating by May of 2006, so much that journalists staged a walkout at a Harper press conference. Not long afterward, Harper himself announced he would have nothing more to do with reporters working in the parliamentary press gallery. "Unfortunately the press gallery has taken the view they are going to be the opposition to the government. They don't ask questions at my press conferences now. We'll just take the message out on the road," the prime minister said. Many reporters were arguing that press conferences were part of the public-service part of the prime minister's job. Harper's office, however, appeared to see them as marketing opportunities—"getting the message out."

Buckler, in her March meeting with the gallery executive, had seemed genuinely perplexed that journalists wouldn't see things that way. On more than one occasion, Buckler had assured reporters that she was sensitive to their needs for eye-grabbing pictures and juicy stories, seeing these as marketing needs, too. The problem, however, rested in a classic collision between public service and marketing. Many of the press gallery reporters were long-serving denizens of Parliament Hill who saw their role as part of the democratic process, not as representatives of a business.

Buckler's explanation about the importance of images, like Luntz's speech, would prove to be an accurate forecast of the style of government to come, one that would go to great lengths to micromanage its every presentation before the public, with great attention to props, backdrops and staging. Like Liberal governments of the past, the Harper government would become very attached to the ad business. Spending on government advertising climbed from $41.3 million in 2005–06 to $136 million in 2009–10. Much of this was spent plastering billboards, construction sites and highways with big "Economic Action Plan" signs: bold blue and green upward-pointing arrows telling Canadians where their tax dollars were being spent. One such sign was even thrown up in Charlottetown to boast of a doorknob replacement, much to the outrage of the opposition. "This is not a government, it is a propaganda machine," Liberal MP Pablo Rodriguez thundered one day in the Commons. "Just look at all the money being wasted to put up signs. A doorknob is changed and a sign goes up. A doorbell is repaired and a sign goes up. A sign has probably already gone up to announce the upcoming installation of another sign."

Meanwhile, the steady increase in communications operatives, which had already begun in earnest under the Liberals in the early part of the twenty-first century, continued apace within the public and political service. A public-service survey in 2008 showed a 23-percent increase in the number of communications personnel working for the government between 2003 and 2007. Even more tellingly, that same survey showed that over a third of the PMO's staff was involved in communications work, while only 8 percent were working on policy. A rough count by the Ottawa-based *Hill Times* newspaper in 2011 found more than 1,500 communications staff people working in federal offices, including a whopping 87 alone within the Prime Minister's Office and the Privy Council Office.

A search through the federal government's electronic directory in the Harper years would reveal roughly three hundred public servants with the word "marketing" in their titles. Some of these were explicable, for people whose jobs involved government over-sight of marketing operations in the private sector. But plenty of others appeared to be tagged on to roles that were once simply called "communications" or "public affairs." The all-powerful Privy Council Office had a couple of jobs with the title "analyst, advertising and marketing." The proliferation of marketers within the halls of the public service spoke to the growing sense that when it came to talking to the citizens, the conversation would be between marketing experts and consumers of the government "product."

No one in the media was shocked at this dramatic rise in atten-tion to communications at the top levels of government. Where journalists had been accustomed to freewheeling access to cabinet ministers and MPs in past governments, Harper's government maintained a strict discipline over every utterance from its spokespersons, elected and unelected. Other governments had issued "talking points," for instance, to keep everyone toeing the party line in public pronouncements, but under Conservative rule, these were scripts from which no one could veer. The talking points were also sent out as friendly emails to Conservative bloggers and online personalities, to make sure the chorus was as large as possible. Media inquiries to ministers' offices would yield terse, generally fact-free emails, which read more like advertising slogans than replies. "Our government believes in accountability," for instance, would be a typical reply to a question for more information or transparency. These replies were usually generated from within the PMO, which required staff to clear all communications at the "Centre." The same kind of slogans would then be cycled through the statements in the Commons, then regurgitated on political TV shows every evening. The MPs or ministers who were best at repeating the talking points, adding inflection or enough drama to make it seem like they thought up the lines themselves, were the most promising salespersons in this marketing-fixated government.

Harper's government was also the first one to really have to contend with the new communications universe on social media—blogs, Facebook, Twitter, YouTube, all of which only came to be popular in Canadian politics after the 2006 election. On the one hand, these fast-moving modes of communications were a boon for a government that wanted to get around the traditional media "filter." Marketing messages could be delivered directly to citizens, whether it was a PMO-produced video or a 140-character tweet. In its later years in power, Harper's PMO began to distribute its own mini-news program, called *24 Seven*, which presented updates on government activities in the way Conservatives wished they would be broadcast on regular news. On the other hand, the fragmentation of the audience made it even more of a challenge to stay on top of all the communications through all channels. There was the irony: the more democratic political communications became outside Ottawa, the more control that had to be exercised from the "Centre."

Thanks to social media, individual voices were now more significant, and maybe more powerful, than any group in modern Canadian politics. Voters who wanted to get involved in the political debate at one time would have had to get in touch with their local MP or party riding association, and then go to a meeting to chat about their views. Or they could contact the media and drum up interest in their causes and concerns. Through Facebook, Twitter and blogs, now every person could be a publisher, and there was no need to test one's views with the editors or in the crucible of brokerage-party debates. Angry about the gun registry or how the government handled foreign policy? Throw your opinion online, gather your own constituency. Think your party chose the wrong leader? Write a blog or a Facebook post, get immediate feedback. The lesson in all of this was that there was no mass-market audience for communications, at least not in the ways that had existed for previous governments. Every Canadian could be a micro-target.

Customer Satisfaction

As soon as the swearing-in was over, the Conservative government got busy keeping all those consumer-friendly promises it created in the platform overhaul of 2005. The accountability act was unveiled with much fanfare. The child-care agreements Paul Martin's government negotiated with the provinces were wound down, and parents began to receive their $100 cheques in July of 2006. On June 30, 2006, Harper made a large show of living up to his GST promise— or, at least, the first half of it. The big prime ministerial entourage pulled up at a Giant Tiger discount store in the south of Ottawa, and Harper announced that Canadians were just a day away from happier moments at the cash register. With the help of some cardboard props, Harper stood at the checkout counter in Giant Tiger and flipped the

"7-percent" sign to show "6 percent" instead, the new rate effective on Canada Day. At the end of December 2007, Harper sealed the whole deal, appearing at the same Mississauga store where he unveiled the original election promise, flipping more signs to announce the new 5-percent tax, effective on New Year's Day.

It was hard to find an economist in Canada who thought this was a good idea. The huge cut to the treasury, amounting to billions a year, would plunge the budgets back into deficits within a couple of years. Stephen Gordon, a professor of economy at the University of Laval, repeatedly warned that sound economic policy had given way to love of consumption—by the populace and by Canadian politicos. "What is revealing here is not that the cut was popular, but that no one in federal politics dared suggest reversing it," Gordon said. "The winning electoral recipe—on the left and on the right—is to offer free money. Gone is the sense that there are trade-offs and costs that have to be shared with the benefits."

The Conservatives were using other tax measures for marketing purposes, too—an idea inspired, in fact, by Bill Clinton and the small, micro-targeted tax breaks he offered to Americans during his time in office, such as for school uniforms. These tax measures even had a cute retail name: "boutique tax cuts." Need to buy hockey equipment or ballet shoes for your kids? The Conservatives would give you tax credits of up to $75 a year for each child. Are you a tradesperson who needs to buy tools? Here's a tax deduction for you, too. Do you volunteer as a firefighter? Take this $3,000 tax credit, as thanks for your service. Canada's tax laws suddenly started expanding with all these pockets of very carefully targeted measures, aimed at the market segments the Conservatives wanted to attract in the electorate. All those "Dougies" out there working in the trades were expected to remember the cash-back-for-tools discount, for instance, when they went to the voting booth.

This micro-targeting was also behind the steady stream of small, sometimes obscure funding announcements emanating from the government. Why, for instance, did the Conservative government feel it necessary in 2011 to give $256,675 to a snowmobile club in the Pontiac riding of Lawrence Cannon, just across the river from Ottawa? Because the marketing strategists had been combing through poll numbers and realized that people who drove snowmobiles fit the profile of potential Conservative voters. Again, in any number of ways, the government was shaping its "product" around its market research.

The Conservatives, like their Liberal predecessors, also kept a keen eye trained on multicultural segments of the Canadian population, and remained ever ready to accommodate them. The Liberal party had traditionally been the home for newcomers to Canada, largely out of habit or the various ways in which the Grits historically pitched themselves as open to immigration and multiculturalism. But Jason Kenney was given the job of luring these communities to the Conservative fold once the party gained power, and he set about the task with a whirl of tours to festivals, churches and local gatherings. He realized that Conservatives could connect to these citizens the same way that they reached Canadians who were born here—through their consumer and pocketbook concerns.

"At the end of the day, people choose to immigrate to Canada not because they want to live a seminar on diversity, not because they have particular grievances related to their country of origin," Kenney would say. "They come here for opportunity. They come here with the expectation that if they work hard, they'll be able to have a higher standard of living, and pass on their future to their kids, significantly more prosperous than what they could have had back home."

Music and Pictures

Dimitri Soudas ended up doing nine years at the centre of communications for Harper, in opposition and in government from 2002 to 2011. Patrick Muttart stayed only for the first few years of Harper's government, working quietly behind the scenes in the PMO before departing Canada to take up a marketing job with a large American firm. The real communications manager, the real brander-in-chief was Harper himself, Soudas said. "People try to analyze who are the strategists, the brains, this, that—it's him." And no one should underestimate Laureen Harper's influence on the branding effort either, according to Soudas. With her own background in graphic design and a creative flair, Laureen Harper was Harper's "number-one adviser," especially when it came to presenting the public face of the prime minister. It was Laureen Harper, for instance, who kept communications lines open to select reporters, sending periodic emails about events in the Harper household: the adoption of a new cat or the acquisition of a new blue motorcycle for the doyenne of 24 Sussex Drive.

As a favour to his wife, Harper also made a surprise appearance at the National Arts Centre in 2009, to play the piano and sing the Beatles tune "With a Little Help from My Friends," accompanied by internationally renowned cellist Yo-Yo Ma. That was such a public relations success that Harper went on to do more occasional musical appearances, such as when he sang "Sweet Caroline" and another few old favourites at the Conservative Christmas party in 2010. With increasing frequency, the PMO would also issue photographs depicting the prime minister in musical pursuits. Canadian rock star Bryan Adams thought he was going to 24 Sussex to discuss copyright legislation, only to find himself thrown into a "photo op" with the prime minister. "Quite disturbing," he later told *Maclean's* magazine. Alex Marland, the Canadian political marketing expert, studied these photos to see what messages the Conservatives were trying to convey with their PMO-issued images. Marland tallied up all the photos released in 2010, and came up with a scorecard. More than 82 percent of the 2010 photos showed Harper in business dress, often attending to meetings or paperwork. More than 35 percent of the photos included Canadian flags. And more than 7 percent included Harper in scenes with the military, police or courts.

Another 8 percent featured hockey or curling, just like Canadians' favourite commercials for doughnuts and beer.

Once upon a time, established media outlets might have turned up their noses at using photographs generated by the government's publicity machine. But the explosion of demand for content on the internet, as well as the cash-strapped state of media outlets, made it harder to refuse photos that reporters couldn't get anywhere else. The name of Harper's official photographer, Jason Ransom, began to appear more and more in the photo credits for mainstream and other media outlets.

Harper, says Soudas, was perfectly placed to pitch to ordinary Canadians, because he himself was an average guy from the middle-class suburbs—unlike his predecessors, who had more elite backgrounds from the halls of powerful businesses or leading Canadian law firms. He was the first prime minister since the 1960s, in fact, who didn't have a law degree (with the exception of Joe Clark, the political science graduate who served briefly from mid-1979 to early 1980). Even after becoming prime minister, Harper fiercely guarded his average-guy pursuits—whether it was going to movies or holding low-key gatherings with friends and family.

"We don't know the score, but Prime Minister Stephen Harper was spotted Tuesday playing a round of miniature golf in New York state," Canadian Press reported in the summer of 2011. "Harper and more than a dozen guests reportedly dropped by at the Broadway Driving Range and Miniature Golf Course in Depew, outside Buffalo. Owner Tom Straus tells YNN cable news in New York state that he was notified a day earlier that an important dignitary planned to play at his course. Straus said the prime minister paid for his group's round of golf."

From the very beginning, Soudas said, Harper's government went out of its way to keep communications simple, ordinary and non-elitist. One way of doing that, for instance, was to keep big dollar signs out of press releases and speeches. "Find me one press release during my time in PMO where the press release had a dollar sign. Never," Soudas said. "You know why? People have never seen $300 billion. They've never seen $10 million. They've never seen $1 million. Look at PMO press releases. They always talk about what we are doing, not how much we are paying to get it." The same thing held true for Harper's speeches, Soudas said—far better for the prime minister to be talking about what people were getting for their money, not the money itself.

As for the so-called visuals, the Conservative government remained unapologetically, aggressively attentive to staging, backgrounds and props. Press releases were frequently issued with the warning "Photo op only" so that the prime minister or his ministers could hold events with no questions from reporters and a picture would be the only public record. On this front, the tension with the press gallery was a constant undercurrent. Harper and his ministers balked at using the old National Press Theatre, objecting to its old-fashioned desk and stage. At one early point in the ongoing press–PMO struggle, Harper's office advised the parliamentary press gallery that government ministers would use the theatre if it was renovated to allow for high-tech screens, which could project the requisite visual images to serve as backdrops for announcements. The press gallery eventually obliged, installing the screens and renovating the stage to accommodate a podium, but even after two terms in office, the prime minister had only darkened the door of the press theatre a couple of times.

The main method for Conservative stage management was the so-called message event proposal—a standard-issue, highly bureaucratic form that had to be completed by anyone in government who was planning a public event. Then the forms would be put into a chain of approval, usually with the Prime Minister's Office having the ultimate say over whether the plan could proceed. The headings themselves on the MEPs revealed a scrupulous attention to marketing detail. Under "The Event," for instance, would-be public performers had to say whether this was their own idea or a response to an invitation. Under "Messaging," there were requests to provide "desired sound bites," "desired headlines" and "desired picture." Under "Logistics," the form asked how long the speech would be and even what the person or persons were planning to wear. The final sections of the form dealt with "rollout," including "marketing follow-through"—basically all the details of how the message landed. If nothing else, these forms demonstrated just how much planning was going into the slightest communication from this government, with not a thing left to chance.

Canadian Press was able to lay its hands on more than a thousand pages of these forms in 2010 by using an Access to Information request. "We discussed every single issue and micromanaged every news release—everything," one former official from Harper's government, who wanted to remain anonymous, told Canadian Press. "Pretty much any event, or any rollout of an announcement, would have an MEP that would lay out the strategy." Canadian Press offered a few snippets from the forms it unearthed. The July 15, 2007, announcement of $12,360 for a retirement centre in Edmonton was approved by the Privy Council Office for its "friendly and celebratory" tone that would help MP Laurie Hawn "highlight Canada's New Government's contribution to helping seniors." An August 2008 MEP envisioned Defence Minister Peter MacKay and Public Works Minister Christian Paradis standing on the back ramp of a Chinook helicopter as the "ideal event photograph" for the announcement of new military copters and drones—a "proactive opportunity" to highlight the federal government's commitment to provide life-saving equipment to the Canadian Forces. A 2008 request from an Ottawa journalism student for an interview with CIDA on its Canada Fund for Africa generated a detailed two-page MEP—even though there was only "remote potential for sale of the article to a Canadian magazine or weekend feature section of a national daily."

Marketing was everywhere in Harper's Ottawa. Tim Naumetz, a reporter with the *Hill Times*, picked up on the marketing lingo in early 2011 when he heard Soudas sending reporters at a press conference over to his colleague Sara McIntyre and her handful of press releases. "Sara has the product over there," Soudas said. Naumetz also reported on an interview he heard with Health Minister Leona Aglukkaq, on CBC Radio's *As It Happens*, when she was asked why government hadn't acted sooner to warn about carcinogenic chemicals in plastic baby bottles. "We issued a product..." Aglukkaq started to say, before using the more standard term, "news release." Naumetz, in his story, noted that this was all in keeping with a government that was highly interested in marketing and "retail politics."

Outside the corridors of Parliament, too, strict attention was paid to image and props. Conservative MPs showed up at community announcements with giant cheques to pose for the old-fashioned "grip-and-grin" photos with grateful recipients of government largesse. The problem, however, was that some of these cheques were emblazoned with the Conservative party logo instead of the official Government of Canada word mark (which was red)—a subtle suggestion that the money was coming as the result of partisan favour.

The idea for the big cheques reportedly came from former cabinet minister John Baird when he was head of the Treasury Board. Baird, in his various jobs in cabinet, repeatedly showed his own acute attention to visuals. When he took over as foreign affairs minister in 2011, for instance, one of his first acts was to order photographs of Queen Elizabeth II to be displayed in every Canadian mission abroad and in his ministry's headquarters on Sussex Drive in Ottawa. Baird also caused a mini-stir when news reports that same year revealed that he had ordered gold lettering on his new business cards and removed the name "Lester B. Pearson Building" from the address field, presumably to excise any reminder of the Liberals on a Conservative calling card. Baird also presided over ceremonies to rename Ottawa landmarks after former Conservative prime ministers. The old city hall became the John Diefenbaker Building and a stretch of scenic road beside the Ottawa River became the John A. Macdonald Parkway. The historic Bank of Montreal building on Wellington Street was also named after Canada's first prime minister.

The Conservative government became fond of slapping advertising-type names on pieces of legislation, with politically friendly terms or loaded words. Thus, a package of Criminal Code reforms was called "The Safe Streets and Communities Act." The bill to abolish the Canadian Wheat Board was the "Marketing Freedom for Grain Farmers Act." A crackdown on human trafficking was called the "Preventing Human Smugglers from Abusing Canada's Immigration System Act." The budget was not simply a budget anymore: it was an "Economic Action Plan." In early 2012, the Conservatives were caught fiddling with one of their legislative labels, obviously trying to do some marketing on the fly. A controversial bill to allow for internet surveillance was printed up and sent to the Commons as the "Lawful Access Act" for introduction in mid-February. But at the last minute, with grassroots opposition already building to the intrusive potential of the bill, the name was changed to the "Protecting Children from Internet Predators Act."

It all felt a little obvious, an affront to people who didn't see politics as marketing. One of Canada's top lawyers, Edward Greenspan, and a leading Canadian criminologist, Anthony Doob, assailed the bill-labelling practice in a hard-hitting *Toronto Star* commentary in 2012. Some of the titles on the "law-and-order" bills, they said, were at best misleading and at worst, just plain wrong. "Criminal justice policy is a product being shaped by the 'need' to attract votes. Conservative criminal justice policy is developed not to serve public or societal needs but to help market the Conservatives to specific constituencies," Greenspan and Doob wrote. Allan Gregg, now well at a distance from this brand of conservatism, also spoke out against the labelling, calling it part of an overall "assault on reason." In a major speech delivered at Carleton University in September 2012, Gregg called it "Orwellian."

"By obfuscating the true purpose of laws under the gobbledy-gook of double speak, governments are admitting that their intentions probably lack both support and respect," Gregg said. But lawyers and academics were not part of the target audience. Conservatives were aiming a lot of their governance at people who didn't care so much about government or politics at all: the 10 percent of shopping voters that Muttart had identified as crucial to the party's electoral fortunes.

Thierry St. Cyr, a Bloc Québécois MP, also openly called out the political marketing slogans on legislation in a spirited address to the Commons in November 2010. St. Cyr noted that the opposition had been complaining for a while about the Conservatives' penchant for slapping slogans on legislation, only to be mocked for focusing on unimportant matters. That very day, the Commons was debating the "Cracking Down on Crooked Consultants" legislation. (This was a bill that would make it illegal for anyone to charge fees to would-be immigrants, dangling the promise of acceptance to Canada in exchange for the right price.)

"Why does the government insist on giving its bills stupid titles?" St. Cyr asked. "This happens not just in the justice area but everywhere. They talk about cracking down on crooked consultants or protecting Canadians against something or other when the bill does not even do that. They talk about ending early release for dangerous criminals when this does not exist. These titles are complete lies… The government does it for political marketing reasons." But St. Cyr, in this rant, also appeared to acknowledge that Canada's busy consumer-citizens were ripe targets for such marketing techniques—that it didn't matter whether the political class was offended:

> Obviously, the people at home are not going to get a copy of the bill and look at the changes it makes to the Criminal Code. They have obligations and work to do. They are very busy with

families, children, jobs and homes. I understand that we cannot all study this country's laws. So what will the average person rely on to try to form an opinion? The average person will rely on what he is told the bill does. If he is told the bill protects people against murderers, he will say it is a good bill. Who is opposed to protecting people against murderers? The answer is obvious. But the public is being deceived and fooled by the government. I think that is insulting to the public.

Recall that old advertising battle over how to view consumers—the choice between Barnum and Powers? St. Cyr was effectively saying that the Barnum view—a sucker born every minute—was prevailing in Canadian politics. St. Cyr, incidentally, lost his seat in the 2011 election.

On top of its penchant for catchy labels on bills, the Conservatives would organize the legislative schedule around themed debate weeks: democratic reform week, jobs week or focusing-on-the-economy week. This was pure communications, said Yaroslav Baran, who worked as an adviser behind the scenes in the Conservative House Leader's office. "The thinking was that there is so much noise on Parliament Hill, whether it's breaking stories, the day's Question Period headlines, scandals of the day and so on, that the only way you can possibly use your legislative program to any communications benefit is to hammer the same theme repeatedly," he explained. "If one day you debate a budget bill, next day you do park boundaries, third day you do modernization of law enforcement techniques, and the next day is a supply day, then it all gets scattered and diluted."

Red, Blue and Green

Conservatives would constantly present the government's actions as consumer-friendly. Like a constant drumbeat in the background, the Conservative government also regularly issued bulletins to proclaim the various ways in which Canadian consumers could be assured that their concerns were top of mind in Ottawa. These missives were usually issued from the offices of Finance Minister Jim Flaherty, and with each year in power, the list of consumer-friendly boasts got a little longer. When the government intervened in the Air Canada labour disputes of late 2011 and early 2012, ordering striking employees back to work, it argued it was acting on behalf of Canadian consumers. Conservatives brought in a raft of measures to tighten up rules over credit cards, for instance—though not on high interest rates, as the New Democrats were demanding. Even the public service, which was already awash in talk of "clients" in the late 1990s, was talking the shopping language more and more with a marketing-sensitive prime minister in power. One government-commissioned study, called "Citizen Compass," was rolled out in early 2013 with a clear directive to public servants: "The research revealed that mobile devices, social media and other technology innovations are changing citizens' expectations and governments must raise their game to match the customer experience of banks and retailers."

Significantly, the Conservatives also rolled out a "taxpayers' bill of rights" with much fanfare in 2007, to warm the hearts of all those consumer-citizens who believed that government was something they purchased with their tax dollars. The fifteen rights were basically good-service promises. "You have the right to receive entitlements and to pay no more and no less than what is required by law," the bill said. "You have the right to privacy and confidentiality." A "taxpayers' ombudsman" was added to government in 2008 to handle citizens' complaints about the service they were getting from Revenue Canada.

Meanwhile, the word "taxpayers" steadily marched into more common usage in official government communications as the years wore on with the Conservatives in power. In 2007, for instance, it appeared just five times in press releases or background papers on the Government of Canada website. By 2012, a search for the word "taxpayer" on the site would yield hundreds of results—not just from

Revenue Canada, but from cultural institutions, too. "The Museum takes very seriously the need to control spending and manage tax-payer dollars effectively," proclaimed a corporate plan from the Museum of Nature.

When a marketing-oriented government is in power, everything becomes a transaction. And no detail is too small, or insignificant, when you're trying to seal the deal on those transactions. Even the colour palette of the government got a marketing makeover, for instance, from Liberal red to Tory blue. Dr. Ken Cosgrove, a US pol-itical marketing expert, has noticed that Canadian politicos appear far more attentive to party colours than Americans are. Though red and blue are also the colours, respectively, of the Republicans and Democrats in the United States, it is possible for a Democrat to show up in a red tie at a party event, and vice versa. In Canada, says Cosgrove, partisans are far more attached to their colours: Liberals, red, New Democrats, orange, and Conservatives, blue.

By 2013 most of the government's websites were a sea of Conservative blue—a result, the government insisted, of consumer preference rather than political persuasion. Government web spe-cialists, according to Treasury Board documents, had conducted "usability" studies and reviewed government websites in Canadian provinces, Britain, the United States and Australia, finding that blue or green was the primary colour in 75 percent of them. "Blue was chosen to complement the red maple leaf and provide sufficient contrast," Treasury Board officials explained in a summary of the rationale for the web overhaul (provided to the author on request). What's more, Conservative MP Andrew Saxton delightedly told the Commons in 2013 that blue was a favourite colour of marketers. Quoting from the website www.about.com, Saxton said, "Blue is a favourite colour of both men and women of all ages. It may be the calming effect of the colour blue that makes it a popular colour for both men and women or it could be the association of some shades of blue with authority figures, intelligence and stability."

In the first years of Conservative power, the Government of Canada website started to feature bold splashes of blue, eventually giving way to blue as the main colour, and yes, even as the Conservative government was branding itself as "new." On Canada Day 2007, blue was the primary colour of the stage on Parliament Hill, and in subsequent years the politics of colour would continue to play out in the national capital. At Christmas 2011, roughly six months after the election that reduced the Liberals to third-party status, the lights on the bushes in front of Parliament were festooned in Conservative blue and New Democratic orange—not a Liberal-red bulb in sight. The spectacle prompted a Rick Mercer comedy sketch featuring a hapless customer trying unsuccessfully to buy faulty, flickering red "Liblites" at his local hardware outlet. "We have seven thousand strings of the blue ones if you want. They're very popular," the clerk advises Mercer. Even the prime ministerial plane, RCAF-1, was transformed from drab military grey to bright red, white and blue during Harper's tenure.

Patrick Muttart and Doug Finley made no apologies for keeping the Conservative government on a constant war footing against the Liberals during the first two minority governments. If Canada could be plunged into an election at any moment, it was crucial to show Liberals that the Conservatives were ready to do battle at a moment's notice. Battle-readiness, in fact, was a large metaphor in the Conservatives' marketing efforts, evidenced not just in the government's increasing financial support of the military, but in Harper's constant appearances in military venues. Very deliberately, his first foreign trip was to Afghanistan, to show support for the Canadian soldiers embroiled in that war effort. In 2012, the thirtieth anniversary of the Charter of Rights and Freedoms was marked with a terse statement, but the Conservatives spent $28 million that year to mark the two hundredth anniversary of the War of 1812. Inside the political offices of the government, wearing red on Friday to support the troops was very popular, encouraged even. So attached were

Conservatives to the military that it began to feel like every day in Ottawa was Remembrance Day.

But no battle consumed as much attention as the battle against Liberals. In this way, Canadian politics was introduced to the "permanent campaign." Although other parties in Canada had dabbled occasionally in advertising outside election campaigns, it was the Harper Conservatives who made attack ads a constant on the political airwaves—election or no election. Not long after Stéphane Dion became the new leader of the Liberal party in late 2006, Muttart placed a call to the New Democrats' then-chief of communications, Brad Lavigne. He wanted to meet him for coffee. Lavigne was one of the young, new faces of the NDP backroom, a former activist for the Canadian Federation of Students who had risen through the party ranks in BC politics. He was typical of the kind of people that Jack Layton had attracted to his inner circle: pragmatists, not ideologues, focused on winning. That inner circle had what it called "the project," an ambitious plan to move the NDP into the mainstream of Canadian politics and eventually to power. Lavigne had always liked Muttart and admired his political smarts; they were very similar, in fact, in outlook and age. So he happily agreed and the two strategists met. It turned out that Muttart had something he wanted to hand over to Lavigne: a DVD. That night, when he got home, Lavigne popped it into his TV system and settled back to watch. His jaw dropped: on the screen was the attack ad the Conservatives were intending to release in early 2007, mocking Dion's fitness to be a leader. Lavigne realized that Canada was about to enter a whole new chapter in political marketing with the advent of attack ads in a non-election period, and particularly harsh ones to boot.

The Conservatives had lifted segments from the Liberal leadership debates in the fall of 2006, particularly one in which Dion, in a slightly pleading voice, asks aloud, "Do you think it's easy to make priorities?" The quote had come in reply to a challenge from his Liberal rival Michael Ignatieff about why the party "didn't get it done" on meeting environmental targets. Jason Kenney, then secretary of state for multiculturalism and Canadian identity, unveiled the ads to the media in late January 2007, just before they were unleashed on viewers of that year's Super Bowl—a highly expensive ad slot for any company, let alone a political party. Kenney didn't reveal the price the Conservatives were paying, but estimates ranged anywhere between $100,000 and $1 million. All Conservatives were doing with these ads, Kenney said, was allowing Canadians to judge the Liberals by the stark evidence in front of them. "His own words— and those of his colleagues—demonstrate that he is a weak leader," Kenney told reporters.

Though the ads were deemed an outrage by many in the political world, they weren't aimed at the cognoscenti. It was just like the howls of protest over the labels on legislation; the government shrugged off the views of "elites." True to Muttart's marketing wisdom of the 2005–06 campaign, the permanent, blunt-edged offensive against the Liberals was created with checked-out voters in mind: those who didn't get their political knowledge from the traditional news media or pundit class. Using the powerful weapon of emotion, and casting Dion in negative emotional terms, the Conservatives were setting out to make sure that no one was tempted to view the Liberals in a positive light. Awash in cash, the Conservatives could afford to place the ads in whatever TV spots they wished—favouring sports broadcasts or any other shows that were favourites of Tim Hortons Canadians.

And from that first Super Bowl ad onward, every couple of months through Dion's leadership, the Conservatives would release more ads against the Liberal leader, who was looking increasingly beleaguered no matter how loudly the party was saying that sticks and stones wouldn't hurt them. In the fifth volley, in late 2007, Dion was pictured on one side of a cash register, as the enemy of consumers because he would allegedly roll back the cuts the Conservatives had made to the GST. "That's right—you'll pay more GST for his lack of priorities," the ad proclaimed. "Stéphane Dion. Not a leader. Not worth the risk."

When the election finally came in 2008, then, the anti-Dion ground had already been well tilled in the population at large. Still, the Conservatives were quick off the mark with another wave of attack ads against Dion. The opening barrage played on a gambling theme, showing craps games, slots and a "scratch 'n' lose" card imprinted with Dion's face. The wording was directly aimed at voters' consumer concerns. "Can you afford to take a gamble on Stéphane Dion? Because with Dion, you always lose. Can you afford a hike in the GST? You lose. Can you afford to lose the $1,200 child-care benefit? You lose again. Can you afford a permanent new carbon tax that will drive up the cost of everything? You lose again, big time! You've got too much at stake. Don't lose it all on Stéphane Dion." Jennifer Wells of the *Globe and Mail* tracked down one of the operatives in the Conservative war room, who explained (anonymously) the need for such a swift advertising assault: "You've only got thirty-seven days to make the sale." What that sales metaphor omitted, however, was all the advance advertising that had been carried out for eighteen months beforehand.

Remember that old memo that Allister Grosart wrote to Conservatives back in 1953, about why political ads weren't like product ads? Political ads, the Tory ad executive had advised, didn't have the luxury of time to work their persuasion with the public. Now, however, in the "permanent campaign" mode of Canadian politics, Conservatives had all the time they needed to "get their message out" to voters. The formal election period itself was just the final flourish on an advertising battle that had been conducted for the better part of two years beforehand. Nobody seemed to like this, least of all the Liberals, of course, but nobody seemed to know what to do about it, either.

During the 2008 election, Advertising Standards Canada took the unusual step of issuing a public notice about political ads, even though the private-sector body has no authority over the political parties. Pointedly, ASC issued an advisory that reminded Canadians that the politicians had more leeway to do negative advertising than the commercial sector did: "While ASC hears from members of the public throughout the year, public interest in advertising clearly peaks during the course of federal and provincial elections. At these times, ASC receives numerous complaints expressing concerns about election advertising. In their complaints, members of the public tell ASC that they find advertising by political parties is often misleading, and that it unfairly disparages and denigrates individual candidates or party leaders."

Just to underline the difference between the public and private worlds of advertising, the ASC advisory included some clauses from its code of conduct to assist citizens in being more educated consumers of the political ads they were seeing. These "pertinent" clauses included:

- Advertisements must not contain inaccurate or deceptive claims, statements, illustrations or representations, either direct or implied, with regard to a product or service. In assessing the truthfulness and accuracy of a message, the concern is not with the intent of the sender or precise legality of the presentation. Rather, the focus is on the message as received or perceived, i.e., the general impression conveyed by the advertisement.

- Advertisements must not omit relevant information in a manner that, in the result, is deceptive.

- Advertisements shall not demean, denigrate or disparage any identifiable person, group of persons, firm, organization, industrial or commercial activity, profession, product or service or attempt to bring it or them into public contempt or ridicule.

The advisory, carefully worded as it was, still served to show how wide a gap had opened between the world of political and consumer advertising, even as politicians were trying to borrow lessons from the private marketplace. Put simply, Canadians were getting business-style persuasion without business-like limits.

Moreover, in this world where consumer-citizenship met political marketing, the Liberals had gone into the 2008 campaign with another disadvantage. Dion had organized the Liberal platform around the so-called Green Shift, a comprehensive, wide-ranging proposal to wed the environment and the economy—two areas of perceived Liberal strength, if you believed the polls. But consumer politics doesn't sit easily with environmentalism, which asks citizens to limit consumption. Nor is it easy to persuade consumer-citizens of any policy that sounds like it will hit them in the wallet. This situation was pointedly true amid the clouds of global economic worries hovering over the 2008 election. The worldwide meltdown, as it was called, had been triggered by the collapse in the United States of the very forces that had powered the consumer-economy growth of the 1950s: the housing market and the automobile manufacturers.

General Motors and Chrysler were in big trouble in 2008, staring down a very real threat of bankruptcy, which would trigger millions of job losses in the United States and Canada, particularly in already beleaguered manufacturing centres in both countries. To ward off this potential disaster, they were asking for bailouts to the tune of billions of dollars from the US and Canadian governments (which they would receive late that year). And this was all against the backdrop of a financial crisis gripping North America. Starting in 2006, the US was seeing a sharp increase in the number of mortgage defaults and foreclosures. Eager home buyers had been getting into debt they couldn't afford, with mortgages offered to them at interest rates below the prime rate. These "subprime" mortgages were sometimes offered to people who had little or no money to put down as a deposit. Banks stopped lending to each other for fear of getting stuck with bad subprime-mortgage debt. And all these bad debts for the banks started to roil the international markets, too, sending the shockwaves into Canada as well. Even as the political leaders were campaigning in the fall of 2008, the stock markets in Canada were rapidly falling in value. Voters were seeing massive losses in their registered retirement savings plans and other stock market holdings. It all put Canadians in an extremely risk-averse mood, which Conservatives used to artfully craft sentiment against Liberals: "Not worth the risk."

Don't Worry, Think Hockey

So whether by accident or design, Canada had a government that was conducting its affairs of state with striking devotion to the lessons that Frank Luntz had provided to the Civitas group. One could even see it as a checklist. Clear messaging, constant repetition, the framing of the government–citizen relationship in "tax" terms—check, check, check. Oh yes, and that advice about hockey? The Conservatives were already on that one.

In the summer of 2005, even before the election, word leaked of a new project for Stephen Harper: a hockey book. *The Globe and Mail* parliamentary reporter Jane Taber, in her much-read column, was the first to deliver the news, saying that Harper's hockey obsession, complete with his love of hockey trivia, had been escalated into a real, live book project. A scant five days before the election, the *National Post* reported that Harper was still committed to his hockey opus, though if he became prime minister he would have less time to work on it. In power, though notoriously stingy about sharing details of his private life with the media, Harper managed to get the news out of his visits to the hockey rink for his son Ben's practices, and every now and then the media would get reports on the progress of the hockey book. He was apparently carving fifteen minutes out of his busy schedule each day to work on the project, and eventually got it onto the shelves through Simon & Schuster Canada in 2013 as *A Great Game: The Forgotten Leafs and the Rise of Professional Hockey.*

With such a hockey-loving PM, then, few people were surprised when the logo for the men's hockey team was unveiled a few months before the 2010 Vancouver Olympics. It bore a remarkable resemblance to the Conservative logo—yes, that same logo that Harper and his team had so colourfully conceived back in their opposition days. The men's team at Vancouver would sport a large "C" on their sweaters, with a small maple leaf inside, just like the Conservative logo. "There's no question there [are] some similarities," Minister of State for Sport Gary Lunn acknowledged to reporters, insisting that it was just a coincidence. "In fact, I talked to the CEO of the Canadian Olympic Committee yesterday and he said… 'You know, that would never have crossed our mind.'" It was a nice coincidence, though, for a government and a prime minister who stayed ever alert to any opportunity to cast the Conservatives in the same frame as hockey.

The prime minister even found some time to write the introduction to a hockey book by Paul Henderson, the player who scored the winning goal in the 1972 Canada–Russia series. Harper's memories of that series, as he wrote in the Henderson book, were actually a revealing glimpse into how well that series, even decades later, remained a touchstone for all those consumerist values drilled into the Canadian psyche in the postwar and Cold War periods. It remained, in Harper's mind, the fusion of sports, politics and the military—values held dear by Tim Hortons voters. It also demonstrated how well the Vickers and Benson advertising firm had done its job back in the 1970s, searing memories into the mind of a young Toronto man—memories that remained with him forty years later, as he wrote in the introduction:

> It really became a proxy for war and that puts it on a completely different level. The Cold War has been over for twenty years now and no one who was not alive in 1972, and certainly no one who

was not alive during the Cold War, could know the feeling that existed between the two different ways of life in the world at the time. It was as if the freedom of Canadians versus the repression of the Soviet system was being showcased in the individualism of the Canadian players as opposed to the regimentation of the Soviet players. It was there for everyone to see.

It was also interesting to see how much of the Harper marketing, like Tim Hortons marketing, was rooted in nostalgia for a Canada that existed in the 1950s through to the 1970s, when mass-marketing, the Cold War and one-size-fits-all politics were still the fashion. Like Tim Hortons, Harper had attached his brand to iconic symbols of the military, sports and consumerism. At many times, it seemed like Harper was trying to recreate the world that existed when he grew up in the Toronto suburbs—a simpler place, before the advertising and polling experts had carved up the Canadian landscape into micro-targets in the electorate. That nostalgic frame, a harkening back to the era when everyone wanted a car and a home in the suburbs, was being repeatedly evoked by politicians on the right-hand side of the Canadian political spectrum in the 2000s, even if the car companies and the housing markets were crashing.

Although Toronto and Canada had radically changed since the 1950s, it no doubt said something about the enduring forces of that era—heavily consumerist, heavily suburban—that the country's politicians could use those nostalgic marketing pitches to win power. Yet however old-fashioned their pitches, these political campaigns were built on very modern tools and ideas about the citizenry, which were far less visible among the ever-proliferating images. Political marketing, thanks to technology, had become an incredibly precise science, capable of carving up the mass electorate into tiny constituencies. And like all good marketers, the Conservatives would pay close attention to building their data files about their consumer-citizens.

9

SLICED AND DICED

B ack in the days when the commercial world was smaller and simpler, keeping your customers happy and loyal was largely a matter of human relations and fair pricing. Customers wanted to find what they were seeking in the stores, with courteous service and at a cost that made sense. If you knew the store owner or the shopkeeper, perhaps as a bonus you could get some advice on what to buy, or merchandise specially obtained for you. Perhaps your local car dealer sponsored your child's baseball team. Maybe you could even get a discount. As the shopping world grew bigger and more complex, though, it was more likely that the people in front of and behind the cash registers were strangers. So, purveyors of goods were looking for ways to make customers feel they were still getting special attention, ever-vigilant to their particular needs. To pull this off with large groups of clientele, retailers needed superhuman skills—the kind they could get with technology, particularly databases.

"In today's world of mass advertising and 'big box' retail store chains, it is impossible for merchants to know each customer in this individualized fashion," Ron Kahan, a Denver marketing expert wrote in a 1998 article in the *Journal of Consumer Marketing*. "Only with the aid of sophisticated marketing database technology can we capture, analyze and act on the same interpersonal marketing opportunities first identified in these earlier and simpler times." All those customer-loyalty cards, such as Air Miles and points-accumulating credit cards, started proliferating in the consumer marketplace because the private sector had realized the superpower of sophisticated knowledge about customer preferences and was treating them as special clients. You, the customer, would get points, and the companies would get information about what you liked to buy and where you shopped. It was called "micro-targeting"—shaping the product not around mass consumers, or even groups of consumers, but one unique person: you, the target customer.

Apple's iPod had been a runaway success, basically killing the concept of record albums, because it allowed music lovers to build their own custom playlists and collections. All iPods may look the same, but the contents, the "brains" of the products, were as unique as the consumer. Everywhere, manufacturers were figuring out ways to customize their products, aided by the speed in technological communications and manufacturing methods. *Time* magazine, reflecting this spirit of the era, named "you" as the person of the year for 2006, designing the edition's cover to resemble a mirror. As *Time* explained, "The tool that makes this possible is the World Wide Web... The new Web is a very different thing. It's a tool for bringing together the small contributions of millions of people and making them matter." Consumer databases, loaded with micro-targeted information about clientele, were the commercial world's way to keep on top of this fragmented marketplace, filled with shoppers who wanted products designed with their individuality in mind. It only made sense that this kind of commercial thinking could also be useful to political parties.

Of course, as always, Americans led the way. The Republicans, under the direction of über-strategist Karl Rove, began to explore databases in earnest after the razor-thin election finish between

George W. Bush and Democrat Al Gore in 2000. Rove's work in this area would earn him the nickname "The Architect" from a grateful, re-elected President Bush. Rove was reportedly skeptical when initially approached by Alex Gage, founder of a data collection company Target Point. Gage had worked with Republican pollsters such as Robert Teeter (who had also worked with Gregg and Canadian Conservatives, we'll remember), but had left politics in the 1990s and had mainly been working in the private sector. While in the commercial realm, though, Gage saw the potential for crossover intelligence. Gage said that if Republicans could gather a wealth of consumer information, they could get a more accurate picture of the American electorate, and where potential support could be found. "Micro-targeting is trying to unravel your political DNA," Gage told the *Washington Post*. "The more information I have about you, the better."

Rove was eventually sold on the idea, and Republicans plunged deep into this brave new world of micro-targeting. Six months and $3.25 million later, amassing thousands of "data points," they realized that the old way of sorting voters, according to their income or neighbourhood, wasn't all that helpful. Matthew Dowd, the chief campaign strategist for the Bush team in the 2004 presidential election, gave an illuminating interview to PBS radio's *Frontline* about how consumer and lifestyle data turned old political assumptions upside down. "People used to sort of divide it by income, and it was like, lower-middle-class, poor people were Democrats; upper-middle-class, rich people were Republicans. That's sort of gone... You could be a wealthy Democrat as easily as you could be a wealthy Republican today, or you could be a lower-middle-class Democrat as [easily as] you could be a lower-middle-class Republican," Dowd explained. "What we learned early on in 2001 and 2002, through some analysis, was that 85 percent of Republican voters don't live in Republican precincts... It means there's a whole bunch of Republicans that live in traditionally Democratic precincts around this country, and the only way to find them is individual profiles or calling or doing all that sort of thing."

Magazine subscription lists turned out to be a wealth of information for the Republican micro-targeters, Dowd told PBS. "Their social or household habits will tell you a lot. If somebody gets *Field and Stream*, they're much more likely to be a Republican voter than a Democratic voter. If somebody gets *Mother Jones*, they're much more likely to be a Democratic voter, or *Rolling Stone*, for example, they're much more likely to be a Democratic voter." The same thing was true with TV viewership. "Somebody that watches *CSI* is much more likely to be a Republican. Somebody that watches a soap during the day is much more likely to be a Democrat. All of these things aren't completely 100-percent true, but when you go through it all and you factor it all out, you can find Republicans fairly quickly that way."

Gage sorted voters into clusters such as "Flag and Family Republicans" or "Tax and Terrorism Moderates," which would then help Republican strategists sort where to direct their direct mail and persuasion efforts. And if some marketing-type tweaks to the Bush platform were required, the Republicans obliged. Twenty years after Margaret Thatcher and Ronald Reagan had first demonstrated how to shape a political product to suit the consumer-citizen, it was now common practice for all political parties in the US and Britain. Micro-targeting advocates would argue that this high level of attention to voters' concerns was a way to put democracy back into elite-driven politics in the US. "In 2000, we very broadly talked to people on broad issues," Bush's campaign manager, Ken Mehlman, told the *Washington Post*. "In 2004, instead of talking about what we thought was most important, we talked about what the voters thought was most important." Bush won re-election in 2004, with the help of constituencies his campaign had singled out for special treatment, and so the fervour for micro-targeting got under way.

The Democrats, meanwhile, had been plunging into the online world themselves, especially under the party chairmanship of

Howard Dean. As a one-time presidential hopeful in the early 2000s, Dean had led the way for other politicians of all stripes in the field of online fundraising—at one point, raising more than $800,000 in a single day in 2003. As chairman of the party, Dean also gathered around him an array of internet-savvy advisers, who used the early fundraising successes as a jumping-off point to revolutionize data-gathering for the Democrats and send the first black president, Barack Obama, to the White House in 2008.

Seeing what Rove and the Republicans had accomplished with micro-targeting, especially when it came to voter turnout, the Democrats pulled together a company called Catalist, which assembled masses of data from progressive-leaning organizations and individuals in the United States. The basic idea was the same: if the Democrats could use tiny data points to identify voters who could be swayed to their side, the campaign organizations would know where to concentrate their efforts and, most importantly, how to propel those people to the polls on election day.

On top of this huge database of information on potential voters, the Democrats applied some old-fashioned knowledge of persuasion. Veteran political hands know that voters are most likely to be persuaded by people who think like them or move in the same circles. And this is where the Democrats' huge outreach on social media, such as Facebook, also played a role. Through social media, people reveal their friends and their tastes online, making it all the easier for politicians to tailor their appeals around them. What's more, the Democrats could set up chains of persuasion, assigning committed voters in one social group (an environmental organization, for instance) to lure on-the-fence voters (consumers of "green" products, for example) to Obama's team.

The respected magazine *The Atlantic* devoted a three-part series in 2009 to a dissection of "How the Democrats Won the Data War," including a confidential report from Catalist. It showed that in turnout alone, micro-targeting had pulled off miracles for Obama.

People who were reached through Catalist's data network showed a turnout rate of 75 percent, compared to the 60-percent national average. And the outreach was impressive: Catalist made contact with nearly 50 million voters about 127 million times before the votes were cast in November 2008. Not only was this a powerful partisan argument in favour of micro-targeting, but a democratic one, too. What's not to like about any system that could boost people's participation in the most fundamental of civic exercises?

Voter turnout actually went up in the United States overall in the early part of the twenty-first century, a sharp contrast from Canada, where turnout was in decline at the same time. About 54 percent of the voting-age population cast a ballot in the 2000 presidential election, and by the 2008 vote that figure had climbed to 62 percent, according to the Center for the Study of the American Electorate. In contrast, Canada's voter turnout fell below 60 percent in the 2008 election, for the first time in more than a century. In the 2012 presidential election, America's black voters voted in higher proportions than white voters—a historical first, and a sign of the supremacy of the Democrats' mastery of micro-targeting and data analysis.

US author Sasha Issenberg released a book in 2012, *The Victory Lab*, that gave Americans their first close look at how the data wars were transforming the modern art of politics. In a blog post he penned for the *New York Times* just before the presidential campaign, he lamented how journalists were still covering "horse-race" polls and developments in elections, when the real strategy was being conducted with the use of reams of data and analysis that came down to vote-by-vote persuasion. "Over the last decade, almost entirely out of view, campaigns have modernized their techniques in such a way that nearly every member of the political press now lacks the specialized expertise to interpret what's going on," Issenberg wrote in a September opinion piece on the *Times* website. Fittingly, he chose a consuming metaphor: "It's as if restaurant critics remained oblivious to a generation's worth of new chefs' tools and techniques and persisted in describing every dish that came out of the kitchen as either 'grilled' or 'broiled.'"

The Victory Lab was also an illustration of just how much the American politicos' preoccupation with data had merged people's identities as citizens and consumers. Their consumer data and preferences were being fed into big-data machines in a bid to influence their civic preferences. Issenberg wrote of how Obama, even as he campaigned for the Democratic nomination in 2008, was relying on the help of a firm called Strategic Telemetry, which was matching voter information with as many as eight hundred "consumer variables" to come up with targets for support in the Iowa caucus. Knowing how Iowans shopped, in other words, was crucial intelligence in knowing how and whether they would vote for Obama.

And once you've started comparing people's political preferences to their shopping choices, you can come up with no end of fun findings, too. A firm called Scarborough Research learned that drinkers of Samuel Adams beer were more likely to vote for Mitt Romney for president in the 2012 presidential election, while Heineken drinkers would probably vote for Obama. Another consumer-research firm, Experian Simmons, learned that Democrats were more likely to shop at Bloomingdale's, while Republicans shopped in greater numbers at Belk department stores. Democratic women were more likely to buy shoes at Lady Footlocker, while Republicans favoured Naturalizer stores.

The revelations and lessons in Issenberg's book, meanwhile, were well noted in Canadian political circles. Issenberg paid a couple of calls on Canada after his book was released: first to a sellout crowd in Toronto in November 2012 and then to a roomful of conservative thinkers and strategists at the Manning Centre's annual conference in Ottawa in March 2013. Stephen Taylor, one of the most ardent advocates of digital politicking among Canadian Conservatives, appeared on the panel with Issenberg at the Manning Centre event. In Taylor's view, no party had a choice in the modern era—voters were getting harder and harder to reach, because they were too busy, too tuned out of politics or simply not answering the phone. Gone were the days when you could figure out people's political preferences with simple surveys. Taylor, who spent a lot of time studying digital campaigning techniques in the United States, believed there was a democratic argument to be made for these leaps and bounds in digital political marketing. "If politicians are able to connect with people directly on issues that they care about, one could argue that's closer to the ideal of democracy," Taylor said. "Data brings politicians closer to having an accurate mirror of the electorate, and that's something we should strive toward."

The presidential elections in the United States through the first decade of the twenty-first century, then, would give Canadian politicos yet more lessons in how to do marketing in politics, following a pattern that went all the way back to the previous century. The marketing world would come up with efforts to reach customers better; then, the American political world would borrow and adapt those lessons; and finally, Canadians would import the techniques north of the forty-ninth parallel. The pattern would remain the same for this digital overhaul of campaign methods. Now, though, Canadian students of modern electioneering would require an eye for very tiny details.

Canada, in Miniature

The arrival of postal codes in Canada in the 1970s paved the way for the huge marketing databases of the future, by sorting Canadian households into tidy, small geographic units. Through the 1980s, advertisers and non-profit groups were increasingly using direct mail and postal codes to reach their preferred potential customers or donors. Credit-card companies could target wealthier neighbourhoods to send invitations for sought-after customers, who were able to pay the premium rates they were offering to prestige clients. Magazines could gather up subscription lists and then sell them to companies who might want to know where readers with specialized interests lived. If you manufactured bicycles, for instance, you might want to know who was subscribing to cycling magazines. Then came personal computers, followed shortly by email, which produced a whole new set of addresses and contact information for the population. The clever marketers in these decades would be the ones who knew how to sort this information for their own purposes.

In Canada, one of the first big firms in the data game was one called Compusearch Market and Social Research, which billed itself as the country's "premier provider of geo-referenced demographic, consumer, and business information solutions." Bursting into the marketplace in the early 1980s, Compusearch could supply would-be entrepreneurs with information about their potential customers. Someone wanting to open a restaurant, for instance, could ask Compusearch for an analysis of the best neighbourhoods in which to situate their new venture. And the data Compusearch was accumulating was also particularly useful to the booming direct-mail marketing business in Canada at the time. Sales from direct-mail ads had doubled between 1984 and 1989, from $4 billion to $8 billion, and the sellers with the most detailed consumer-contact information stood to reap the biggest profits. In a 1990 article in the *Toronto Star*, Compusearch's director Michele Sexsmith explained that the firm gathered up information from Statistics Canada and even some municipal and tax records. The researchers then sorted this information to group households by age, income, education and so on. That information, in turn, was used to create direct-mail marketing lists, which were traded among list brokers "like so many baseball cards," according to the *Star* story.

As technology grew more sophisticated and the demand grew for sharper pictures of the consumer marketplace, more of these firms started popping up in the United States and Canada. Environics Analytics emerged as a big player in this business in 2003, boasting when it started up that it could sort Canadians into sixty-six lifestyle types with playful names such as "Cosmopolitan Elite," "Electric Avenues," "Les Chics" and "Lunch at Tim's." A branch of the long-established Environics polling firm founded by Michael Adams, this company's micro-analysis promised to be a much more vivid picture of the marketplace than the kind provided by traditional pollsters. "For years, we've been working with clients to help them understand the social values of their customers. My books and articles are written from about 35,000 feet," Adams said when Environics Analytics launched. "Social values segmentation takes us down to 1,500 [feet]."

No matter how impressive these new Canadian databases were, however, they lacked much of the detailed information available in the United States. In the first place, the United States had a much richer consumer marketplace from which to mine this information. As well, Canada's privacy laws made it almost impossible to obtain data on an individual, household level. So while an American marketer could look at the databases to get precise pictures of specific households, the big Canadian marketing databases were limited, by and large, to postal codes.

Canadian politicos, with rare exceptions, also lagged behind the Americans in micro-targeting. A few smart Canadian political operatives had already been dabbling in data. John Laschinger, for example, had been an early pioneer in accumulating political marketing information when he started "prospecting" private-sector lists in the 1980s to accumulate lists for direct-mail targets for the Progressive Conservatives. The arrival of the permanent voters list in 1993, especially in digital form, saw the Liberals adapting software so they could manipulate the voters list for their own fundraising and get-out-the-vote efforts. The Liberals started to buy demographic maps from Compusearch in 1993, to feed the statistics into their own data about individual ridings and voters in local constituencies. For about $2,000 each, MPs received demographic profiles of their ridings as well as a computer program they could use to link the Compusearch maps to their own rudimentary databases. This particular milestone in data-accumulation politics only came to public notice when news emerged of sixty-one MPs paying for the Compusearch information out of their House of Commons budgets. The MPs protested that these maps helped them do their jobs better, communicating with constituents, but it was also true that the Liberals had election goals in mind. Liberal MP Ronald MacDonald told reporters that the Compusearch maps would help fine-tune the messages that the party wanted to get out to voters as well as help determine which households should be receiving their literature.

But databases didn't really become a major player in Canadian politics until around 2004, when the merger of the old Progressive Conservative party and the Canadian Alliance transformed the machinery of modern election campaigning in this country. The credit for the Conservatives' early database plan has to go to Tom Flanagan, who was serving as Harper's chief of staff before and after the merger. The old Reform Party had organized its fundraising around small donations and in the process had accumulated the contact information for thousands and thousands of individual citizens. Gathered the old-fashioned way, with local poll captains and boots on the ground, this data gave Reformers an intimate knowledge of their local strength. These were their friends and neighbours, after all, many in rural areas. Reform's entire grassroots mentality, heavy on populism, was well suited to gathering the kind of information that would prove essential to a modern database. Through waves and waves of pamphlets and postcards, they obtained valuable addresses of and contact information for potential donors and voters. As the party grew and morphed into the Canadian Alliance under leader Stockwell Day, so too grew the list of donors and members. But the voter-ID and fundraising system, such as it existed, was only as strong as the volunteers on the ground.

By the time Harper was running for the Canadian Alliance leadership in 2002, the party had about 300,000 names on its rolls, including anyone who had been a member of the Reform Party, dating as far back as 1987. With the help of campaign manager Doug Finley and his understanding of marketing technology, Harper and his team first used this database to raise money for his leadership campaign—all told, more than $1 million from 9,500 donors, whose average individual donation was about $116.

After Harper won the leadership, Flanagan realized the value of having an ongoing database, one with more information than simply supporters' names, addresses and phone numbers. For all their skills in gathering the data, the Reform Party and then the Alliance had been in the habit of losing information in between elections, forcing them to start from scratch each time. By happy coincidence, the Canadian consumer world was also seeing a rapid expansion in professionals who were in the business of matching consumers to their data. One of them was an outfit called the Responsive Marketing Group. RMG specialized in direct marketing to help businesses and charities raise money; it had also worked with the Ontario Conservatives to set up an early database known as Trackright. (In 2009, RMG would be honoured by the Manning Centre for Building Democracy for raising more than $75 million for right-wing causes across Canada.)

Michael Davis, then head of RMG, went to Ottawa to sell Harper's office on the idea of a systemized database, such as the one it had built for the Ontario PCs. Jim Armour, then Harper's communications chief, sat in on one of the sessions and like the others was dazzled by the possibilities of this technology. Armour said he felt a bit how our prehistoric ancestors must have felt when they saw the first caveman walking with a torch. Suddenly, a whole new world was opened up to the Canadian Alliance team—a world in which they could quickly and efficiently find the voters they needed, through electronic sorting of phone numbers, addresses and contact information. Instead of relying on their small army of foot soldiers on the ground, they could assemble all this information in one big database.

With the help of RMG's data-building skills, the Canadian Alliance started to put together the information colossus that came to be known as CIMS: the Constituent Information Management System. It's pronounced just like "Sims," the video game in which you build lives and lifestyles for simulated characters, winning points for how well you tend to their needs and desires (just like modern marketing in politics, you might say). In those early days, CIMS was well fed, with information and big money. The Conservatives were spending as much money on CIMS as they were on advertising, in fact. And yes, this machine was being built by the same party that was leading a national crusade against the Liberals' gun registry—the same party that would oppose the mandatory long-form census. Although Conservatives would rail against the "intrusive" government taking names and keeping lists, they were remarkably sanguine about their own political party doing the same—with much more information and fewer controls over the way it was gathered.

For privacy reasons, though, the Conservatives tightly guarded this information, even from each other. Only people at the highest level of the Conservative pecking order had access to the full array of information in this massive Fort Knox of voter contact information. Lower down the chain, partisans were given passwords that opened the door only to the information that had been stored about their local area or polling districts. Reportedly, the quality of information in CIMS varied from riding to riding, depending on how diligently it had been collected by MPs or volunteers. CBC TV reporter Keith Boag was offered a rare glimpse into the database for a documentary he did called "The Data Game" in 2007. Boag gave the CIMS technicians the address and phone number of one of CBC's producers. A frowning face appeared by producer Sylvia Thompson's name; she had apparently been brusque with Conservative callers on some earlier occasion, so she was not viewed as a likely future prospect for funds or support.

The CIMS database was built on a wide variety of information sources. It started, naturally, with the national voters list, the names and addresses of every eligible voter in the country. On this basic layer of data, the Conservatives added information they gained from door-knocking, party membership lists, phone-bank efforts and national and local surveys. The basic Elections Canada list has no phone numbers or birthdates attached; that vital information could be gathered manually or by purchasing phonebook-style lists from data vendors. Everyone, from Conservative members of Parliament to candidates to canvassers, was expected to log information into the system. Well-trained volunteers were also instructed to keep an eye out for toys in the yard or small things such as a National Association of Stock Car Racing (NASCAR) sticker in the window of a pickup truck in the driveway. "We train our canvassers to take note of things that are of interest to us, in terms of them being able to segment [the voter information]," Richard Ciano, a long-time Ontario Progressive Conservative who was elected president of the provincial party in 2012, said in an interview.

CIMS kept track of who had donated or volunteered for the party in the past, and also names and contact information of anyone who had attended partisan events in the ridings. It noted whether you had a lawn sign, either for the Conservatives or for one of its rival parties. If you were generally seen as friendly to the Conservatives, a little smiley-face icon appeared beside your name in the CIMS database. If you angrily hung up on a Conservative seeking your support or slammed a door in a campaign worker's face, a little frowning face was likely beside your name. If you had written a letter to the party condemning a policy issue—the gun registry or funding for the CBC, to cite two popular causes—that too was tracked. And of course, CIMS kept records of people who were undecided or leaning toward the party—and those who were not. CIMS could sort and manipulate all this data quickly to help Conservatives figure out where to fire up their base of support, and where they needed to apply some extra effort. And the more information the party accumulated, the more sophisticated and micro-targeted its efforts would become.

Through a CIMS list, the party knew where to send fundraising letters that mentioned the gun registry or the CBC, for instance. CIMS could also generate digital lists of phone numbers, which could then be supplied to companies such as RMG for Conservatives' telemarketing efforts. During election campaigns, the Conservatives divided up this telemarketing work among a number of companies, not just RMG. The other Conservative-friendly firms in this business over the years included Campaign Research, Voter Track and Margaret Kool Marketing Inc. Other parties had their own favourite firms to do the same sort of thing. The Liberals used First Contact Voter Management and Voter Identification Solutions Inc., for instance.

Ciano, in addition to his political work, helped run Campaign Research, a firm that probed consumer and political preferences, sometimes in the same survey. "Things like hunting, fishing, gun ownership, boating, outdoor sports, NASCAR, major league sports—those are all things that are tracked as part of consumer behaviour," Ciano explained. "We can index that against polling information… That kind of thing is extremely useful to us in prospecting for support and donations." As an example, Ciano said that his surveys might turn up the fact that people who attend National Hockey League games several times a year, or people who buy a certain type of clock, are more likely to vote Conservative. The party then would try to seek out commercially available lists to reach these consumers of hockey or clocks. It's not just the collecting of the data that's important, in other words—it's the *analysis* that makes those connections between shopping and voting.

This was the business that politicians of all stripes had scrambled to keep exempt from the do-not-call list in 2005, in the dying days of Paul Martin's government. And the databases existed in a legal grey area with respect to privacy. Unlike commercial firms in Canada, political parties were under no obligation to tell members of the public what information it was storing about them, nor did they require people's permission to accumulate data on them. So these companies had a free hand, more or less, to keep dialling into the homes of Canadians, often through automated waves of calls, nicknamed "robocalls," and to keep amassing intelligence in the process. Like the pollsters of earlier eras, these telemarketing firms made the lion's share of their money in the commercial world, but their reputation in the political world. And they served as yet another bridge between the consumer and civic worlds—bringing private-sector expertise into the practice of democracy. Technology was making this possible to a degree that previous political marketers never could have imagined.

Stephen Taylor was building online communities for the party in the early 2000s—before, as he says, anyone had heard of phrases like "social media." Taylor founded a website called "Blogging Tories" that served as a one-stop shop for online Conservative opinion blogs. As the party's database became more sophisticated, so did Taylor's focus. He would mine through online data to find out who supported conservative and libertarian issues, to see what data-based characteristics they had in common. An adherent of the "always be testing" school of digital campaigning, Taylor pored through the analytics to see what online methods worked best in getting people to vote, speak out or donate to the Conservatives. Passionate about this new online frontier, Taylor talked the language of digital marketers, sprinkling terms like "metrics," "URLs" and "split-testing" throughout his explanations of his methods.

Split-testing, incidentally, is the means by which web marketers send out multiple versions of a digital message—sending customers to two different versions of a web page, for instance, or sending out two different types of emails to potential customers. The marketer can then test which web page or email had the better effect, by measuring how many web clicks they get or, better yet, how much business they generated. It's not that different from TV commercials that urge buyers to call a 1-800 number and ask for Operator Number 222 or 537. There are usually no such numbered operators—it's just a way for the advertisers to figure out who saw the ad in question, on which TV show and at what time, for instance. In this way, whether on television or online, marketing messages are constantly being tweaked and modified to maximize their potential audience or success. Political parties are no different from commercial marketers in trying to figure out what messages work best, according to Taylor. Taylor does the same kind of digital-analysis work for the commercial clients of Fleishman–Hillard, a worldwide public relations and marketing firm. Taylor has a foot in both worlds—the political world and the consumer world—just as Martin Goldfarb had in the 1970s and Allan Gregg had in the 1980s.

Taylor would tell partisans and business clients the same thing about the need to do data mining: "If you aren't showing up with this, we know someone else is. If you cede that competitive advantage on anything, someone else will fill that breach and take advantage of it." In 2010 Taylor became director of the National Citizens Coalition, the same organization that was once headed by Stephen Harper. The NCC had come a long way since those bags of mail sent to founder Colin Brown, or even the mass-market billboard campaigns that Harper and Gerry Nicholls managed in the 1990s. With Taylor's help, the NCC started to pay a lot of attention, just like marketers, to micro-targeting and to custom-designing its product appeal.

But Taylor and other data specialists weren't holding their breath for the day Canadians would learn what kind of beer or doughnuts that Liberals, Conservatives and New Democrats favoured. Canada's privacy laws didn't allow for the sharing of that kind of micro-data, and Elections Canada didn't keep records of how often, or for whom, people voted. Nor did Canadian political parties, under strict campaign spending limits, have the money to pay for the dazzling kind of consumer-data analysis that the Americans could get their hands on. "If I were a political entrepreneur, I think I would be more likely to see a more wide-open and more vibrant market for my wares in the United States than I would in Canada," Taylor said. Still, though, Canadian political entrepreneurs, especially Conservatives, would keep trying to plunge ever further into this brave new world where consumer and political data merged.

Swimming in the Blue Ocean

In 2005, a few years after he left elected politics, former Reform Party leader Preston Manning set up a think-tank/political training school called the Manning Centre for Building Democracy. Based in Alberta, this centre conducted conferences, seminars and research on how to build the small-"c" conservative base in Canada. Its stated vision was, "A free and democratic Canada, where conservative principles are well articulated, understood, and implemented."

In that quest, Manning, the former management consultant, liked to look at ways in which business lessons could be applied to the cause of growing the conservative movement. He became a big fan of a book called *Blue Ocean Strategy*, a manual on how to find new customers in not-so-usual places. The title comes from marine lore and the book, translated into more than forty languages, had become a bit of a bible for marketers. In places where sharks are fierce competitors, the book says, the seas are dyed red with the blood of their battles. But there are quiet areas of the ocean, free of shark fights, where the water is calm and blue. These uncontested fields are where real entrepreneurs can make their mark. Canada's Cirque du Soleil, unlike any other kind of circus, is a prime example of this attitude toward competition, according to the manual. Rather than compete with the circuses already out in the market, Cirque created a whole different style of three-ring entertainment heavy on acrobatics and free of animals.

Manning urged other Conservatives to read the book and see the political parallels. Not that he thought Canada needed another circus, but he did think Conservatives had to go looking for blue areas free of fighting sharks, and to expand choice rather than intensify competition. Manning's old US consultant friend Frank Luntz had told the Civitas group in 2006 that *exurbia* held the same potential. Harper's marketer, Patrick Muttart, had also been intent on creating a political base where no politics had existed among the Tim Hortons Canadians. To help locate the blue oceans among the electorate, the Manning Centre commissioned a 2012 study with another retail bent. "Reaching Near Customers" it was called, and it was delivered by a demographics whiz named Mitch Wexler.

Wexler unveiled some of his findings at a 2012 Manning Centre conference in Ottawa. Not surprisingly, perhaps, his demographic analysis revealed that Conservatives' hopes of growth continued to lie among the segments of the population who cared more about their consumer concerns than they did about politics. Wexler calls them "bread-and-butter" Canadians, the same term used long ago when US pollster Lou Harris was trying to tell Liberals where to pitch their political product. "They don't identify with any particular party. They work hard, they want to enjoy their family, they want to put food on the table for them, but they don't want to have to be bothered, or have things get in the way, that have to do with government," Wexler told the Manning conference.

Wexler himself is an entrepreneur at the leading edge of the merger between consumer and political databases. His company, Politrain Consulting, has developed a whole array of political marketing software for the modern campaigning professional. One of his systems is called PollMaps.ca, which shows detailed poll-by-poll election results and analyses on colourful maps. Another is Spectrum Electoral Demographics, which adds demographic data to the mix, showing polls in all their sociological splendour—neighbourhoods categorized by average age, household income, family size, ethnicity and so on.

It was Wexler's demographic analysis that showed Toronto mayoralty candidate Rob Ford where to look for his support in the 2010 election. Ford, though a conservative-style politician, didn't have access to the CIMS database because he was in a municipal

campaign. But he did have Wexler's array of data to build his electoral crusade against the "gravy train" in Toronto. That was a pitch,
Wexler found, that resonated in the ring of suburbs around downtown Toronto, where everyday working men and women were feeling
simmering resentment against elites and the establishment in 2010.

Wexler got involved with Conservative politics in 1993 and is
proof of the old maxim that your first job in politics will turn out
to be your enduring interest. His entree was the federal Progressive
Conservative leadership race that gave Canada its first woman prime
minister, however briefly. He volunteered to help Kim Campbell's
leadership campaign with something known as "delegate tracking"—
keeping an eye on the number of supporters that Campbell was
bringing to the convention. After the federal Conservatives' spectacular loss in the 1993 election, Wexler, like many Conservatives, drifted
to provincial politics, working in Mike Harris's Ontario for cabinet
ministers such as Al Palladini and David Johnson. Wexler also did
stints in the private sector, always with an eye to software and data.

Around the time the Conservatives came to power in Ottawa,
Wexler started to strike out with his own company, confident he had
found a smart-market niche for detailed, data-rich political maps.
Wexler jokes that his business matches his personal disposition. He
calls himself a "completist": one of those people who starts collecting
things and isn't satisfied until he has the whole set. So once he started
gathering up the data for his poll maps, he still thought that he
needed more—demographic information, such as the type available
to sophisticated private-sector firms. Knowing it would be too costly
to accumulate that information himself, he started looking for a business partner. Through a mutual friend, he was introduced to Zhen
Mei of Manifold Data Mining Inc., who had just the kind of data
that Wexler needed. Within one meeting over coffee, the two men
forged a partnership, fusing political and marketplace information.

Zhen grew up in China, but obtained his degree in Germany.
During a visit to Canada for a conference in 1996, he and his wife

fell in love with Toronto. They were amazed by its diversity; the subway was a marvel to behold. Almost immediately, they decided that Canada would be their future home. So the couple applied to emigrate to Canada and in 1997 settled in a city rich in the kind of demographic data that Zhen was good at accumulating and analyzing. He figured that businesses would pay to understand what kind of customers they needed to attract, and where they needed to be located.

Zhen, much like Patrick Muttart or Martin Goldfarb or the people at Environics Analytics, breaks down the population into consumer types. "Nest builders," for instance, are "typical, middle, urban Canadians" who spend nearly three times the average amount on home renovation and investments. Here's what else Manifold Data Mining knows about this group: their average income is $83,900, their house is valued at about $346,300 and there are precisely 2.85 people on average in the home. They are better educated than most, and they work in jobs related to administration, management and the natural and applied sciences. They are more likely to live in Edmonton or Calgary, and they trace their ancestry more than average to British, Polish, Dutch and Italian heritage. When they're not renovating their homes, they play golf and favour reading about business, mystery, sports and gardening. They're more likely than most Canadians to be buyers of camping equipment and fireplaces.

Zhen purchased his raw data from Statistics Canada, and also from a source rich in consumer-type information—the Bureau of Broadcast Measurement (BBM) surveys. These lengthy questionnaires, called "diaries," are conducted regularly to provide ratings for TV and radio. But they also gather up all kinds of lifestyle information from participants. BBM doesn't sell the names, addresses or individual information from its surveys, but it does sell its results, which companies such as Manifold can then sort into postal codes. Zhen also mines data from Citizenship and Immigration Canada, which releases statistics about immigration and settlement patterns.

He gathers financial and economic data from the Canadian Bankers Association, real estate market stats from the Canada Mortgage and Housing Corporation, and surveys from associations in multicultural communities. He puts all these numbers through something he calls a "data-fusion" technique, which matches the patterns in all the numbers to postal codes in Canada.

Mix Manifold's information with Wexler's electoral data and what you get are maps that serve as vivid portraits of the consumer-citizen marketplace—a "360-degree view of customers' needs and desires," as they bill it. The maps PollMaps provide to candidates are dense, tight, fact-filled portraits of ridings across Canada, loaded with household information sorted by individual polls in the ridings. Basic political information is there: how certain neighbourhoods voted in past elections or where the pockets of strength and weaknesses are for each party within that riding. Then there's all the demographic information available from Statistics Canada: average age, income, education, family size and so on within these polls. The most comprehensive of the maps contain consumer and lifestyle information, too. For Wexler, the real power of all this information lies in its ability to help him create "voter profiles." These are essentially charts, in which Wexler analyzes voting patterns for each party based on typical voters from specific constituencies. He can then pick a demographic group—South Asian immigrants, for instance, or single-parent families—and see where parties need to devote extra time or persuasion.

Wexler has also worked as a campaign director for the Conservatives in provincial and federal elections, and he used CIMS and his own maps to organize the vote-getting strategy. CIMS helped him find the names and addresses of past donors and supporters, so that he knew where to dispatch lawn signs and where to hunt for volunteers and donations. His own poll maps helped him figure out how to fine-tune his direct mail to target constituencies and their lifestyles. In the 2011 election, for instance, Wexler knew which neighbourhoods in Brampton would get the Conservative pamphlets about family-friendly policies, and which ones would get the mail written with seniors' concerns in mind. He knew the pockets of the riding that would be more likely to be impressed by a promise to give tax credits for children's art classes, and which ones would not. In this way, the Conservatives knew where to find the vote-shopping customers for their "boutique" policies—which is why they had those policies in the first place.

Wexler also believes that these sophisticated tools and maps can serve a higher purpose, in improving voter participation. If political parties can identify where turnout has been weak, for instance, they can analyze the data to see what may be keeping people away from the ballot box or, more importantly, what can be done to make those pockets of voters more engaged in the civic life of the country. On election day, they can dispatch more volunteers to ferry such people to the polls, for instance. Above and beyond all these arguments for database politics, who could argue with a technological innovation that forces politicians and their strategists to know their voters better? Isn't that democracy in action?

Taking Names, Making Lists

Not all Conservatives happily went along with their party's data-collecting frenzy. Inky Mark, who served five terms as a Manitoba MP from 1997 to 2009, regularly bristled at orders from party central to update the database. He told Canadian Press interviewer Jennifer Ditchburn, "I always knew that I had to do my own thing, because… they can control you 100 percent, and that's exactly what happened with CIMS." CIMS first leaped into major public attention late in 2007, after Garth Turner, a member of Parliament for Halton, just outside Toronto, was booted from the Conservative caucus for being a little too open on his much-read blog, the Turner Report. Turner sat for a while as an independent, then joined the opposition Liberal caucus.

Once freed from any remnants of Conservative discipline, Turner started documenting the things that had bugged him while he was trying to be a loyal party MP. He was particularly incensed by the order for all Conservative candidates and MPs to log their dealings with voters into the massive, central database called CIMS. But what bothered him even more, he said, was that MPs, in their capacity as elected representatives, were asked to keep filing information into the machine—even if their constituents were dealing with them on a non-partisan basis. Turner took up the cause during Question Period in the House of Commons in the fall of 2007: "Millions of Canadians may have had their privacy breached and their trust misused by members of this House. This is due to CIMS, a database run by the Conservative party, which each party MP has installed in his or her office. Unknown to millions of constituents, personal information is routinely fed into this database, which experts are calling a 'chilling' breach of ethics."

No matter how much the Conservatives deflected the charges about CIMS, the revelation about an all-knowing, Big Brother–style database could actually explain a lot. How had the Conservatives known to send greeting cards to members of cultural communities, celebrating their holidays? Reports kept surfacing about these unexpected, at times unwelcome, bits of mail from the Conservative government. Members of the gay and lesbian community were startled in 2012, for instance, when they received an email from Immigration Minister Jason Kenney boasting of what the government had done for gays and lesbians abroad. It turned out that he had obtained the emails from a petition sent to his office in 2011. Some Canadians felt a bit creepy about the idea of the population getting sorted into lists this way. Michelle Kofman, a Jewish Canadian who lived in Thornhill, a Liberal-held riding the Conservatives coveted, wrote a letter about her concerns to the *National Post*, which was published on September 29, 2007:

On Monday, I received a postcard from Stephen Harper. The front of the card featured his lovely family, and on the back, my family was wished a "Happy New Year." Besides the fact that it was ten days later than the actual Jewish new year, this card raises the question: How does the prime minister know I'm Jewish? Did his office acquire this information from the most recent census? If so, is this an appropriate use of this information? Is this gesture strictly for political gain?... This public relations initiative appears to be using my ethnicity to win support in the pending federal election. Does the PMO really think there is any sincerity there? I hope the development, printing and mailing of this card was paid for by the Conservative party, and not the Canadian taxpayer. And if the intentions were purely genuine, then I expect a beautiful Hanukkah card in my mailbox this December.

That wasn't the first such letter printed in the *National Post* either. A man with the surname Lee wrote of how he had received a Chinese New Year card, even though he had no Chinese origins. What kind of Conservative direct marketing was this? Where were the ruling Conservatives getting the data that allowed them to send out these greeting cards to target audiences? Suspicions immediately ran toward the database—technology run amok. Former Conservative party and Parliament Hill staffer Michael Sona, who would eventually go to prison in the controversies over the CIMS database and "robocalls" in 2012–13, said it was part of his job working in MPs' offices to feed constituent information into the Conservative database. This was true for other staffers, too, he said. However, the party also had lots of volunteers to sift through names and come up with these lists, according to Richard Ciano. "That's the advantage that we have, that volunteer labour to do that stuff. I know that sometimes the output of it concerns people, but at the end of the day, it's stuff that we're observing in public."

Moreover, the Conservatives aren't alone in doing this kind of cultural outreach. There are services that supply analytic software to databases to help decipher the cultural origins behind names on the voters list. Pitney Bowes, a British firm, supplies one such system, called Spectrum, that boasts that it can do "name matching" from more than two hundred countries to help databases get their spelling correct. The Liberals, with their own historic ties to cultural communities, bought this software to augment their own database, called Liberalist.

The use of these databases also further entrenched the reality of the permanent campaign in Canada. Where once parties only made occasional forays to people's doorsteps, through doing periodic door-knocking or distributing pamphlets through the mailbox, now the political offices had the technology and resources to make voter contact a full-time job, whether an election was in progress or not. It also meant that when an official campaign got under way, parties didn't have to waste precious time identifying where possible support would lie. Thanks to these databases, the campaign honchos already knew where they should fine-tune and concentrate their "customer relationship management" at the micro-level in all the ridings. Political parties were increasingly seeing Canadians as potential consumers of their "product," twenty-four hours a day, seven days a week. The Conservatives had applied this permanent-campaign technique to advertising, and the same would be true for its direct-marketing efforts.

Call Display

What's most amazing is how the booming database industry popped up in the very heart of Canadian politics without much notice from the media or even some of the political players themselves. That would start to change late in 2011, when the extent of the direct-marketing business in politics started to register on the public radar. Irwin Cotler, a Montreal Liberal MP, was shocked to find that a scant few months after the 2011 election Conservatives were busily phoning people in his riding, testing to find which of his constituents would switch from the red team to the blue team if he stepped down. He apparently was unaware that in marketing politics, the campaign never stops.

Residents of the Mount Royal riding received calls in the fall of 2011 that began with a preamble about "rumours" of a Cotler resignation. If that happened, the callers asked Cotler's constituents, what party would you support in a by-election? The calls were traced back to a firm called Campaign Research, owned by two Conservatives: Richard Ciano and Nick Kouvalis, the latter having helped Rob Ford get elected as mayor in Toronto and who served as Ford's first chief of staff. Cotler, incensed by the calls, had no intention of stepping down and was furious at the way this bit of direct marketing had made his constituents doubt his commitment to the job he had campaigned to win only months earlier. Cotler made several vigorous protests to the House of Commons about this interference in his duties, and Speaker Andrew Scheer eventually ruled that the tactic was "reprehensible." But Conservatives, who openly acknowledged hiring Campaign Research to do this job, were unapologetic. One party official anonymously told the *Globe and Mail*, "If the Liberals spent as much time doing voter ID instead of complaining about political parties doing their work, they'd be in better shape than they are today."

Kouvalis made a rare TV appearance in late 2011 to defend the practice and was similarly unabashed. He claimed that the Conservatives had learned from Liberals how to play hardball politics, and that these calls were part of the playing field. "My job is to end Liberal politicians' careers. That's what I get paid to do. It's not pretty, it offends some people, but that's what I get paid to do," Kouvalis said. "We're a service provider and we're good at what we do and we follow the rules."

Not long after the Cotler controversy died down came another, larger potential blow to the political parties' direct-marketing efforts.

In an explosive front-page story by Postmedia reporters Stephen Maher and Glen McGregor, news emerged in February 2012 of a major Elections Canada investigation into fraudulent phone calls in Guelph during the 2011 election. Recipients of these calls, mainly past Liberal voters, were wrongly informed that their polling stations had moved and that the calls were coming from Elections Canada.

The calls, according to the ongoing investigation, came from automated lists generated by one of the big direct-marketing firms that worked for the Conservatives: Rack Nine Inc., which also did robocalls for nine other Conservative candidates in their ridings, including Stephen Harper. This wasn't unusual. Every modern party has a database that can generate automatic dialling campaigns. What was unusual about this effort was that it involved keeping voters away from the polls, not marketing to potential customers. It's called "voter suppression" by the tacticians. It's also called illegal by Elections Canada, which takes a dim view of denying people their fundamental democratic right.

In subsequent days and weeks, the headlines exploded with more reports of fraudulent calls, not confined to Guelph. By the spring of 2013, Canada's chief electoral officer, Marc Mayrand, would report that more than 1,400 separate investigations were under way in 247 ridings across the country. The Council of Canadians launched a Federal Court challenge to annul the results in six ridings across Canada because of robocalls, too. Although the council didn't achieve their goal in the final ruling, Federal Court judge Richard Mosley found in the spring of 2013 that there was evidence of a determined campaign to suppress votes using robocalls and the Conservatives' database. "Misleading calls about the locations of polling stations were made to electors in ridings across the country," Mosley wrote in his ruling. "The purpose of those calls was to suppress the votes of electors who had indicated their voting preference in response to earlier voter-identification calls." Mosley went on: "The most likely source of the information used to make the misleading calls was the CIMS database maintained and controlled by the CPC, accessed for that purpose by a person or persons currently unknown to this Court."

Also in the spring of 2013, former Conservative staff member and campaign worker Michael Sona was formally charged in relation to the fraudulent robocalls in Guelph, and was sent to prison in 2014—though he insisted throughout his trial that he was being made a scapegoat. Sona said in one television interview that the robocalls scheme was a "massive" one, but he did not know the perpetrators. The Conservatives weren't the only ones who had been playing fast and loose with robocalls, either. In Guelph, again, Liberal MP Frank Valeriote would be fined by the CRTC for massive waves of phone calls that his campaign conducted against Conservatives, for failing to properly identify the calls as coming from the Liberals. The Wildrose party in Alberta was similarly fined $90,000 in the spring of 2013 for wrongful robocalls in the 2012 provincial election, and the Ontario Progressive Conservative Party was fined $85,000 for its wrongful use of robocalls.

In total, the CRTC levied $369,000 in fines in May 2013 for misleading robocalls, and every major political party took a hit: the New Democrats had to pay $14,000 for some automated calls they made in Quebec, while the federal Conservatives were slapped with a $78,000 fine for calls they made to protest against riding-boundary changes in Saskatchewan. Liberal MP Marc Garneau, Canada's first man in space, was fined $2,500 for calls he made during his unsuccessful campaign to lead his party. While there were some demands for an outright ban on robocalls in the wake of these controversies—from Democracy Watch, for instance—the big political parties were aware that too much was at stake here. Speaking to a room full of Conservatives attending the Manning Centre's conference in Ottawa in early 2012, Richard Ciano of Campaign Research warned that the scandal could undo fifteen years of progress in political marketing:

Since the 1990s when customer relationship management approaches became widespread, conservative parties have moved quickly to implement this essential business process into electioneering. And for the last fifteen years we have amassed a considerable lead on the Liberals and NDP in this area, as evidenced by the numbers on our direct response fundraising programs. Why? Is it because we had people with more technical savvy? Is it because the Liberals were stupid? Or lazy? Personally I prefer stupidity as an explanation, but it's immaterial. The fact that the Liberals and NDP couldn't get their act together on CRM approaches and direct contact is not our fault. It's theirs.

In Ciano's view, the Conservatives' rivals were whipping up the robocall controversy in a bid to destroy their competitor's advantage. "Why do the Liberals and NDP want to remove direct contact from Canadian elections? Because, put it bluntly: they suck at it." Actually, Ciano was only half right. While the Liberals were indeed far behind the Conservatives in the data game at this point, the NDP had been playing a furious game of catch-up on the marketing front. It was starting to look like "customer relationship management," at the micro-level, would spell the difference between success and failure in Canadian political salesmanship.

THIS LITTLE PARTY WENT
TO MARKET

Marketing manuals are loaded with advice on how to handle fierce competition. One familiar refrain is, "Don't just imitate, differentiate." That means if you own a restaurant suddenly losing customers to a fast-food outlet, you don't simply overhaul your menu to offer the same fare. Smart marketers know how to learn from their rivals' strength, borrow examples when necessary, but offer consumers something distinct. The smartest marketers know how to turn this purchasing choice into a lifestyle statement, like those Apple-versus-PC ads that used to run on television, framing computer buys as an epic showdown between the cool kids and the nerds. So here was the situation facing the Conservatives' political competitors in the years after Stephen Harper became prime minister and elevated marketing to a tool of winning power and keeping it, too. How could they adopt marketing practices and do them better than the Conservatives? Could they market at all? And how willing were they to imitate the Conservatives' pitch to consumer-citizens? Who would end up as the cool kids, and who would end up as the hapless nerds?

From Lemon-Aid to Orange Crush

In the late 1980s and early 1990s, Canada was given a sneak preview of the future strength of the New Democratic Party, though it would take a couple of decades to unfold in full. Brian Topp, a Montrealer and former student journalist at McGill University, was the owner of a print and graphics shop called Studio Apostrophe. Some of his more political friends were dabbling in the NDP, at the margins of the back-and-forth between Liberal and Conservative dominance at the time—and using Apostrophe to print their pamphlets and posters. Through these friends, Topp met a man named Phil Edmonston, an American-born founder of the Automobile Protection Association and author of a popular series of car-buyers' manuals called *Lemon-Aid* guides. Edmonston decided to run for election in Montreal in 1988, and eventually won a seat in a Chambly by-election in 1990. He became the first New Democrat elected in the province of Quebec, pulling off that feat with the help of a strategic organizer named Ray Guardia. Edmonston lasted only one term as an MP, and Topp went on to work as an adviser to provincial NDP governments in Saskatchewan and Ontario. But this early mix of these individuals' particular strengths—consumer advocacy and Quebec-organizing talents—foreshadowed a recipe that would vault the NDP to unprecedented heights in the twenty-first century, and an "orange crush" of an election in 2011.

Jack Layton, who had become leader of the NDP in 2003, was in many ways the ideal person to drag the party into the modern age of marketing. Sharp, fast-talking, always "on," Layton had the perpetual optimism and extroverted demeanour of a salesman. (His critics would regularly disparage him as a "used car salesman.") A former Toronto councillor, he had gained his political experience in the city that was ground zero for the Canadian ad and marketing business. His own 1991 campaign for the Toronto mayoralty was seen as slick and sophisticated, complete with camera-ready photo opportunities and reams of policy papers. Although Layton spent far more money than his rival, June Rowlands, he went down to defeat. Still, Layton's political education at the municipal level, which tends to revolve around more practical concerns, gave him a window into the "bread-and-butter" concerns of the average citizen. As NDP leader, Layton would surround himself with people who were eminently practical about putting the party on the map, and Brian Topp was at the heart of the circle.

Layton loved gadgets and data, all the hardware that political parties need to practise marketing in the digital age. Layton adored his BlackBerry and often surprised friends and acquaintances with unexpected missives, even late at night. He regularly reminded his team that well-run political parties operate on three priorities: people, money and data. After every NDP-hosted gathering, he exhorted staffers to gather contact information from attendees, so they could be tapped later to help out the party, either with cash or maybe even by serving as candidates. "He loved asking people for money," said Anne McGrath, who started working alongside Layton when he was running for the leadership and she was rounding up supporters for him at the Canadian Union of Public Employees (CUPE). "And he was always recruiting candidates."

McGrath was recruited to work in Layton's inner-strategist circle in 2005, joining other loyalists working on the "project" of modernizing the NDP. She would serve as the anchor to Layton in her years as chief of staff, a voice of quiet, calm competence. The others who would drive the project included Topp, as well as Drew Anderson, a talented writer and communications strategist, and Brad Lavigne, the former BC student activist who quickly rose through the NDP ranks from communications adviser to national director of the party. Ray Guardia, still plying his strategic trade a decade or so after first working with Edmonston, was in charge of building the Quebec operation. Oddly enough, the rapid succession of federal elections in Canada from 2004 through to 2011, though volatile to the country, would be a stabilizing force to this group, repeatedly testing and sealing their allegiance with each run at the polls. Layton, as leader, went through four elections before his untimely death from cancer in 2011, and each campaign taught this tight-knit group lessons they would use for the next go-around. None of these people were romantics or ideologues about the "project." They were well aware of the marketing universe in which they were working. Topp, particularly, had a clear-eyed view of Canada's consumer-citizens and what it took to reach them in a multi-channel universe. "Many people make their decisions about leaders and candidates in the first ten seconds they look at them. Images are more powerful than words," said the man whose early graphics-shop experience taught him about the importance of those images.

The transformation to a market-friendly NDP began in earnest right after the 2008 election. Layton's team emerged somewhat dispirited from that encounter with the electorate, even though Harper had been kept to a minority for his second mandate and the Liberals were further enfeebled, knocked down to seventy-seven seats. Sure, the NDP had picked up ten more seats, giving them thirty-seven MPs. But when Layton's strategists looked more closely at the numbers, they realized that their share of the popular vote had only climbed by 0.7 percent. Worse, 75,000 fewer people had voted for the NDP than in 2006. If this was the base, it was shrinking. The NDP strategists realized that they'd gone about as far as they could go in attracting the traditional ideological supporters of the party— all those people who liked the NDP's well-known stands on labour unions, the environment and other progressive issues.

The more optimistic people around the table at the party's Laurier Avenue headquarters in Ottawa turned their eye to another number: 104. In more than one-third of the ridings across Canada in the 2008 election, the NDP had placed either first or second. Now they had to persuade Canadians that they were more than just the "conscience of Parliament," which had always been a nice way of saying the New Democrats were also-rans. The NDP needed Canadians to see the party as a serious option for government, too, as capable as Liberals or Conservatives at running the country.

In marketing language, this is called expanding the "consideration set." Those busy Canadian consumers, shopping 24-7, are constantly sifting through all the choices out there and narrowing them down to a manageable number of options. There may be fifty cans of tomatoes on the shelves of their supermarket, but browsers usually waver between two or three labels presented for their buying consideration. In political terms, then, the NDP's challenge was to climb into the ranks of those two or three "brands," the ones voters viewed as serious options for government. One way of doing this would be to build a solid campaign in Quebec, where the party had been shut out since Edmonston's brief shining moment in the 1990s. Another way was simply to keep telling the people and the pundits that the NDP was intent on being more than an opposition after-thought. Layton had been saying for some time that he was running for prime minister. Official Ottawa may have laughed, but NDP-commissioned focus groups had been saying that they believed him: "What else would he be doing?" participants would ask.

After the 2008 disappointment, Layton's inner circle realized it was time to take the NDP into the marketing-friendly world of twenty-first-century Canadian politics. They would imitate the Conservatives with strict, top-down discipline and in micro-targeting the electorate, zeroing in on consumer concerns. After all, while marketing-style politics had been championed by the right wing through history, from Thatcher to Reagan to Harper, Tony Blair's New Labour experiment in Britain showed it could be pulled off on the left, too. If they wanted to get more voters in the next election, they would have to find what they called the "next tier" of NDP supporters: all those people who might see the NDP as a second choice. Like Blair, the NDP would start looking for its future among the disengaged voters—the same Tim Hortons Canadians or "bread-and-butter" voters that the Conservatives had

been successfully courting for the past few years. So they commissioned a polling firm, Viewpoints Research, to paint a demographic
portrait of people who might be swayed to the New Democrats
with the right marketing effort. As a polling exercise, it was a mix
of Allan Gregg–style "typologies" of voters, organized by political
leaning, and the pop-psychographic look at consumer tastes and
lifestyles favoured by Patrick Muttart and Martin Goldfarb. It was
also the first time that the NDP spent the bulk of its research dollars
learning about non-NDP voters.

According to Viewpoints' results, this next tier of potential NDP
support consisted of people who were slightly older and a bit more
well-heeled than traditional New Democrat supporters. They lived in
medium-sized cities, were as likely to be male as female, and they were
in that so-called sandwich age group simultaneously worrying about
their children and their aging parents. Most of all, these potential
NDP converts were turned off politics. They didn't have any ideology and didn't rely too much on political news, either. From what
they did know of federal political events, they weren't crazy about
Harper—they felt they couldn't trust him. They didn't really like
Ignatieff either—something about his demeanour turned them off.
Although they liked Layton, they thought his workplace, Parliament,
was dysfunctional and tuned out of their everyday concerns.

In this target audience, not that far removed from Tony Blair's
Basildon Men, John Howard's "battlers" in Australia or Stephen
Harper's Tim Hortons voters, the NDP had found the new direction
for the "project." With market research in hand, Layton and his advisers set out to overhaul the New Democrats' product, transforming
not just its image, but its policies to capture these disengaged voters.
Like the Conservatives, they would come to see the voters as beleaguered consumers with very personalized complaints, whether it was
credit-card rates or not being able to find a family doctor. The NDP
would shed its reputation for being solely the voice of groups—students, unions and protesters—and get far more precise about talking

to voters as individuals. Ever practical, his eyes on the long game, Brad Lavigne was an unapologetic proponent of taking policies to the level of transactional politics. "This approach offered the voter, as consumer, a tangible benefit in return for voting for us," Lavigne said.

Still, this approach required a bit of a leap for the NDP rank and file, heavily invested as it was in its view of society as a collective and its optimism about the basic unselfishness of the "ordinary" Canadian. And not everyone was happy about the shift in thinking. James Laxer, a political economist and one-time leadership candidate for the party in the 1970s, was probably the most vocal critic of the party's marketing transformation as it was under way. "The NDP has evolved into a party much like the others," Laxer wrote in a stinging critique on rabble.ca. "There is little political ferment. Riding association meetings, party conferences and provincial and federal conventions are not occasions for basic debate and education about the state of society and what needs to be done, but rather [should] focus on fundraising, holding raffles and showcasing the leader for the media."

Brad Lavigne and Brian Topp shrugged off criticism such as this, believing it represented a tiny anachronistic fragment of the New Democrats, the kind who were happier to remain as a protest rump on the Canadian political landscape. The NDP wanted to play in the big leagues with the Conservatives and the Liberals, and it would have to start seeing people as these major parties had through history—through the prism of their everyday consumer wants. Bill Clinton in the United States and Blair in Britain had already proven that citizens' material "aspirations" were neither right nor left, merely the opening to a conversation between the politicians and the voters.

The difference was obvious almost immediately after the 2008 election. Layton began to focus his rhetoric in the Commons more sharply on consumer concerns, including a crusade for lower credit-card rates and lower home-heating costs. When Harper's newly re-elected Conservative government tabled its spring budget in 2009, for instance, Layton and the NDP came out against it, making explicit the kind of voters they were trying to reach. Layton accused the Conservatives of being more concerned with the "board-room table than the kitchen table." He said Harper's government was "picking the pockets of the hard-working consumers across the country, those who are trying to buy some gas, or trying to take their money out of the bank or trying to pay their credit cards." Layton wanted Ottawa to set upper limits on the interest charged to credit cards and to remove the goods and services tax from homeowners' gas or oil bills.

The pundits started to notice. Don Martin, writing in the *National Post* during the NDP's 2009 convention, complimented the party for being in touch with voters. "Keep in mind that on issues important to many Canadians—pension protection, employment insurance reform, credit-card gouging, salvaging the auto sector, escaping Afghanistan and even attacking a carbon tax—the New Democrats lead the charge, bringing those concerns to the House of Commons floor with the Liberals playing catch-up," Martin wrote.

Topp was keeping a close eye on how the Conservatives had tried to capture the Tim Hortons set. He read with interest, for instance, an interview that Patrick Muttart did with the American Enterprise Institute in 2010, in which Harper's marketing whiz explained how he had framed Conservative policies to suit the Tim Hortons crowd. Topp thought this was smart "political engineering" but fundamentally dishonest, given that conservatives, historically and around the world, had been much friendlier to wealthy constituencies. "It is Orwellian double-talk," Topp wrote in his online *Globe and Mail* column. "The Conservative agenda seeks to impoverish all of Tim Hortons' clients and to transfer their savings and income to people who view Starbucks as pedestrian." New Democrats, Topp believed, had to take back the language of populism and turn it on Conservatives: imitate in approach, differentiate in substance. He also thought that the left had fallen into talking about itself in elitist tones, or as he scathingly put it, "Thirty years of impenetrable, internally-focused, liberal, academic, bureaucratic, entitlement-driven, self-absorbed 'progressive' language."

To that same end, the New Democrats set about removing references to "democratic socialism" from its party constitution, simply because this wasn't a phrase that spoke to ordinary Canadians anymore—if it ever did. The NDP brass portrayed this constitutional amendment as a mere cosmetic update, but it also represented a party shift away from talk of collectives and ideology and more toward individuals and pragmatic consumers. Or as Lavigne has argued, "the party, as with commercial marketing, needs to continue to keep pace with language and concepts that Canadians are comfortable with in their day-to-day activities. The core values of the party remain, but the language used to articulate them is constantly updated."

Around the campaign-planning table at the Laurier Avenue headquarters in Ottawa, the NDP strategists looked closely at what other marketing lessons they could import to the project. McGrath and Lavigne believed that good marketing was all about effective communications and knew that the Conservatives had managed this with highly centralized control from Ottawa and terse, clear language from everyone up and down the chain of command. The NDP, they realized, was going to have to be tighter in its discipline over its public pronouncements, and it was going to have to simplify its platform message as well. They got out their scissors and started paring down the lengthy list of promises from the 2008 platform. Not coincidentally, they settled on a neat five commitments, or guarantees, just as Tony Blair and Stephen Harper had done, all of which were eminently pragmatic:

- Hire more doctors and nurses. "We'll start training more doctors and nurses and give doctors that have left Canada incentives to come back home."

- Strengthen your pension. "We'll work with the provinces to double your public pension and offer you more choice over your retirement savings."

- Kick-start job creation. "We'll give small businesses a two percentage points tax cut and bring in targeted tax credits for companies that hire here in Canada."

- Help out your family budget. "We'll cap credit-card fees at prime plus five [percentage points], take the federal sales tax off home heating and give consumers control over cellphone bills."

- Fix Ottawa for good. "We'll stop the scandals and commit to work with other parties to get things done for you."

These were simple, easy-to-understand promises, limited in scope and ambition, in part to reassure anyone nervous about the NDP's reputation for favouring sweeping social change. The five "Practical First Steps," as they were called, were also designed to be viewed as the opposite of what the Conservatives were promising. If the Tories were going to give tax cuts to big business, the NDP would offer tax cuts to *small* businesses. Language was also crucial. The NDP's promises were sprinkled with consumer-friendly words like "choice" and references to lower prices. It was through that powerful consumerist "choice," too, that Layton was going to smash through stodgy old ideas about Liberals and Conservatives being the only real options for government. The NDP leader would say repeatedly in election ads, "People will try and tell you that you have no choice but to vote for more of the same. But you do have a choice." It became as much of a motto for him as his old favourite, "Don't let them tell you it can't be done."

NDP Vote

Under Layton, the NDP also got very serious about collecting data, as he had so often urged his team to do. The party had had a rudimentary database kicking around since the late 1990s—one they built in-house called NDP Vote. But the more the New Democrats plunged into marketing, especially after 2008, the more sophisticated they became about collecting and sorting information about Canadians, right down to individual postal codes.

The NDP database collected intelligence from everywhere, from old-fashioned phone calls and canvassers' meetings on doorsteps, to the big "telephone town halls" they were increasingly conducting with citizens. All parties were getting into this game: phoning a mass of voters and asking whether they wanted to take part in a giant conference call with the leader or, on other occasions, a high-profile member of Parliament. It was a way to take modern politics into people's living rooms—instead of asking them to come to you—with the added bonus that the calls yielded a treasure trove of relevant information to be collated and sorted later. It worked like this: while on the call (which sounded a bit like a radio show), participants were asked to press buttons on their phones in response to questions. "If you think you are paying too much for home heating, press one," for instance. Later, thanks to the technology that tracked the responses, the NDP would have a detailed record of how long people stayed on the call and how they had felt about the questions posed. All these records would then be fed into the database, so the party knew which voters should receive direct-mail postcards in future or other follow-up advertising specifically targeted to their policy concerns.

The NDP also bought all the data it could find to stuff into the machine—anything to help the party learn more about where to find potential support. The director of operations for the party in the 2011 campaign was Nathan Rotman, a long-time NDP aide who had first worked as Layton's assistant in Toronto for Layton's wife,

Olivia Chow, at Toronto City Hall from 2004 to 2006. Rotman was the person largely responsible for overseeing the data collection and sorting machine, and he cast his gaze wide, looking for every speck of information the party could gather on what was important to voters. Much of it was consumerist in nature. Just as the Progressive Conservatives' John Laschinger had done in the 1980s, going to the "list brokers" for direct-mail contacts, the NDP purchased data from several data-selling organizations, including from Environics Analytics. The dozens of demographic "clusters" from Environics, loaded with consumer data, would prove useful to the party in its bid to talk to people about their ordinary concerns. For example, the NDP knew the neighbourhoods where people were paying the highest cellphone costs, and so knew which homes would be most receptive to demands from Layton to bring down the cellphone charges. Here's the kind of thing that the NDP was telling cellphone customers in the 2011 election:

> New Democrats have been there from the beginning—fighting all forms of usage-based billing, and standing up for open, accessible internet for everyday Canadians. It's time to give hard-working families a break. And that includes stopping the gouging from the big internet companies. New Democrats will also bring broadband to rural areas, and give consumers more control over their cellphone contracts by unlocking cellphones. Together, we can bring Canada to the leading edge of the digital economy. This election, let's make it happen.

NDP strategists could also use the database to find neighbour-hoods where there were plenty of seniors or parents with young families. Instead of sending these voters a mass-market pamphlet with the NDP's policies listed chapter and verse, they could give them specific literature on their concerns. The New Democrats, unlike the Conservatives, didn't use smiling or frowning faces to classify potential support, preferring instead to rank them with numbers from one to four. Rotman was convinced that it would become more and more important to build electronic profiles of voters in future, for a very simple reason: "People are harder to find." The old days of trying to locate voters through simple mass communications, either around the same channel on prime-time TV, or even on their home phones (many people only have cellphones) are long gone, at least in most parts of Canada. Rotman realized that political parties need to find out where the voters' interests lie, merely to stay connected with them.

The NDP also used its data-collection techniques to design its advertising campaign. In the 2011 election, the NDP bought ads in specific time slots to reach the voters they didn't have yet. They bought TV time during *Grey's Anatomy* or *The Amazing Race* because those shows, the data said, were watched by "sandwich generation" Canadians, caring for children and older parents, who might be open to voting for the New Democrats. The ads themselves were also pitched at the voters they didn't yet have. One of the NDP's more successful ads of the 2011 campaign featured a hamster spinning on a wheel as a metaphor for politics-as-usual around Ottawa. Another featured noisy dogs barking: the sound of aimless debate from the same old revolving world of Conservatives and Liberals running Canada. The "next tier" of NDP supporters strongly believed that politics was broken in Parliament, so Layton would make that point at every opportunity on the campaign trail. "Ottawa is broken. We'll fix it," was a handy slogan for the 140-character Twitterverse.

The NDP also had an internal database called "National Field" to connect all the partisans. Rotman had first seen it while looking over campaign technology south of the border. National Field, which boasted on its website that it's all about "people plus data," was basically a sophisticated networking site that organized conversations being held across a large team. Through this internal network, the party office in Ottawa could stay on top of raw intelligence being gained on the ground across Canada. If, for instance, a local campaign manager was encountering voters who were troubled by a recent NDP policy announcement, he or she could throw a warning shot into National Field, and the party could decide how to respond. None of this would have been possible without highly centralized control from the top, imitating the Conservatives' strong marketing head office in Ottawa. Under Rotman's direction, the NDP dismantled the party structure that linked federal operations to the provincial branches. They hired organizers specifically dedicated to the federal NDP and gave Ottawa central control over the membership and fundraising. This is the contradiction of marketing-style politics, as we've seen: the more fragmented that the "market" becomes, the tighter the discipline needs to be at the top.

Election night on May 2, 2011, gave the New Democrats a historic breakthrough. For the first time ever, it had become the official opposition in the House of Commons, winning 103 seats. But for all the attention the NDP strategists paid to marketing, it was far from clear that this was the approach that had sealed the deal for the party. Almost two-thirds of their seats came from Quebec, in ridings that had not been micro-targeted or singled out for special attention by the NDP's market researchers. A couple of the new Quebec MPs had not campaigned that much at all (one, Ruth Ellen Brosseau, was famously vacationing in Las Vegas before she won the riding of Berthier–Maskinongé).

In short, the NDP didn't win Quebec because of modern marketing techniques. As a matter of fact, the NDP's victory in the province came as a result of more traditional political strategies, the kind that existed before the arrival of market-researched platforms or segmenting the population into consumer bits and bytes. The NDP found an old-fashioned mass market in Quebec, organized around the appeal of the leader, "*le bon Jack*," the Québécois term for a good guy. Layton had capitalized on that image with a much-praised mid-campaign appearance on the popular Radio-Canada show *Tout Le monde en parle*. While the rest of the country's TV audience had shattered into fragments, Quebec's political audience remained an outpost of old viewing habits in the country. It was a still a province in which politicians could count on having a large, influential mass of viewers, much like the CBC's *The National* could boast in its heyday.

In the rest of Canada, the NDP's gains were more modest, rising from thirty-six seats to forty-four seats outside Quebec after the 2011 election, reflecting an increase of roughly 24 percent in the popular vote. Without the big mass-marketing success in Quebec, in other words, the NDP's 2011 election story would have been a tale of how their strategists' new approach to micro-targeting efforts yielded slow but steady progress. The NDP cobbled together its impressive 2011 election results, therefore, by playing a new marketing game in the rest of Canada, but an old, retro one in Quebec. Or as Brian Topp would put it, "The Quebec result demonstrated that a truly big win comes from speaking to feelings, themes and goals that are very broadly shared among all demographics and regions."

Layton's death from cancer, less than four months after the election, threw a question mark over whether the NDP would continue to march down the marketing path under new leadership. Topp stepped forward as a candidate, but he was defeated in March 2012 by former Quebec Liberal cabinet minister Thomas Mulcair. As Mulcair moved into the opposition leader's office, many of the people at the centre of the Layton "project" stepped to the sidelines: Lavigne, McGrath and Anderson went on to other jobs. Topp took up a post with the British Columbia New Democrats.

But they left Mulcair with one parting gift: a TV ad, loaded with marketing wisdom gained from their extensive research after the 2011 election. Within a couple of weeks of Mulcair's victory, an ad was launched to "introduce" the new NDP leader to Canadian TV viewers. Every frame of the ad, every word, every character in it, had been carefully chosen to appeal to target demographics. Olivia Chow appeared in the ad to assure the NDP base about continuity under new leadership. The words "fight" and "cares" had been inserted into the text because focus groups had been saying that these were positive traits associated with Layton. Plenty of women appeared in the ad, to thank them for supporting the NDP in expanded numbers in 2011. But the ad also featured shots of power tools and a workboots-sporting man climbing into his truck with his dog, because the NDP was now reaching out to yet another "next tier" of support: men, particularly rural men. With their eyes on the 2015 election, the NDP researchers had now identified seniors and men as their new targets among the electorate. So instead of airing this ad during *Grey's Anatomy*, it went into heavy rotation in sports broadcasts. The NDP spent quite a bit of money—"seven figures" was all they would say—to make this political marketing investment.

One more demographic group was at the front of NDP thinking when it made the meet-Mulcair ad: Liberals. After seeing how the Conservatives had pulverized two Liberal leaders with negative advertising, the New Democrats were adamant that the same thing wouldn't happen to them. Now that they had a leader sitting in the Commons chair once occupied by Stéphane Dion and Michael Ignatieff, the NDP vowed that Mulcair would not succumb to the same death by a thousand advertising cuts.

Video Killed the Liberal Stars

Advertising was once the Liberals' best friend. It helped turn Pierre Trudeau into a gunslinger and it sold a large part of the country on the constitution, complete with scenes of flying Canada geese. Liberals liked to try to solve problems with advertising, whether it was fighting inflation in the 1970s or separatism in the 1990s. But in the wake of the advertising and sponsorship scandals during Jean Chrétien's reign, the long-time allegiance seemed to rupture. Indeed, that old friendship between Liberals and advertising started to look more like a curse in the twenty-first century. No matter where the federal Liberals turned from about 2003 onward, it seemed their fates were being undone by ads, and even more so by slick marketing.

Nowhere was this more evident than in the Conservative ads that felled Dion ("not a leader") and then the subsequent wave that greeted Ignatieff when he was crowned leader, uncontested, after the 2008 election. Ignatieff, a former Harvard professor and international journalist, was seen as the new best hope for putting the Liberals back in power. His urbane, freewheeling intellectualism would serve, many in the party hoped, as a natural foil to Harper's strange but potent blend of populism and strict communications discipline. But that was not how the battle shaped up at the front lines of the marketing wars, where the goal is to master the art of the "brutally simple."

The Conservative attack lines on the two former professors were similar and aimed at people's emotions, not their heads. Ignatieff would be pilloried for his "selfishness" and lack of patriotism. "He didn't come back for you." As with the Dion ads, the choice of attack lines came from extensive focus-group testing among the Canadians who didn't pay much attention to politics, and who were suspicious of elites. Out rolled the "just visiting" campaign against Ignatieff, portraying him as an effete dilettante who had spent most of his working life abroad, only to return to Canada expecting to become prime minister. The ads began showing in the spring of 2009, not long after Ignatieff became Liberal leader. "Why is Michael Ignatieff back in Canada after being away for thirty-four years?" the ads asked. "With no long-term plan for the economy, he's not in it for Canada... just in it for himself. It's the only reason he's back. Michael Ignatieff: Just Visiting."

Perhaps because the Liberals had previously been so in awe of the power of advertising, they responded to these ads over the years with a mix of paralysis and ambivalence. They argued among themselves, often in public, on blogs or political TV panels, about how to reply. They alternated between defensiveness or sticks-and-stones-won't-hurt-us rhetoric. "They're not attacking our family care plan or our early learning and child-care plan," Ignatieff said after a new wave of ads was launched against him in early 2011. "It's the same stuff they've been throwing at us for years, and it's exactly what Canadians are tired about with Stephen Harper."

Money was also a factor in the Liberals' reluctance to grapple with the Conservatives' attacks on their leaders. It costs a lot to wage an ad war, especially on prime time in non-election periods, and Liberals didn't have the fundraising clout of the Conservatives anymore. Their traditional financial strength had been concentrated on attracting big corporate donations, and when these were put under strict limits by Chrétien in 2003 and then banned outright by the Conservatives, the Liberals were caught short on the cash-flow front. They had not yet learned how to tap the grassroots for money on hot-button issues, as their rivals had done. In 2011, the numbers told the tale: while the Conservatives tapped more than 95,000 individuals for donations, the Liberals had barely one-third that number of donors—just over 32,000.

In the absence of a plan to match ad fire with ad fire, Ignatieff and the Liberals then tried other replies. Ignatieff published a 2009 book, *True Patriot Love*, which read like a protest-too-much reply to his detractors. But people who were persuaded by the Conservative attack ads, Muttart's 10 percent of unengaged voters, were not likely to buy or read a book written by an academic. Nor were they following political developments all that closely, and the Liberals' whole strategy seemed organized around the Ottawa "bubble." The book spoke only to converted Liberals.

Ignatieff was surrounded by people highly connected to the formidable Liberal machine of the twentieth century. His first chief of staff was Ian Davey, son of the legendary "Rainmaker," Keith Davey. His second chief of staff was Peter Donolo, the communications expert who had turned Jean Chrétien's image around in the 1990s. In theory then, at least, Ignatieff's circle was built on the glory of past

Liberal marketing successes and should have been expected to march into the new era. Much had happened in Canadian political marketing, though, since Keith Davey's time, and even since Donolo's first stint in the 1990s. Most importantly, the Liberals were no longer in power, and they were still being pummelled by the Conservatives.

US consultant Frank Luntz, in his 2006 speech to the Civitas group, had urged the Conservatives never to let up on the Liberals. "I want you to do something for me because I know you might be able to make this happen," Luntz said. "Your Liberal government was corrupt. It was disgusting. The way they wasted your hard-earned tax dollars was a disgrace. I want you to leave here committed and insisting that the Conservative government hold that previous Liberal government accountable... so that every Canadian knows and will never forget and will never allow another government to steal more from them." Harper wasn't in the room when Luntz gave that advice, but he clearly shared some of his views. A Canadian website called openparliament.ca tracked "favourite words" of Canadian politicians based on what they said in the House of Commons over the years. Repeatedly, it found that Harper's most oft-repeated word was "Liberal."

All in all, it seemed abundantly clear that while their opponents were practising increasingly sophisticated marketing against them, Liberals themselves were tethered to what had worked for them in the past. They continued to see themselves, for instance, as defenders of the institutions they used to run. Former Ontario premier Bob Rae, who left the NDP to join the Liberals and seek the 2006 leadership, would politely chide reporters who used the word "taxpayers" in questions about how the Harper government was spending money. "They're not taxpayers, they're citizens," Rae would say. Inside Ottawa, similarly, there was a lot of Liberal outrage over how Harper had twice shut down Parliament and withheld information about detainees in Afghanistan and the costs associated with the G-8 and G-20 summits in Canada in 2010. Liberals remained fired up on

what they saw as abuse of democracy, holding regular press conferences and seminars to denounce the affronts to institutions, but none
of these issues appeared to resonate with Tim Hortons Canadians.

And the Liberals would repeatedly invoke the rule of law as a
favoured reply to the gut appeal of marketing politics. Liberal senator
Dennis Dawson tried to fight back against the Conservatives' ad
blitz with earnest legislation, introducing a bill in 2011 that would
clamp down on any party flooding the airwaves with ads in the three
months immediately before an election. Dawson's bill proposed to
make any ads airing in this time period count toward the official
limits imposed during formal election periods, to address what he
saw as a growing loophole in the laws. "For decades now, political
parties have always waited for the election call before launching their
official campaign. But now, the Conservatives are trying to impose
on Canadians permanent campaigning, the same way it is done in
the United States," Dawson said when he introduced his bill. "The
Canadian way is to debate ideas, not to throw money around all year
long to try to discredit your opponents. The Canadian way is also to
work and govern between each election, not to spend most of your
time campaigning against the other political parties... Do we want
to be in permanent electoral mode as the Conservatives are trying to
do, or do we want to preserve the Canadian tradition of having fair
elections, where ideas prevail over money?"

Dawson was asking reasonable questions for another era in politics, but the world had moved on. The days of the Commons as a
legal debating society had started to fade back in the 1980s, when
the number of lawyers on the MPs' benches was being matched
and then overtaken by people with business backgrounds. Many
Conservatives liked to boast that Stephen Harper was not a lawyer,
the first prime minister in decades who wasn't groomed for office in
the courts or in one of the country's big law firms. So while Liberals
were inviting citizens to peer more closely into the halls of lofty
institutions, to see the world through the same legal frame that they

did, their chief opponents were out talking to those same citizens in the shopping aisles. The Liberals seemed to lack the language or the motivation to pursue hard-sell political marketing. It was an echo of that long-ago 1957 federal election when the Liberals hewed to their plodding, institutional brand of politics while Dalton Camp and the Conservatives ran advertising rings around them.

One other large impediment stood in the way of Liberals becoming a true marketing party in the twenty-first century: a strong central head office in Ottawa. Historically, the Liberal party has functioned as a loose federation, with strong provincial wings and various other commissions in charge of youth, women or aboriginal members. Political marketing, as the New Democrats and Conservatives had learned, requires tight control from the centre, which the Liberals lacked. Herding Liberals into tight message discipline was like herding cats. Not a week would go by without a disgruntled leak from the Liberal caucus, or a Liberal blog post bemoaning the state of the party. Up until 2007 or so, the party didn't even have a national membership list or any central fundraising apparatus. Various party presidents and executive directors had been trying to address this situation, but short of blowing up the entire Liberal organization, the party was stuck with a structure ill-suited to impose the discipline and marketing control of their rivals.

One Country, One Mass Market

Ignatieff took to the road in the summer of 2010, on what was called the "Liberal Express" tour. His bus would make frequent stops at Tim Hortons on its travels across the country, to prove his down-to-earth Canadian credentials. But the leader's heart didn't seem to be in this idea of wedding politics to consumerism. "It's something I actually don't like about the Conservative vision of the country. I don't think there's a division between a Tim Hortons nation and any other nation," he told the *Toronto Star* in an interview in 2010. "I don't think there's a division between people who've lived outside the country and people who've lived inside. I don't think there's a division between people who go to Tim Hortons for their coffee and people who go to Starbucks for their coffee. I see one country, right?"

This was the nub of the problem. Neither Ignatieff nor Liberals in general had the appetite to do the kind of scrupulous micro-targeting that the Conservatives and the NDP were capable of doing. That Liberal bus was travelling mainly through friendly territory for the party, and not into the terrain of those disengaged voters who increasingly decide elections, as the Conservatives had learned through market research. This wasn't just a case of squeamishness on the part of the Liberals. Modern marketing methods, many in the party believed, sat directly at odds with the traditions of Liberals as a mass-appeal voice of the moderate middle.

Before becoming party leader, Justin Trudeau, son of the prime minister who presided over the Liberals' golden age of advertising and polling, expressed uncertainty about the Liberals' readiness to embrace a segmented view of the nation, or even that it would work for a middle-of-the-road view of politics. "Parties that are positioned on the left or right of the political spectrum can take advantage of certain constituencies that are more engaged with activism or protest," Trudeau said in an interview in the fall of 2012. "Because we don't have those natural constituencies, because we are trying to appeal to that broad swath of regular folks, the micro-targeting just doesn't appeal to us." In Trudeau's view, breaking down the electorate into component parts is a departure from a national vision. "We've sort of bound ourselves as a party to saying the same things from one end of the country to the other, saying the same thing from one room to another, and trying to govern for all the people, not just the people who voted for us."

But when Trudeau campaigned to become Liberal leader and eventually won the job, he would be forced to grapple with the con-undrum of how to sell that one-nation, mass-market concept in a micro-targeted universe. In an interview with Canadian Press, days before his leadership win in April 2013, Trudeau acknowledged he was taking a gamble with this approach. "I refuse to win in such a way that would hamper my ability to govern responsibly for the entire country," he said. Yet even if Trudeau and his Liberals were not sold on the idea of breaking down the electorate into micro-targets, they seemed to recognize that they would have to arm themselves for the data war, in which they had somehow fallen perilously behind their rivals in the twenty-first century.

Red-Listed

Despite their laggardly progress to micro-targeting, federal Liberals had not been sitting out the revolution in database politics in Canada, at least not in the early days. They were actually among the first to see the possibilities of matching the national voters list to customized maps provided by Compusearch in the early 1990s and then a system called ManagElect about a decade later. They also engaged the services of direct-dialling firms such as First Contact Voter Management to fundraise, identify support and get out the vote on election days, just as all the other parties were doing.

In 2009, after Ignatieff became leader and Toronto lawyer Alf Apps became the party president, the Liberals became very serious about getting state-of-the-art technology to keep up with their Conservative rivals. They were well aware of the power of CIMS and wanted to stay in the game, even beat the Conservatives in this race for sophisticated research of the electorate. Fundraising was a primary goal, of course. Liberals were still trying to adjust to the new political-finance reality in the country, which rewarded the parties who were best at gathering small donations from a wide pool of the electorate. They needed a super-powered machine to catch up to the Conservatives and the New Democrats as well as a dedicated staff to oversee the effort. Ignatieff asked Issie Berish, a former Liberal staffer extremely familiar with databases, to serve as director of digital operations.

The next job for the party was to find the best database out there. After some shopping around, they landed at NGP VAN, which was the main voter-management machine for the US Democrats and Barack Obama's 2008 presidential campaign. The Liberals liked this system because it was capable of tracking people according to their concerns about issues. So they imported NGP VAN to Canada, with a few customizing tweaks, and dubbed it "Liberalist." In many ways, this system was similar to CIMS and NDP Vote. When it comes right down to it, after all, most political parties have the same hardware requirements for fighting election campaigns, raising money and getting out the vote. So it isn't surprising that their party machines would be outfitted with the same gadgets. In perfect keeping with the consumerist nature of these databases, they often work with the same kind of barcode-scanning machinery that merchandisers use for products. All the databases are constantly updating their software to work with new generations of technology, such as smartphones and iPads. They all keep track of people who agreed to lawn signs or donations or volunteer duties in the past. They all try to sort people by their top-of-mind interests. In Liberalist, a person who tells the party about his or her concerns about employment insurance, either with an email or a phone call or a conversation at the doorstep, will have that interest logged into the database. Later, party workers could search the database for people with the same interests and target them for mass mailings or one of those "town hall" conference calls.

But the Liberals' system had several interesting differences, which served to highlight the party's ambivalent relationship with modern micro-targeting and marketing, at least as it was being practised by their rivals. In the first place, Liberals didn't go out and purchase consumer data. Berish said he wasn't sure it would be all that useful to the party database, even if the Liberals had the money to buy the information. Knowing what kind of car a voter buys did not give the party any clue as to whether this person would vote Liberal. A Volvo owner in Toronto might vote Liberal, for instance, but the same may not be true for a Volvo owner in Calgary. Berish said he could point to any number of voter profiles, identical in their lifestyles and consumer choices, but one would be Liberal and the other would be Conservative or NDP. Geography and tradition, rather than buying decisions, were usually stronger indicators for Liberals in looking for possible votes. The Liberals did purchase some database software from Pitney Bowes, which helped them sort last names by cultural origin, but that was a reflection of the Liberals' long-term association with immigrants and multicultural communities.

The Liberals' system was also wide open to view online. Anyone could log on to liberalist.ca to see how the machine ran. The actual details about voters, naturally, were privacy protected, but the workings of the database, including the user manual, were posted online. Liberalist didn't categorize voters, either, with smiling or frowning faces like the Conservatives do, or with numbers, as the NDP does. The system had the capacity to sort neighbourhoods for canvassing, to identify which houses were worth visiting and which houses were not. This is a handy device in the United States, where there are registered voters for the parties in advance, and where it's a waste of time for Democrats to visit registered Republicans and vice versa. But Berish claimed it hadn't proven that useful for federal Liberal volunteers, who appeared to favour canvassing all houses in a block or polling district, regardless of whether some doors were useless prospects: "We're not at that level where we say 'only selectively knock on doors.'"

The most important difference between the Liberals' database and those of their big rivals, though, was one that would be more troublesome to the party. The machinery itself was state of the art, but the wealth of the data, even after two years in Liberal hands, was substandard. By 2011, when they were knocked back to third place in the federal election, the Liberals had only entered data into their system about a paltry 1.3 million voters, and not very thorough information at that. Conservatives and New Democrats didn't give out comparable figures on their data rolls, but they are widely assumed to be larger than one million. This was an enduring frustration to party president Alf Apps, who wrote in his post-mortem of the 2011 defeat:

> Rank and file Liberal supporters need to understand what the party is up against. The same political party that prefers to govern the country without reference to data and evidence has in fact pioneered a form of campaigning in Canada that turns politics into a highly sophisticated science, based almost exclusively on data and evidence, with its political messaging based on detailed individualized and aggregated intelligence. The CPC is able to calibrate its voter contact to each voter's profile with laser-like focus… LPC is flying half-blind and well behind when it comes to election technology and digital know-how.

Apps was highlighting a strange irony in Canadian politics. The ruling Conservatives displayed an almost visceral distaste for government-run databases—they dismantled the long-gun registry established by Chrétien's government and they made the long-form census no longer mandatory in Canada in 2010. The Liberals, in reply, proclaimed themselves the party in favour of facts, evidence, records and science. Yet in terms of political-party databases, the situation was flipped. The Conservatives, for the most part, seemed to love CIMS and accumulating all the data they could. They were hard at work on a second-generation database after the 2011 election, too, reportedly turning CIMS into a new system called "C-Vote." The Liberals, however, seemed to have deep reservations about loading Liberalist with information, perhaps because of the skepticism about micro-targeting that Trudeau and Ignatieff also voiced. It also could have been that the Liberals, in power for so long through the twentieth century, had just not cultivated the grassroots energy to be in opposition.

Bought, but Not Totally Sold

The 2011 election, which reduced the Liberals to third-place status in the Commons for the first time in history, was the most vivid illustration of the party's inability or unwillingness to come fully into this age of micro-targeting and marketing. It continued to see itself as the voice of the mass-market middle in a fragmented, polarized world. It was not as if the party was averse to seeing voters as consumers. The Liberal platform was carefully crafted around this approach, and even named after a fast-food consumable: "The Family Pack." With their own market research, the Liberals cast themselves as the friends of Canadian families, just as Conservatives and New Democrats were trying to do. And in a direct nod to the success of the Conservatives' 2006 platform, the Liberals were waving their own cheques for families in this campaign—up to $1,350 a year for anyone caring for aged or ill relatives in their homes. It was the same strategy as the Conservatives' "choice in child care" promise from 2006, except that the Liberals' cheque giveaway was aimed at the other end of the demographic spectrum, toward older voters.

Ignatieff, launching the 2011 Liberal campaign, was even careful to sprinkle some colourful, shopping-friendly words in his opening statement to reporters. "Folks, in the election that's coming up, there is a blue door. You go through the blue door and you get jets, you get jails, you get corporate tax cuts, and you get miserable knock-offs of the real article. But, you go through the red door and you get compassion, you get fiscal responsibility, and you get a government relentlessly focused on the real priorities of Canadian families." And then Ignatieff added, fatefully, "There are only two choices."

Choice is a big deal to consumer-citizens, so any suggestion that their choice is limited is probably ill-advised. Sure enough, Ignatieff's remark played right into the hands of the New Democrats, engaged as they were in expanding the "consideration set." Layton was able to portray Liberals as people who didn't believe in choice at the ballot box. "People will try and tell you that you have no choice but to vote for more of the same," he would say. Meanwhile, the NDP could busily keep pursuing its campaign to reposition Canadian politics for the next election as a whole new kind of colour choice: between the blue door and the orange door. After May 2, 2011, the House of Commons was painted blue on the governing side, orange on the opposition side, with a mere splash of Liberal red at the margins.

Hardcore political marketing, especially as it has been developed in the United States, works best in polarized, partisan climates. It thrives on that vaunted consumer virtue of choice, but it has to be a sharp, well-defined choice: left versus right, good versus bad, no ambivalent middle. To do micro-targeting with any kind of success or efficiency, the electorate has to be separated into "people who may vote for us" and "people who will never vote for us." All the better if those differences turn up in their consumer choices, too: buyers of *Field and Stream* magazine versus *The New Yorker*, for instance, or Tim Hortons versus Starbucks. Parties can then concentrate their efforts on prospective voters and forget about the others. This type of sorting is more difficult to do for parties that are still trying to be all things to all voters, as Canada's Liberals continued to believe they could be. Up against the political marketing colossus of the Harper Conservatives, one party, the NDP, went to market and another, the Liberals, mostly stayed in their traditional home.

Even after Trudeau won the leadership in April 2013, he said his party's aim was to once again be the home, as it had been in his father's time, of the mass-market middle class in Canada. "I say this to the millions of middle-class Canadians, and the millions more who work hard every day to join the middle-class. Under my leadership, the purpose of the Liberal Party of Canada will be you. I promise that I will begin, spend and end every day thinking about and working hard to solve your problems," Trudeau said in his victory speech.

So the question in 2013 was whether the Liberals, under new leader Trudeau, could play a mass-market game, albeit with the tools that their rivals had used to do micro-targeting of the electorate.

Whether the Liberals liked it or not, they were going to have to amass the data to compete with the Conservatives and New Democrats. Some of that work was done through the Trudeau leadership campaign itself. One of the main missions of the Trudeau leadership team was to accumulate as much data as possible on potential Liberal voters for the 2015 election. And at several points during the campaign, the Trudeau team also consulted with US Democrat experts to see whether there were lessons to be learned from Barack Obama's example. Mitch Stewart, a "battleground-states" director for the winning Obama campaign in 2012, was one of the Democrats who gave the Trudeau strategists some advice. Trudeau's Liberals were particularly interested in how Obama had won votes of people who had never cast ballots before.

At each of the well-attended Trudeau events across the country, volunteers were on hand with sign-up sheets, pursuing names, numbers and addresses of attendees. With a spending limit of $950,000, the Trudeau campaign was not able to pay for many things, but it did fork over money to pay people to enter names and contact information into the database. "My hands are getting cramped," one young student mildly complained as she sat at Trudeau's campaign headquarters in Toronto with her fellow data-entry workers, putting the information into the computers at a rate of roughly forty to fifty forms an hour. It was an apt illustration of the Liberal party entering the age of digital campaigning.

The party overall had made this digital quest a little easier by setting up a system that allowed people to sign up as "supporters" of the party and vote for the leader in April 2013. This "supporter" class did not have to pay membership fees, but they did have to supply their contact information. Trudeau's campaign team also created their own separate class of membership—"volunteers"—who committed themselves to some level of active participation in Liberal politics and thus also added their names to the burgeoning data files the party was amassing. By the end of the campaign, Trudeau's team had amassed more than 150,000 supporters and 10,000 volunteers. In terms of direct marketing, it had been a runaway success. And like Ronald Reagan's Republicans, Margaret Thatcher's Conservatives or Tony Blair's Labour Party, the Liberals were in pursuit of the disengaged, floating voters who had proved to be the most valuable commodity for political marketers since the 1980s. More than a decade into the twenty-first century, after more than fifty years of borrowing the market's tactics to deal with the public, all parties seemed to have no choice but to treat people as shoppers. Politics just wasn't that important to people's lives now, but their lives had become very important to Canada's political marketers.

11

READY

Four human resource workers are sitting around a boardroom table in Room 115 of a nondescript office building, reviewing job applications. "Let's talk about Justin," an older man says, taking off his glasses. The group then goes over a file folder containing Justin Trudeau's photo and credentials, which they're finding to be flimsy. "Nothing about balancing a budget or making a payroll," one woman offers. As the group chats about all the ways in which Liberal leader Justin Trudeau may not be fit for office, another woman declares, "People, being prime minister is not an entry-level job."

Her colleague agrees, though with a tiny hint of regret: "I'm not saying no forever, but not now." One man picks up the file folder and looks again at Trudeau's photo: "Nice hair, though." As the camera zooms in on the folder and photo, Trudeau's job application is rejected with three words, underlined with a big red marker: "Just Not Ready."

This one-minute-long advertisement, launched by Prime Minister Stephen Harper's Conservative party in the spring of 2015, captured a significant moment in the long story of political marketing in Canada. When it rolled out on the airwaves, it was looking like Trudeau and his Liberal party were indeed not ready for politics as it was being played in the twenty-first century. Once again, the big Conservative campaign machine was steamrolling over another Liberal leader through the force of advertising and deep market research. The "not ready" ad was the product of extensive focus-group findings over the previous couple of years, which showed that while people liked Trudeau (and his hair) they had some serious reservations about his fitness to run the country. The New Democrats had similar focus-group findings. In fact, the Conservative ad bore a striking resemblance to an ad the Manitoba NDP ran against provincial Conservatives in 2011. It also featured four people around a boardroom table, talking about Conservative leader Hugh McFadyen as "too big a risk" for the job of premier. It even featured a kicker line: "Nice suit, though."

The federal NDP, meanwhile, had their own reasons to feel confident about their chances against the Liberals when the Conservatives' "not ready" ad started rolling across TV screens throughout the country. Although Thomas Mulcair had been slow to catch on in popularity after he took over the leadership in 2013, the NDP was climbing in the polls two years later, in no small part because of a surprise victory in Alberta in May. When Rachel Notley became the first-ever NDP premier of Alberta, defeating a forty-four-year-long Conservative dynasty in the province, it was starting to seem that all things were possible in the tumultuous, unpredictable world of twenty-first-century Canadian politics. That would turn out to be true—just not in the ways that anyone expected as the 2015 election loomed.

Everyone loves a comeback story. The tale of how Trudeau and his Liberals got into the game of modern election campaigning—and then changed that game—would turn out to be one of the biggest comeback stories in Canadian political history. Moreover, how the Liberals pulled off this feat would be a whole new chapter in the evolution of political marketing in Canada. It started with a leader and a team with a keen appreciation for two of the most important tools in the modern political marketers' toolbox: advertising and data.

The Conservatives' "not ready" ad had failed to mention that Trudeau, while inexperienced at running a country, actually had some hard-won experience in the modern political arts of advertising and imagery. He knew as much about these arts as Harper did, arguably more. Trudeau saw advertising, in effect, as cultural anthropology. "I have long said that if archaeologists of the future want to understand the late twentieth century they could do worse than to look at advertising," Trudeau would say in an interview much later, as he reviewed what he'd learned about being at the centre of an advertising war in the lead-up to the 2015 election.

Harper had come to his appreciation of advertising and images by looking at them and carefully studying what worked, before and during his tenure as prime minister. Trudeau understood images by spending a lifetime at the centre of them. Where Harper was an astute consumer of images, Trudeau had been an active *producer* of images from the day he was born—Christmas Day 1971 to a popular prime minister and his photogenic young wife. Being in the picture was not a skill Trudeau would have to learn on the job.

Trudeau can't precisely pinpoint the exact moment when he realized his life was part of the news, but he does remember a couple of times when the reality of fame was driven home to him in childhood. A 1982 photograph of Justin and his brother Sacha roughhousing on the tarmac of an airport while they waited for their father to return from an official trip, showed the younger Sacha, eight, delivering an upper cut to his ten-year-old brother's chin. Young Justin eventually got the better of his brother in that scuffle, but the photo made it look like Sacha was the superior fighter. "I got teased for that mercilessly by the kids in my school," Trudeau said. It was also a valuable, early lesson in how what you see in the media may not exactly align with the bigger story behind the picture.

When Trudeau assumed the leadership of the Liberals in 2013, the party was in serious need of a shakeup behind the scenes. It had fallen woefully behind the Conservatives and the New Democrats in assembling a modern electoral machine. Worse, it wasn't entirely clear whether Canada needed a middle-of-the-road political party anymore. All the political leaders were looking for support of the famed "hard-working middle class." Yet politics in Canada seemed to be polarizing between Conservatives on the right and the NDP on the left. The polarization of politics matched well with more pronounced economic divisions between rich and poor: income inequality was on the rise in Canada, too. Even in the consumer marketplace—inspiration for so many political innovations of the past half-century—mid-market retailers were having a tough time. Consumer-trends writers were noticing that buyers were flocking to high-end luxury items or deep-discount, online bargains, but not so much to the stores offering mid-priced goods.

The phenomenon was laid out in the 2006 US book *Treasure Hunt: Inside the Mind of the New Consumer*. "At the high end, consumers are trading up, paying a premium for high-quality, emotionally rich, high-margin products and services. At the low end, consumers are relentlessly trading down, spending as little as possible to buy basic, low-cost goods and services," author Michael Silverstein wrote.

Yet here in Canada was Trudeau and his team, trying to revive the fortunes of a mid-market, centrist Liberal party sitting in third place in the House of Commons. Gerald Butts, seasoned in government as an adviser to Ontario premier Dalton McGuinty in the early 2000s, had been friends with Trudeau back in their days at McGill University in Montreal. They both studied English literature, which may not be the most obvious path to political life, but as former New York governor Mario Cuomo famously said, politicians campaign in poetry and govern in prose.

"I don't write poetry. I'm not a poet," Trudeau said, but "to understand poetry you really have to dig into the meaning of every word, not just what it says but why this word and not another word… You look at poetry of the past, you look at good rap now, you look at advertising now: [it's about] how to put maximum message into a limited package."

For Butts, advertising was fundamentally storytelling. "The best ads have simple messages with great stories told compellingly," Butts said in a post-election interview. "That's what we try to do in everything. One idea in every ad." In this view of advertising as poetry and prose, Butts and Trudeau found a kindred spirit in David Rosenberg, partner and chief creative officer at the Bensimon Byrne ad firm in Toronto. Butts admired Rosenberg's lack of cynicism, a rare find in the ad world, and the two would spend many hours crafting the Trudeau brand into advertising messages throughout the roller coaster of the 2015 campaign.

Rosenberg and Jack Bensimon, head of the firm, said they had never encountered a politician who understood advertising as well as Trudeau did. "We tended to write for Justin in short, declarative sentences," Rosenberg said. "He wasn't afraid to say things simply and powerfully and we tended to write for him that way." Trudeau also cared about the details; he would insist that words he spoke in the ads sounded like his own voice. He called this "wordsmithing."

"That's what I do. The big speeches, but especially the advertising, anything that I record I will wordsmith because the words matter. And they have to be mine and they have to be the right ones," Trudeau said.

The Trudeau team had landed at Bensimon Byrne thanks to David Herle, campaign manager for former Liberal prime minister Paul Martin in the 2004 and 2006 elections. Since the 2006 defeat of the Liberals, Herle had been heading up the Gandalf Group, a market-research firm in Toronto, as well as keeping his hand in political organization and as a part of "The Insiders" panel every two weeks on CBC TV's *The National* broadcast. Herle was one of a small group of trusted Liberals gathered at the Mont Tremblant resort in the summer of 2012 to plan Trudeau's bid for the leadership. In the years since, Herle has been involved in provincial Liberal revivals in Nova Scotia and New Brunswick. His biggest electoral coup came as director of Kathleen Wynne's 2014 seemingly long-shot campaign to win a fourth mandate for the Ontario Liberals. The common thread to all those victories was a carefully considered bid to position Liberals to the left of the NDP.

Herle's Toronto office was housed inside Bensimon Byrne on Wellington Street in downtown Toronto; he and Bensimon had worked together on political advertising through several federal and provincial elections. "We thought they might be looking for something a little different than the conventional political advertising," Bensimon would recall in an interview. Indeed, if being different meant staying away from negative ads, Trudeau and his team were asking the ad firm to be unconventional. Attack ads had become stock items on the shelves of the Canadian political marketplace.

Doing the Math

The "not ready" ad of 2015 was only the latest in a series that the Conservatives had been running from the moment Trudeau became Liberal leader in 2013. In terms of tone and ridicule, it was gentler than the initial wave of Conservative ads, which had mocked Trudeau for his background as a drama teacher in the 1990s. While it was true that Trudeau had filled in teaching drama and poetry while a fellow teacher was on maternity leave at West Point Grey Academy in BC, his main job was to teach French and math. It's harder to mock a former math teacher, though, especially given contemporary political marketing's reliance on numbers and data.

When Trudeau wanted to relax on vacations or long plane trips, he would do logic puzzles or sketch out intricate drawings composed entirely of dots. Riding from one event to the other on the road, Trudeau would often grab the iPad from his aides and plot the best route to the next destination. So the mechanics of modern political campaigning, loaded with tiny points of data plotted on maps, were also his idea of a good time. This would be more than a handy coincidence for a party that was building itself into a modern data-collecting enterprise. The famed "Big Red Machine" of the twentieth century was being massively retooled—all the clunky old hardware transformed into a sophisticated series of data and analytics and poured into a computer program dubbed as the "Console."

The Console, with its maps and myriad graphs and numbers, was the most vivid evidence of how far the Liberal party had come in its bid to play catch-up in the data war with its Conservative and NDP rivals. Call it Trudeau 2.0. Just as the old Rainmaker Keith Davey brought science to the party of Trudeau's father in the 1960s and 1970s, the next generation of Trudeau Liberalism would get seized with data, science and evidence in a big way, too.

And in the grand tradition of Davey, Allan Gregg and all the other political pollsters and marketers who went before them, this new squad of strategists set about dividing Canada's electoral map into target ridings, ranked according to their chances of winning in them. In a twenty-first-century–style campaign, though, the distinctions would be far more sophisticated than simply "winnable" and "unwinnable" ridings. Trudeau's Liberals divided the nation's 338 electoral districts into six types, named for metals and compounds: platinum, gold, silver, bronze, steel and wood.

Platinum ridings were sure bets: mostly the few dozen that the Liberals had managed to keep in the electoral catastrophe of 2011. Gold ridings were not quite that solid, but they were the ones in which the party strategists felt pretty certain about their prospects. Silver ridings were the ones the Liberals would need to gain to win the election while bronze ridings, the longer shots, would push them into majority-government territory. Steel ridings were ones they might win in a subsequent election, and wood ridings were the ones where the Liberals probably could never win a seat, in rural Alberta, for instance.

The Console kept close track of voter-outreach efforts on the ground, right down to the number of doorsteps visited by volunteers and what kind of information they had gathered from those visits—family size, composition, political interests, even the estimated age of the residents. By consulting the Console, campaigners could even figure out what time of day was best for canvassing in specific neighbourhoods or which voters required another visit to seal the deal.

When the Liberal team unveiled the Console to Trudeau, he was blown away. He told his team that it was his new favourite thing. He wanted regular briefings on the contents of the program: where it showed the Liberal party ahead, and where fortunes were flagging and volunteers needed to do more door-knocking. Actually, he wondered, why couldn't he be given access to the Console himself, so that he could consult it on his home computer or on his phone while on the road?

And that, Trudeau would say later, was the last he ever saw of the Console. "My job was to bring it back, not on the analysis side, but on the connection side—on getting volunteers to go out, drawing people in, getting people to sign up," Trudeau said. Clearly he was doing something right on that score—Liberal membership numbers had climbed from about 60,000 to 300,000 within Trudeau's first eighteen months as leader.

Volunteers for the party would learn—often to their peril—that the leader was fiercely serious about turning his crowd appeal into useful data. Trudeau wasn't known for displays of temper, but the easiest way to provoke him was to fall down on the job of collecting data from the crowds at campaign stops. Few things made him angrier, for instance, than to see Liberal volunteers surrounding him at events instead of gathering up contact information. "That was what I demanded. If they wanted a visit from the leader they had to arrange that or else I'd be really upset," Trudeau said.

Back at headquarters in Ottawa, the primary force in the data-collection enterprise was Katie Telford, Trudeau's campaign manager, whose friendship with the leader dated back to the 2006 Liberal leadership contest. Telford had worked with Butts at Queen's Park when she was chief of staff to Education Minister Gerard Kennedy. When Kennedy decided to run for the federal Liberal leadership in 2006, Telford was the national campaign director. Thanks to his old friend Butts, Trudeau was thinking of supporting Kennedy, but he wanted to meet Telford. They hit it off immediately—and unexpectedly in Telford's case. After she and Trudeau had a spirited discussion about the state of Liberal politics, he got up to leave the restaurant. Trudeau looked over his shoulder, smiled and said to Telford, "I'm not quite what you thought I was, am I?"

Telford preferred to stay out of the limelight, carefully picking her moments to speak publicly. One of those was in a December 2013 video sent out to Liberal partisans in which Telford laid out the party's challenge as one of numbers—urging everyone to view numbers the way she did, as "competitive" and "addictive." She said her favourite email each day contained a spreadsheet tallying up the funds raised or support recruited. "Numbers tell stories," Telford said. At every campaign-strategy meeting she convened, Telford asked participants to arrive prepared to deliver a number—any number that would tell the story of how the Liberals were faring.

In one fun-with-numbers story, the Liberals decided to see in late 2014 whether the Canadian political universe was still sharply divided along the lines of coffee preference. The survey found that although Conservative voters were slightly more likely to be loyal Tim's drinkers, Liberals still led by 34 percent to 29 percent among all patrons of the patriotic doughnut-and-coffee chain. In yet another sign that Canadian politics was blurring those sharp, Starbucks-versus-Tim's distinctions, Thomas Mulcair unapologetically told a CTV interviewer during the 2015 campaign that he preferred Starbucks for coffee, but Tim Hortons for the Timbits. "The espresso at Starbucks has really been fuelling this campaign," Mulcair said in the CTV interview. "For the Timbits, okay, fair enough, after a really busy night when we finish at eleven at night, we can be seen sneaking off to Tim Hortons for a box of Timbits." So much for the great coffee divide in Canada's political market. In 2015, things in the consuming world of politics were extremely fluid.

Committing Sociology

Political operatives still like to talk about campaigns in military terms: the "air war" and the "ground battle." The air war is the one fought in the media and the horse-race polls—the big, overarching narrative of the campaign. The ground battle is all the work done to amass votes, volunteers and funds. One of the Liberals' campaign mottos was "Hope and Hard Work." Hope was the air war and the ground battle was hard work. Advertising was the tool they would use for hope. Data and digital strategy could do the hard work of the ground campaign.

The man overseeing the story of the numbers was Dan Arnold, a long-time party loyalist who had been famous in the early days of political blogs writing as "Calgary Grit." Arnold, who had degrees in statistics from the University of Calgary and the University of Alberta, first drew the Trudeau team's notice while he was working with Pollara, the firm run by the Liberals' 1990s pollster Michael Marzolini. In 2014 Arnold was hired to be what was called "lead research strategist" for the Liberals. In creating this position, Liberals were following a pattern increasingly being seen in political parties. Rather than rely on outside polling companies—firms whose attention is divided between commercial consumer research and pure political data—modern parties prefer to internally conduct and analyze their own polls. As a practical bonus, it's much less expensive than paying an outside pollster to gather and analyze data.

Arnold would be looking at Canada's political map in a far different way than Harper's in-house marketing strategist, Patrick Muttart, had done when he worked for the Conservatives in the early years. Where Muttart scoured the map for pockets of deep support, Arnold and the Liberals had to cast their view more widely.

"We were coming from a position where we needed to double our share of the vote, quintuple our seat count," Arnold said in an interview after the election. "We weren't going to do that with ten thousand votes here and twenty thousand votes there. So just from necessity, we needed a much broader message, something that would appeal to most Canadians. We also had a much larger pool of people who were open to the Liberals."

So while Trudeau had registered his strong opposition to segmenting the Canadian marketplace as a matter of principle, it was also a practical matter. Liberals needed to see Canada as one mass market, and it was Arnold's job to find multiple "paths to victory," as they were called in the Liberal backrooms.

Bringing polling into the heart of the political operation coincided with an important turning point in the story of political marketing—a shift away from reliance on consumer data and toward purer sociological information. A decade of big-data politics in the United States had already blazed the trail that the Liberals were now following. Where Republicans gained an early advantage in the data game by amassing consumer-type information on US voters, the Democrats had surpassed the Republicans by focusing on data far more specific to voting intentions. Why bother learning who owns snowmobiles when you should be keeping track of the things that really influence voters—their families, their communities, their political interests or their jobs?

"We didn't use any consumer files," said Tom Pitfield, director of the huge digital operation the Liberals launched after Trudeau won the leadership. "We had limited time, so we had to decide which pieces of data would help us assess whether someone was a supporter.

Knowing whether they bought red shoes or drank beer didn't mean-
ingfully tell you whether they were going to vote for you." Pitfield had
known Trudeau since childhood, when his father, Michael Pitfield,
was the clerk of the Privy Council in Pierre Trudeau's government.
The two sons would remain lifelong friends, spending holidays and
vacations together. Pitfield's wife, Anna Gainey, was elected president of the Liberal party at the party's Montreal convention in early
2014. It was Pitfield who forged some early connections between
the Trudeau team and American digital strategists who had worked
on Barack Obama's presidential bids—people such as Teddy Goff
and Jen O'Malley Dillon at Precision Strategies, and Dan Wagner at
Civis Analytics.

Digital campaigns in Canada and the US had come a long way
since the early days of mixing politics with the internet. No longer
just the "techies" in the basement, the digital experts had seats at
the big strategy table, coordinating the online campaign with the
leader's tour, the advertising experts and the armies of volunteers
and field workers. Digital campaigns could be far nimbler. For all the
time and energy it took to do one big-production TV ad, the digital
team could distribute dozens, even hundreds, of online advertisements. Even better, with sophisticated analytics they could dispatch
this advertising only to the desired targets. An ad about Trudeau's
child-benefit program, for instance, could be sent only to people
with kids. When Conservatives started saying in ads that Trudeau
would end income-splitting for seniors, the Liberals could reply with
an online retort that would go to people fifty-five years of age and
older in target ridings.

"We knew which types of people would benefit from the Canada
Child Benefit, and which types of people would benefit from the
middle-class tax cut, and which types of people would benefit
from transit investments," Arnold said. "Based on that, we'd send
direct-mail pamphlets to those areas that were more likely to have
parents or more likely to have commuters. There was a bit of that in

terms of tailoring the message." The Console could also give advice on where to place more traditional ads. On one day, Trudeau walked into a radio studio and recorded forty different ad scripts, each written with a particular community's interests in mind: from rush-hour gridlock to water quality.

Canadian politicians of all stripes were learning, as the Americans had learned, that Facebook was maybe the most important digital tool they had. In the 2012 election, Obama's thirty-three million Facebook friends connected him, through their own networks of friends, to 98 percent of Americans on Facebook. In the 2015 campaign, Trudeau hit many similar mileposts on the digital front. The Liberals' digital outreach stretched to about thirteen million voters on Facebook—more than four million in just one day. Those thirteen million Facebook users had been deliberately wooed by the Liberals in competitive ridings. Trudeau also would become the first leader in Canada to use Facebook to unveil his election platform.

The real power of Facebook is its ability to reach people who are not necessarily connected to politics, as well as their networks of friends. Liberals were not just looking to take votes from the other parties, but to reach new voters and non-voters, too, particularly among Canada's youth and indigenous people. The Occupy movement on income inequality and the aboriginal Idle No More protests in 2011 and 2012 had awoken nascent political interest in these constituencies and it wouldn't be an accident that the Liberal campaign platform would include their issues. (The proposal to increase taxes on the wealthy 1 percent, for instance, came straight from the language of Occupy and its "We are the 99 percent.") In 2015, social-media platforms were also a way to make contact with voters who weren't tuned into the old, traditional political channels. The Liberals had also found new, more finely tuned methods to use social media in a way that Obama's team had not been able to do in 2012—by identifying individual voters through responses to the party's "calls to action" on Facebook, Twitter and Instagram. In the digital business this technique is called "conversion," generating leads for business through social media.

Digital advertising is a cost-effective way for politicians to raise money and test various appeals for support. Liberals could send out slightly different versions of a fundraising email and then measure which one pulled in the most dollars. A flurry of by-elections between 2013 and 2015 had also presented the Liberals with many chances to test and measure what worked and what didn't in the digital realm. In the 2014 by-election in Whitby, Ontario, Liberals learned that NDP voters between the ages of eighteen and thirty-five were more likely to respond to appeals to vote strategically against the Conservatives.

Kate Purchase, director of communications for the campaign, used social-media analytics to refine how Liberals were selling their wares to the public as the 2015 election loomed. Initially, for instance, they had billed their child-benefit program as a $2-billion invest-ment for Canadian families. They thought that huge figure would show just what a big-ticket piece it was within the Liberal platform. After the promise was first unveiled in the spring of 2015, Purchase noticed it wasn't making much of a dent in social-media conversa-tions. She realized that the $2-billion figure was just too abstract to ordinary voters. (Harper had made a habit of not putting big figures in his prime-ministerial announcements for the very same reason.)

Purchase went looking for new ways to make the numbers real to voters, breaking them down to show how much would end up in the pockets of individual families. To see how this was working, she'd watch to see how much the information circulated on Facebook or Twitter. Eventually, the Liberals would figure out a way to turn their child-benefit dollars into a visual image, loading up two grocery carts with goods valued at roughly the same amount as the child benefit.

"Talk Like People Talk" was the motto that Purchase would scrawl at the top of every whiteboard during meetings on communi-cations strategy. Purchase also monitored social media carefully to measure the reaction when the Liberals did occasional forays into negative advertising. In one of these experiments with the darker side, the Liberals created two nearly identical ads featuring a list of indictments against the Harper government. One was in full colour, one was in a darker grey-scale. The darker ad provoked backlash: Liberals were accused of playing dirty; grassroots Liberals themselves were not pleased. Lesson learned: the grey-scale ad was pulled.

Liberals, incidentally, weren't alone in leaning on the lessons learned from US Democrats. The New Democrats had their own advisers from the old Obama team, such as Jeremy Bird from 270 Strategies. Some NDP candidates, such as Jennifer Hollett in the Toronto riding of University–Rosedale, had spent some time in the US learning state-of-the-art campaign tactics. "We're definitely going to see a lot of Obama tactics at play," Hollett had said even before the 2015 campaign got under way.

All parties had also been refining their software from the 2011 campaign and making their technology mobile—a trend perfectly aligned with the consumer marketplace of Canada in the early part of the twenty-first century. By 2014, about 68 percent of Canadians owned smartphones, and Canada's retail and political marketers were trying to keep up with consumers and citizens who were connected 24-7 to their digital networks. The Conservatives' Constituent Information Management System (CIMS) had a portable component called C2G (short for CIMS-to-go). The New Democrats had scrapped NDP Vote in favour of a new program called Populus. Trudeau's team had kept the bare bones of the Liberalist system, which had gained some new features from US election innovations, but exponentially added to its contents. As well, Liberalist could now be updated by a mobile system known as "MiniVAN"—a nickname that originated in the NGP VAN database software the party bought from the Obama Democrats. It meant that Liberal campaigners could carry devices door to door and feed information into the database.

Gathering the data was only the tip of the big-data iceberg. The real art, or science, was knowing how to sort all this information into useful material for political campaigners. Behind the scenes, clever data people were building algorithms—the fancy word for a computer equation—to create categories of likely supporters as well as the issues or interests that could move their votes. All parties could then concentrate their efforts where they were most likely to have an effect. The Liberals' algorithms were developed by a man named Sean Wiltshire, a statistical whiz from McGill University who liked to describe himself as a "serial problem-seeker." His job was to find the significant patterns in the voter database. Voters were divided into ten categories based on their likelihood to vote Liberal. No metallic names for this system, though—just a numbered ranking from one to ten with ones being the least likely to cast a Liberal vote and tens as the committed partisans. Throughout the campaign, most of the Liberals' digital outreach would be focused on the numbers in the middle—the "persuadables," as they're called in the business.

Here was the state of voter profiling in 2015. A decade earlier, Harper's campaign strategists had created fictional "Zoe" and "Dougie" profiles to figure out where Conservatives should shop for their votes. In 2015 the Liberals were making direct contact with real, live people in their database. By election day, 2015, Liberal volunteers had knocked on more than twelve million doors across the country. And if all this seemed very similar to the Conservatives' big-data operation, that's because it was. Trudeau had been promising that Liberals wouldn't do micro-targeting or "boutique" policies as Harper's party had done. But that didn't mean the Liberals were averse to accumulating data at a microscopic level and retail politics on a grand scale. "The Tories' methodology wasn't the problem," Butts said. "It was what they were putting it in service of. They used it to pull people apart, but it could be used to bring people together."

As the election loomed ever closer in the summer of 2015, though, it was starting to look like all this talk of pulling people together was extremely optimistic, maybe even dangerously naive when it came to the state of political marketing in Canada. Trudeau was still pulling out impressive crowds on the road while his campaign workers were amassing data on attendees. But the New Democrats had a solid first-place lead in the polls and people were now talking about the very real prospect of Thomas Mulcair as the next prime minister. Canadians' long-held reservations about seeing an NDP government in Ottawa seemed to have been put aside.

As well, the political market was overcrowded with "change" labels. Liberals were running as "real change" and the New Democrats' slogan was "ready for change." In French, the two, progressive-leaning parties' slogans were even more easy to confuse: "*Ensemble pour le changement*" for the NDP and "*Changer ensemble*" for the Liberals. Eric Blais of the Quebec-based Headspace marketing firm said in an August newspaper interview, "If this was for a service brand in the private sector, you can be sure that one of them would be rethinking their positioning and brand narrative ASAP."

The NDP's former campaign chief Brad Lavigne, who had been writing speeches for Mulcair, was noticing an eerie echo coming from the Liberals, too. Mulcair would list off all the ways in which Canada's middle class was economically stuck, and then Lavigne would hear Trudeau or Liberal spokespersons rattling off the same list days or weeks later. "I was developing a keen ear for language that was being appropriated by the other side," Lavigne said. Finding original ways to talk up the middle class in this 2015 election wasn't an easy task. While the consumer marketers may have been experiencing "death in the middle" in the retail world, every political pitch in Canada's election, across party lines, was organized around revival of the country's middle class.

One word that the Liberals were guarding as their own, though, was "real." The most prized trait in contemporary politics was this whole idea of authenticity. People wanted to know that politicians were "real" people, the kind of people who would say what was on their minds. No matter how low Trudeau was in the polls, no matter how many verbal gaffes he'd committed, Liberals believed that their leader could be presented as more authentic than Mulcair and certainly more of a "real" person than the remote, often aloof Harper. If the election turned on perceptions of managerial competence, this would be a problem for Trudeau. In Arnold's focus groups, Harper was still scoring much higher than Trudeau on the question of who would be the best economic manager. "He looked like a manager and he'd built up this aura of being the guy who guided us through the downturn," Arnold would recall in an interview later, "and you couldn't shake people from that."

The "not ready" ad was landing with enormous effect in the weeks after it launched, apparently justifying the millions of dollars that Conservatives were clearly spending to keep it on TV. (Conservatives, like the other parties, did not disclose exactly what they were spending on advertising, but anyone in the vicinity of a TV knew how frequently the ad was popping up at commercial breaks.) A Forum Research poll in early September showed that nearly half of Canadians polled, about 47 percent, agreed that Trudeau was not ready to be prime minister.

"The weight of the Conservative ad buy had penetrated into every market, every demographic group. 'Not ready' was everywhere," said Brad Lavigne, who had come back to the NDP in January 2015 to advise Mulcair on communications. After writing his 2013 book, *Building the Orange Wave*, Lavigne was hoping 2015 would prove to be a sequel, or even a triumphant new story about the NDP's path to power in Canada. The widespread reaction to "not ready" was fuelling that hope. Liberals were seeing the "not ready" damage in their internal research and focus groups, too. Even likely Liberal voters were telling Arnold in focus groups that they worried about Trudeau's readiness to govern. No one needed to break the bad news to Trudeau. He was hearing the same thing. A friend's nanny said the children under her care would automatically repeat "just not ready" when they heard Trudeau's name. Trudeau himself heard kids saying he had "nice hair." A lot of people around the Liberal leader were getting nervous, including his wife, Sophie Grégoire. Trudeau would repeatedly reassure her, "I've got this."

For a couple of months, Herle had been arguing that the "not ready" charge needed an aggressive reply from Trudeau. Why not have the Liberal leader address the charge head on? The Liberals had flirted already with direct-reply ads; one early one in 2013 showed Trudeau sitting in a classroom and turning off a TV that was showing the flickering image of the Conservatives' latest attack ad. But generally in politics, the rule is that you should never repeat an allegation made against you. Richard Nixon's "I am not a crook" defence during Watergate is the oft-cited example. But this "not ready" business seemed to cry out for a radical response. Trudeau was ultimately persuaded that the damage had already been done and it was hard to imagine it getting any worse. "We were in no danger of further amplifying it. Everyone had already seen it twenty times," he would say later.

So on one of the hottest days in Ottawa that summer, Trudeau and the Liberal ad makers descended on Major's Hill Park just a stone's throw from Parliament Hill and filmed the ad that would be known simply as "Ready." Three blue shirts were hanging on the branch of a nearby tree, for Trudeau to sweat through successively while walking over and over again toward the camera, looking into the lens and saying his lines. "Stephen Harper says I'm not ready. I'll tell you what I am not ready for," Trudeau said, going on to elaborate on how he would be all the things that Harper was not. It took a few hours and several changes of the blue shirts, but the team finally wrapped up filming with Trudeau uttering the closing line: "I'm ready to bring real change to Ottawa." In the 2011 campaign, NDP leader Jack Layton had been the sunny salesman promising to fix where Ottawa was "broken." With the "Ready" ad, Trudeau was picking up where Layton left off.

Once the ad was done, it was sent to Toronto for focus-group testing. For this sneak preview, Arnold gathered up small audiences composed largely of middle-aged or older men, who were proving to be the most skeptical about Trudeau's readiness for office and also most receptive to the Conservatives' "not ready" ad. Butts was amazed as he sat in on the focus groups. People asked to see the ad again; they said Trudeau looked "prime ministerial." One of the few women present in the room said that she would think of the ad every time she saw those Conservative interviewers on TV reviewing Trudeau's job qualifications. The men liked that the Liberal leader was fighting back. Butts emailed Telford: "We need to spend $4 million on this ad. It is as good an ad as I've ever seen."

Arnold was also surprised by the focus group's reaction. "It was probably the most effective ad I've ever seen in terms of undoing or changing opinions of people," he would say in an interview later. It was around this time that Butts and Arnold started to feel in their guts that the Liberals were going to win the election, even if the polls weren't showing it yet. Why did the ad work so well? Butts liked to call it a feat of political jiu-jitsu, turning the force of the Conservatives' own attacks back on them. And as everyone in political marketing knows, politics often mixes well with sports and feats of athleticism. Harper had attached his brand to hockey. And the Liberals, in the 2015 election, found their fortunes tied to baseball and the Toronto Blue Jays in particular.

With equal doses of luck and canny foresight by Bensimon Byrne, the Liberals decided in late July to purchase ad time with the Blue Jays. At that early point in the summer, it was not certain that the Jays would be in the playoffs come October. The regular season would end, after all, just before the election's key final weeks. Still, the ad team decided to buy up as much time as they could, anticipating that the Conservatives or New Democrats would do the same. Because they were making the purchase so far in advance, they were given deep-discount rates—about $6,000 for a thirty-second spot.

It was an election that would prove an endurance test for all the political players. On August 4, Harper went to the governor general's residence and formally kicked off Canada's forty-second election. It would last seventy-seven days, more than double the usual length of Canadian election campaigns, and the vote would be held on October 19, 2015. In the meantime, the campaign would require other athletic activities. When Rosenberg first met Trudeau in a quick, get-to-know-each-other session in an airport lounge, he had been struck by what he called his "physicality"—Trudeau's easy movements, his ease with himself. In advertising, you work with your product's strength, especially as it stands against your competitors. So Rosenberg featured Trudeau on the move whenever possible in the advertising, with the unspoken, implicit question: Would either Harper or Mulcair do an ad like this? When Rosenberg was pulling together an ad for British Columbia audiences, for instance, he assembled clips of Trudeau climbing a mountain trail in North Vancouver, the famous Grouse Grind, a 2.9-kilometre uphill hike billed as "Mother Nature's Stairmaster." Trudeau, not even winded by the climb, talked about his deep roots in BC as the ad cameras rolled.

Rosenberg had also been looking for a way for Trudeau to do an ad about the stagnation of the middle class. He came up with the idea of the middle class trying to climb upward on a down-ward-moving escalator. Why not put Trudeau in that picture? After some spirited back and forth among the campaign team—some were worried about the prospect of ridicule—Trudeau said he wanted to do it. The ad team scouted out a perfect, sun-drenched set of escalators in the Metro Toronto Convention Centre. They filmed the ad in mid-August and were happy with the way it was all coming together. But suddenly on August 25, one statement from NDP leader Thomas Mulcair would force some major changes in the ad's script and, as it turned out, the entire course of the election campaign.

In the Red

Thomas Mulcair was in Hamilton making a campaign stop at a company that manufactured playground equipment. He made a fateful pronouncement while talking to reporters travelling with the campaign. "Our first budget will be a balanced budget," Mulcair said, an intended reassurance to all those who might have feared that an NDP government would usher in a new era of free-spending social-ism in Ottawa. "We know, because we've got a lot of experienced people, that governing is about priorities." It was the only answer that Mulcair would have been expected to give. No politician in Canada had dared to veer from balanced-budget orthodoxy for at least twenty years. A good politician was one who would keep the country in the black. This was doubly true for anyone from the pro-gressive side of the spectrum, painted by the Conservatives as free spenders and a danger to Canadians' pocketbooks. As recently as July, Trudeau had been adhering to this orthodoxy himself while talking to a party rally in Markham, Ontario. "I've committed to continu-ing to run balanced budgets," Trudeau said at the rally. "In fact, it is Conservatives who run deficits. Liberals balance budgets. That's what history has shown."

The Liberals had some other history in their files, too. Herle had been gathering research for several years showing that Canadian voters could be sold on the idea of increasing the deficit, if per-suaded that in-the-red finances would improve their standard of living. Herle's research had taken note of how the Conservatives had paid no political price for running deficits year after year since the worldwide economic downturn of 2008–09. During the 2012 Nova Scotia election, the Gandalf Group conducted polling to see whether voters in the province would recoil at the prospect of delaying a bal-anced budget until 2017. They didn't. Those findings and others convinced him that the federal Liberals, within cautious limits, could pull Canadian politics away from the orthodoxy of balanced budgets. That had not been part of the Liberal platform, though.

It only became a campaign promise when Mulcair said he would balance the budget. If the Liberals could pull off this about-face with minimal damage, it would give Trudeau a chance to paint Harper and Mulcair as advocates of two identical versions of austerity.

So with Mulcair's promise now on the record, the ad team at Bensimon Byrne also decided they had to do some hasty editing to the escalator ad. It needed to include a mention of the NDP leader as well as Harper. Trudeau quickly slipped back to Toronto's convention centre to film the ad all over again—on a different escalator, less telegenic than the first one. Once again, Trudeau marched on the moving steps and read his lines about how Harper was making it harder for people to get ahead in Canada. As the escalator ground to a halt, the camera zooming in briefly on his shoes, Trudeau now looked into the camera and added, "And Mulcair promises more cuts. Now is not the time for cuts."

On August 27, Trudeau landed in Oakville, Ontario, and said the Liberals planned to run a "modest" deficit if they were elected—putting Canada into the red for three years to finance spending on roads, transit and other infrastructure that would fuel economic growth. "Now is the time to invest in the projects our country needs," Trudeau said, flanked by construction workers in bright orange vests—the NDP colours. Even as he was making that announcement, Trudeau was aware that something game-changing was happening in the 2015 campaign. "I said to Sophie that night, people will look back at today as the day we won the election," he recalled in the interview later. Grégoire wasn't so certain, reading the media reports the next day and the pundits' predictions that the Liberals had made a serious strategic blunder.

Perhaps not a blunder, it was an audacious form of rebranding for the Liberals. In the 1990s, the Liberals had carefully cultivated a profile as deficit slayers and strong economic managers, in no small part to counter the reputation acquired in earlier decades as taxers and spenders. Working for Finance Minister Paul Martin back in the

1990s, Herle had helped shape that Liberal image. In July, Trudeau himself had boasted about that record and promised more of the same. Now in August, Trudeau had pivoted the Liberal brand 180 degrees again, presenting the party as champions of tax increases for the wealthy and proponents of spending the country into a deficit.

Insiders and Outsiders

With some notable exceptions through history, Canadian election campaigns have been fought as domestic affairs with issues and platforms organized around the voters' wallets. That reality had made it easier for politicians to import consumer-style marketing tactics into the electoral arena. The 2015 election would see Canadian politics veering off that familiar territory, though, thanks to events and even individuals far away from Canada. A Syrian refugee child, a woman who wanted to become a citizen while wearing traditional Muslim face coverings and an Australian political operative—three isolated individuals in three totally different contexts—all contributed to a sharp turn in the narrative of this extra-long Canadian election campaign.

The child was a two-year-old named Alan Kurdi, drowned in his family's attempt to flee Syria. The heartbreaking photo of the toddler, lying face down on a beach in Turkey, was still spinning around the world in early September when news emerged that the family was trying to come as refugees to Canada. Suddenly, Canada's election debate began to revolve around whether the country should do more in the Syrian refugee crisis. The Muslim woman was Zunera Ishaq, who had been battling the Conservative government's attempts to ban the wearing of a niqab for citizenship ceremonies. Religious garb had been a hot-button topic in Canada for several years, especially in Quebec where the 2013 introduction of the so-called Charter of Values, with its strict limits on public display of religious symbols, had stirred up often toxic questions about people's openness to cultural diversity.

A Federal Court ruling in mid-September, clearing the way for Ishaq to cover her face while taking the citizenship oath, reignited that debate within the election campaign, forcing all the leaders to declare where they stood on the issue of the niqab. Harper staked out a strong opposition to face coverings, going so far as to say he might also consider banning public servants from wearing the niqab while on the job. Trudeau stood by his father's Charter of Rights and Freedoms. Mulcair, facing backlash in his own Quebec base of support, made clear he stood on the side of religious freedom. The NDP leader said later that this was his proudest political moment, but it was also the beginning of the end of his chances to finish the election in first or even second place. Brad Lavigne, keeping a close eye on internal NDP polls, watched as the numbers started spiralling downward in September, in a circle that started in Quebec but began to radiate outward to Ontario, the Prairies and BC. "It started with the niqab, but then began to chip away at the idea outside Quebec that Mulcair was the best chance to replace Harper," Lavigne would explain.

The blame for this toxic culture war within the Canadian election campaign was laid at the feet of the Conservatives, specifically (though wrongly, as it turned out) an international political operative named Lynton Crosby. Crosby was a hard-nosed Australian campaign consultant known for his role in helping to engineer surprise victories for Conservatives around the world. The most recent victory for the "Wizard of Oz," as he was called, was British Prime Minister David Cameron's unexpected majority win in the spring of 2015. In September, some Conservative sources leaked to reporters that Crosby's advice was being sought to put Harper's campaign back on track.

Crosby's specialty was exploiting hot-button or "wedge" issues to harden support for Conservatives. Campaigns he advised in Australia and Britain had featured immigrant and refugee issues. So when refugees and the niqab became part of the Canadian election mix, speculation ran rampant about the Conservatives' import of "dog-whistle" politics to the 2015 campaign. And when the Conservatives held a press conference to announce the establishment of a special 1-800 line to report "barbaric cultural practices," the backlash was directed at the alleged influence of dark-arts political practitioners from abroad.

Crosby's influence was greatly exaggerated, as it turned out— perhaps even non-existent. Sources close to the war room confided privately that there were no sightings of Crosby at Conservative headquarters, and that his name never appeared in the senders' or recipients' lists of campaign emails. Crosby's business partner, Mark Textor, exasperated by the rumours of his firm's involvement with Canada's Conservatives, took to Twitter to issue denials. He posted photos of himself with a cheeky #notinCanada hashtag and eventually tweeted outright, "It's pretty simple. Neither Crosby nor Textor are there. Nor staff. We don't do bit-part politics." The new twist in hot-button Conservative marketing appeared to be home-grown. In a *Globe and Mail* article after the election, the Conservatives' campaign chief Jenni Byrne would even call it a mistake.

On Stage

If Trudeau and his team were breaking some political communications rules on purpose in this election, Conservatives were breaking them accidentally. Before the first leaders' debate in early August, Harper's campaign spokesman, Kory Teneycke, had set the bar ridiculously low for Trudeau to succeed on the debating stage against his more experienced rivals. "I think that if he comes on stage with his pants on, he will probably exceed expectations," Teneycke told reporters travelling aboard Harper's campaign bus.

The 2015 election featured a marked departure in the old standard of the televised leaders' debates. Back in the summer, Harper's Conservatives announced that they would likely not be participating in the traditional debates held by the big TV networks—the "consortium" debates. For several decades these televised debates, one in French and one in English, had been the centrepiece of every federal election. Conservatives said instead that Harper would be participating in a series of smaller debates with different sponsors. *Maclean's* magazine and Rogers TV would host the first one. Others would be hosted by *The Globe and Mail* newspaper, a consortium of French-language broadcasters and the Munk debates in Toronto. This new approach to debates matched the Conservatives' well-practised approach to politics and marketing, dividing the Canadian political map into smaller targets, segmenting the audience rather than mass marketing. It was a formula that had turned them a tidy profit at the polls since 2006.

Trudeau and the Liberals, though, decided to use the debates for mass marketing, especially through social media. They launched the "Ready" ad on major broadcast outlets on the same night as the *Maclean's* debate, and put in place a huge network to distribute images and sound bites from each debate across the digital universe. That networking operation began hours before Trudeau would utter a word in any debate. He'd start the day with a photo glimpse of how he was spending debate day—practising boxing in a gym or canoeing on a river, for example. Liberal campaign workers back in Ottawa would be writing prepackaged tweets and Facebook posts—"fact checks" or snippets of the The Liberal platform—to keep churning through social-media streams in between blasts of what Trudeau was actually saying in the debate. Liberals also laid out thousands of dollars for what's known as a "promoted trend" on Twitter, meaning that anyone who clicked on a popular hashtag for the Canadian election would see a fifteen-second video ad from Trudeau. This was a tip borrowed from US politics; Obama and his Republican competitors had used it during the 2012 presidential campaign.

None of the debates were producing moments of high drama, but Trudeau kept winning the race of the social-media metrics afterward. After every debate, Trudeau would have drawn the most mentions on

Twitter and Facebook, as well as more searches on Google. One line in the ubiquitous "not ready" ad caught Trudeau's notice from the moment it appeared on TV. It was the part where the woman allows that she is not saying "no" forever to Trudeau, just "not now." He saw that line as a crack in the Conservatives' armour—a flaw in their reasoning with the electorate and an opening he might exploit. "If they're thinking, well, maybe someday, all we have to do is convince them [it's] now," he said.

Trudeau had decided to use the TV debates to prove he was up for the job, and the Munk debate, the final one of the campaign, had to be good enough to carry him through the last month of the campaign. It was held in the final week of September, and speculation was running high that this might be the one in which the Liberal leader stumbled. It was a whole debate on foreign policy—not an area in which Trudeau had shone—and the room was packed with Conservative and NDP supporters. But Trudeau was not intimidated and spent the Munk debate playing to the crowd, a skill he had honed during all that time on the road. "Trudeau soars," read one headline. He later said it was on the Munk debates stage when he realized how the Liberals would nail down the election win: by getting voters to turn that "not now" skepticism into the here and now. "I realized, oh, okay. This is the way it feels and this is where we're going to go."

Better Is Possible

As September turned to October, the NDP had fallen out of first place in the opinion polls. The Liberals, on the other hand, were climbing, an ascent parallel to the Toronto Blue Jays' summer-end romp toward the playoffs. The Jays were becoming must-see TV—and the Liberals, thanks to the clever ad buy in July, had Canadians' attention during the commercial breaks. Their grand advertising finale had been in the works for months. Butts and Rosenberg had been sketching it out back in Major's Hill Park during the filming of the "Ready" ad. It would be an all-out attack on Harper presented in a relentlessly sunny, upbeat fashion. Butts had nicknamed it the "one-slur" ad. It wasn't exactly an attack ad, according to the strict definition, but it would be the sharpest Trudeau assault on Harper and his record to date.

"It was a contrast. It wasn't a personally negative ad. It didn't try to brand Harper with a cute little slogan. It was a contrast ad in terms of visions for the country," Rosenberg would say later. The idea would be to organize a huge Liberal gathering in the suburbs outside Toronto in early October and send Trudeau to the stage with a rally-the-troops speech. The footage could then be used for an ad that would carry the Liberal campaign to voting day on October 19. The ad had to embody the positive, "sunny ways" disposition that Trudeau had been promising to bring to politics, while also demonstrating momentum in the Liberals' direction. But selling hope on a large scale is hard work. "People think the biggest risk we took in the campaign was the deficit announcement. It wasn't. It was staging that event," Butts would confide later.

The Liberals booked the Powerade Centre in Brampton, Ontario, and started firing up the troops from near and far to pack the hockey arena with at least seven thousand people. Buses were booked to ferry Liberals from Hamilton, London, Windsor and even Ottawa, a five-hour journey away. The digital team was bombarded with RSVPs to the emailed invitations: more than two thousand in just seventy-two hours. Trudeau's speech was essentially a greatest-hits package of all his crowd-pleasing lines from the past couple of years. "Stephen Harper isn't afraid of me, my friends. He's afraid of you. And he should be," Trudeau shouted to the crowd. "He wants you to believe that better isn't possible. His job depends on it. Well, we've got news for you, Mr. Harper: this is Canada. And in Canada, better is always possible."

The Bensimon Byrne camera team was in the hall, filming the spectacle with five cameras. Three were trained on the leader, two on the crowd. Late into that Sunday night, Rosenberg and the crew started assembling the footage into an ad that would become the most powerful of the Liberal campaign—some would say the most powerful Liberal ad seen in decades. Big-applause lines from the speech were interspersed with images of Trudeau meeting ordinary Canadians out on the road, punctuated with scenes of the cheering Brampton crowd. In look and feel, the ad bore a strong resemblance to that old Molson "I Am Canadian" ad—no surprise, since Bensimon Byrne had done that ad, too, in the 1990s.

The ad, in keeping with the long US-to-Canada trajectory of political marketing over the past decades, also owed some of its inspiration to former president Ronald Reagan. Harper may have admired much of Reagan's brand of conservatism and modelled his party along the same lines, but Trudeau also found a way to channel the upbeat style of advertising that Reagan brought to America in the 1980s. "Morning in America?" Trudeau said later. "Yeah, we did think about that." Nor was Reagan the only former president on Liberals' minds as they scripted this ad. Trudeau was also a fan of Bill Clinton's 1993 inaugural line: "There is nothing wrong with America that cannot be cured by what is right with America." Trudeau said, "I mean, that kind of messaging, we knew that it connects with people. You just have to be able to deliver it in a way that is true to you. True to what you're trying to do. True to the brand."

Harper, true to his brand, was finishing up the final week of the election campaign waving dollar bills. At each stop, the Conservative campaign would haul out a cache of bills and have them counted on stage to show the alleged cost of Trudeau's promises. With every promise and wad of bills thrown down, a cash-register bell would ring. On the final Saturday of the election campaign, Harper did one of these appearances with the famous Ford brothers in Toronto. And for the final, election-day pitch to Canadian voters, the Conservatives laid out some dollars of their own for—what else?—a major advertising purchase. All Postmedia newspapers in Canada were wrapped in a front-page ad for the Conservatives, in Election Canada's yellow hues, urging people to vote for Harper on October 19.

Ready to Win

The two most senior people in Trudeau's inner circle viewed modern political arts as a way to tell stories. Advertising is storytelling, according to Gerald Butts. Numbers tell stories, Katie Telford likes to say. The story of the 2015 campaign ended, then, with a big advertising flourish and a flurry of numbers churning through the Console. More and more ridings were swinging to the Liberals, rising through the metal-and-wood ranking system. That meant finding new volunteers to seal support in places where Liberals hadn't exactly been in a surplus. The digital team set about identifying more than 840,000 voters in these ridings and making contact with them in the final days of the campaign. Ridings such as Fundy–Royal in New Brunswick, which had gone Liberal only once since Confederation, were turning red.

Many of the graphs and sliding bars on the Console were getting redder, showing that Trudeau's party had a real chance of grabbing nearly 40 percent of the total vote and the magic number of 170 seats—the minimum required to win a majority. Turnout was going up all over the country, too; later the Liberals would find that it had increased a full 7 percent among people they directly contacted during the campaign. The 2015 election saw a huge spike in turnout overall in Canada, reversing a decades-long slide. Nearly three million more ballots were cast in 2015 than in 2011. Liberals were the clear beneficiaries—almost seven million votes in total, four million more than they won in 2011. Many of the new voters may have been drawn in by the advertising, the hope part, but their support had been sealed with the hard work of a modern, digital political machine.

Trudeau had brought the Liberal party into the twenty-first century but also, he would say later, back to an ages-old idea about the purpose of politics. "This is something that the Liberal party has needed for a long, long time, to remember how to connect with people," Trudeau said. "Marketing, the consumer world, what is that? You can't be a politician without connecting with people." In the end, those connections gave the Liberals 184 seats in the new Parliament that Canadians elected on October 19, 2015. Conservatives and New Democrats, who had led the way in modern arts of political marketing for most of the early part of the century, were back on the opposition benches. Trudeau would have four years to shake up Canadian government in the same ways he and his team had shaken up the Liberal party.

SHOPPING: THE SEQUEL

Justin Trudeau became Canada's twenty-third prime minister with a flood of imagery: thousands and thousands of "selfies" with Canadians; a parade of pictures distributed on social media such as Facebook and Instagram, even a photo shoot with *Vogue* magazine. The swearing-in ceremony at Rideau Hall on November 4, 2015, could have been produced in Hollywood—a young prime minister, accompanied by his family and gender-equal, diverse cabinet, walking up to the governor general's residence under sunny skies and a Liberal-red canopy of trees in their fall colours. It all had Canadian commentators reaching for cinematic metaphors. *National Post* columnist John Ivison wrote of the swearing-in, "It almost overwhelmed the senses—like the moment Dorothy entered Technicolour in *The Wizard of Oz*."

No question, it was an abrupt scene change for Canadian politics. For ten years before the shift in power, former prime minister Stephen Harper had presented a very different picture of life at the top of government. In his ads, Harper worked alone in his dimly lit office late into the night, turning out the lights to mark the end of another long workday. If politics was a movie, the scenery change alone in the fall of 2015 would signal to Canadians that something significant had shifted in the culture—from the dark arts of political management to what Trudeau liked to call "sunny ways." Had Canada's political marketing culture really changed, though? Or had the country simply exchanged one kind of picture for the other?

No prime minister in twenty-first-century politics can afford to be indifferent to the art of imagery and the science of data-driven campaigning. Trudeau and Harper, in their own ways, were no exceptions. For a real picture of where political marketing was headed after the 2015 election, it was first worth a closer look at the similarities as well as the differences between the outgoing and incoming prime ministers. The two politicians, though born only a dozen years apart, had distinct approaches to the marketing of imagery. Harper spoke to people who understood the power of images as he did—produced on high and broadcast down to the masses. This was very effective throughout Harper's decade in power, but it was also very twentieth century.

Trudeau, however, appeared far more comfortable among those who had learned that in a digital age, everyone has the power to be a consumer and a producer of images. He was a living example of the democratization of fame, available in the twenty-first century to anyone with a smartphone and access to social media. Trudeau was famous but so was anyone who appeared in a selfie with him, at least while the image was circulating on Instagram, Twitter or Facebook. "I see images as a way to communicate," Trudeau said in an interview in his Parliament Hill office a few months after the election. "Understanding how to use everything you can to connect with people, whether it's my speeches… or whether it's images or advertising, that's a way of connecting directly with people."

How a government connects with the people depends to a large degree on how it sees them: as consumers or citizens, or both. Conservatives liked the phrase "taxpayers"—government as a monetary transaction between the leaders and the led. Harper spent the final week of the campaign literally throwing dollars on a table to show what Canadians would be losing by electing a Liberal government. Trudeau, on the other hand, was not a fan of the "taxpayers" word, arguing in a post-election interview that it was only half the equation of being a citizen. Yet the Liberal campaign often spoke to Canadians as shoppers, offering tax relief for school supplies or loading grocery carts to show families how much they would be able to spend with the new child-benefit program. Those pictures alone would indicate that the shopping relationship between politics and citizens is an enduring one, built in the twentieth century but stretching well into the twenty-first century, too.

All the political leaders in 2015, the New Democrats' Thomas Mulcair included, set their sights on the votes of the middle class in Canada, and in the process evoked a considerable degree of nostalgia for the twentieth century. Harper was fond of presenting himself as a child of the suburbs and the consumer expansion of the 1960s and 1970s. Trudeau only needed to remind people he was the son of the prime minister who led Canada in that era of an ever-expanding middle class. But the Canadian population, and the Trudeau brand, had come a long way since then.

For more than fifty years, Canadian political practitioners had been increasingly adopting the tools of the consumer marketplace as they went shopping for votes. Through the first couple of decades after the Second World War, our politicos were lured by the pitch of the advertising and market researchers, and how their methods could better reach consumer-citizens. It all seemed like good fun—political strategists as Mad Men in their smoke-filled, wise-cracking backrooms. Then in the 1980s and 1990s, the bargaining began on both sides: What price were we willing to pay for mixing civics with shopping culture? Political consumerism marched on, however, hand in hand with rising voter cynicism and a larger mass of "flexible" voters shifting political allegiances election to election. With the arrival of the twenty-first century and the ascent to power of Harper's Conservatives, the marketing deal was sealed. Canadian politics itself, not to mention its parties, people and "products," were being shaped by consumer demand. Voters were not only getting the governments they deserved, as the old saying goes, but also the bare, transactional governance they seem to have requested: deep discounts on their taxes, snappy slogans on their legislation, images rather than policy discussions.

The 2015 election campaign was a powerful reminder of just how flexible the Canadian electorate had become in shopping for their preferred brand of politics. At the beginning of the campaign many voters seemed willing to put their money on the New Democrats, but as the weeks wore on they were increasingly open to what the Liberals were selling. Voters in the twenty-first century are not only flexible but fickle, creating a democratic marketplace so volatile that political parties can go from third to first place, and vice versa, in one election campaign.

Trudeau, before and after he took power in 2015, promised that he would roll back some of the marketing excesses of Harper's years in power. Canadian voters, he said in the post-election interview, were tired of being told for a decade that the only relationship they had with the government was as consumers. Among the Liberals' campaign promises, for instance, was a vow to end partisan advertising in government—a practice that critics had been condemning as far back as the 1980s when Pierre Trudeau's government used images of Canada geese to sell constitutional reform to Canadians.

As important as advertising was to Justin Trudeau's successful campaign in 2015, he also said after the election that he would be in favour of some stricter standards over political ads. "It's ridiculous that political advertising isn't subject to some sort of control," Trudeau said, acknowledging it might be difficult to regulate what he called the politicians' tendencies to "over promise" or exaggerate all the change they were offering. "But flat-out lying? In an ad? You should have your knuckles rapped on that." One way to rein in political advertising, Trudeau suggested, might be to have it subject to the same voluntary code as Advertising Standards Canada oversees in the private sector. Many Canadians might be inclined to agree. If politics is being pitched to Canadians with the same techniques used to sell beer or doughnuts, shouldn't political marketers be subject to the same code of conduct?

The big-data campaign of 2015 also showed just how much Canada's political marketers, like consumer marketers, were relying on digital information and analytics for success. Trudeau and the Liberals probably owed their majority victory to the efforts they made to catch up to their rivals in the sophisticated science of modern electioneering. Yet here again, Canada's political parties were operating as businesses did—without the same rules. As citizens and consumers, Canadians have powerful legal rights to privacy. The federal Privacy Act puts strict limits on how the government collects information about individuals, and gives people the right to see what kind of data the government has accumulated about them. The federal Personal Information Protection and Electronic Documents Act (PIPEDA), meanwhile, offers most Canadians similar reassurances in the commercial sector (British Columbia, Quebec and Alberta have their own similar laws). Citizens have a right to demand informed consent about sharing their personal information, and transparency on the part of the banks, stores and service companies.

The federal political party databases, however, were a glaring exception to Canadian privacy rules in 2015, a good decade or so after they started being built in earnest. They were in a legal limbo, not covered by the Privacy Act or PIPEDA. Canada's chief electoral officer, Marc Mayrand, called the databases a "black hole" in terms of privacy when he started arguing for a crackdown in early 2013. If you wanted to see what the Conservatives or Liberals or New Democrats knew about you, you were out of luck. Was there a happy face or a frowning face beside your name and address in CIMS? The Conservatives didn't have to tell you. Did you want to change the information that was stored about you in Liberalist, on the famous "Console" or in the NDP's Populus database? You had no legal right to see or change that data.

In January 2015, even as his party was loading up the Console for the looming election, Trudeau's most senior adviser, Gerald Butts, was on a conference stage in Ottawa with NDP strategist Brad Lavigne and Conservative spokesman Tim Powers. The election was still months away. Butts told the attendees at the digital-governance conference that political parties and their databases would eventually have to fall under some kind of privacy oversight. His colleagues on the stage were more equivocal. "Let's not kid ourselves, political parties are public institutions of a sort," Butts said, pointing out how parties are allowed to offer tax deductions for donations, or the ways in which they've been exempted through the years from the do-not-call list and access-to-information laws. As well, the Conservatives' Fair Elections Act, which became law in 2014, contained provisions specifically aimed at adding to the information in the databases. Under these new provisions, parties are required to submit their own records of who voted and who didn't—so-called bingo cards—to Elections Canada. "Maybe we have just created a hole in our two bodies of law that allow political parties to exist out there in the ether," Butts said. "I think that is increasingly a problem and it is difficult for me to envision a future where it exists for much longer."

Yet one year after Butts mused aloud about the need to bring the databases under some kind of privacy protection, it seemed that future might go on for some time. Butts's boss, now the prime minister, seemed less enthusiastic about privacy rules for the databases. "We have a strong culture around privacy. I trust Canadians to self-regulate on that," Trudeau said. "I'm worried about being overly heavy-handed [with] legislation." Perhaps it isn't a surprise that once the Liberals caught up in the data game, they would become more guarded about revealing what was in their own database.

"The 2015 election proved that big data is here to stay," said Colin Bennett, a University of Victoria professor who carried out a study of the political databases for Canada's privacy commissioner in 2013. But as 2016 dawned, only one province—British Columbia— was taking steps to force political parties to be more careful about the data they were collecting. Any organization or person who wanted to obtain information from Election BC's list of electors would also have to comply with government privacy policy. "This includes registered political parties, members of the Legislative Assembly and candidates in an election," said the advisory from Elections BC. Bennett, who refers to the databases as a form of democratic "surveillance," was convinced that other provinces, as well as the federal government, would have to follow in British Columbia's footsteps in the years ahead. "We have a tradition in Canada, that unless there are really good reasons—national security, for instance—organizations are not supposed to be constructing secret databases," Bennett said.

Marketing 2.0

Many seasoned political players and observers in Canada were warning in the aftermath of the 2015 election that it would be a mistake to draw too many lessons on shopping for votes: too much of the campaign was unusual and unexpected. In the first place, the eleven-week marathon was one of the longest election campaigns in Canadian history—a long enough campaign to employ marketing tactics that wouldn't have worked as well in a short five-week sprint. Trudeau's ad team, expert though it may have been, was given the luxury of time to rehabilitate his brand. Had the election been held the traditional five weeks after the starting date of August 5, the results most likely would have been much different. In the aftermath, surveying the lessons for the battered NDP, Lavigne liked to joke that Canada actually had two election campaigns rolled into one in 2015.

"The seventy-seven-day campaign was the length of two traditional federal elections. The NDP won the first one. The Liberal Party of Canada won the second one."

In a *Globe and Mail* article published several months after the election, the Conservatives' former campaign chief Jenni Byrne confided her belief that they might have won the election had the party not decided to play politics with the niqab issue. "The party needed the NDP to do well. With the NDP rising in the polls for the first half of the campaign, Stephen Harper was well-positioned to be re-elected," Byrne wrote. "The decision during the campaign to turn our guns on the NDP was a mistake. They were never the party's enemy. The final straw was when the party went after the NDP on the niqab issue. It crushed the NDP in Quebec, but it also removed them as a viable alternative in the rest of the country, something Conservatives needed them to be."

Liberals would say after the election that the 2015 campaign had proven that positive advertising was more powerful than negative advertising, and that they had rewritten the rules book on how to reply to attack ads. Others were not so certain, especially about whether it was now possible to address an alleged smear by repeating it. As Trudeau himself knew, this tactic worked only because he had little left to lose; the widespread damage had already been done by the "not ready" ad. "I'm not sure that would work again," Lavigne said in an interview after the election. "Somebody would have to be in exactly the same position—down with nothing left to lose."

On the value of positive campaigning, though, Liberals may have been on to something. In the United States, where the presidential race was heating up in early 2016, new analysis of political advertising studies showed that positive ads yielded more rewards than negative ones. The authors of one such analysis wrote in the *Washington Post* in late January: "Positive advertising can win voters, although only when candidates air more positive ads than their opponent. Negative advertising, however, had at best no effect on vote totals and may even have hurt the candidate running negative ads," wrote social scientists Shanna Pearson-Merkowitz and Liam Malloy. Canada's forty-second election could have lent some new evidence to their conclusion.

Jen O'Malley Dillon was one of the former advisers to Barack Obama's presidential campaigns who helped out the Liberals in the 2015 election. Sitting in a Washington office adorned with Obama campaign memorabilia a few months after the Canadian vote was over, Dillon was reflecting on what Americans might have learned from Trudeau's victory. Certainly, she said, the Liberal campaign had demonstrated the importance of sophisticated data and field organization, but also the power of a positive message and the importance of sticking to it. "They weren't reliant on external polls. They weren't reliant on just what was being said out there. They had their own data sets and their own anecdotal data," Dillon said. "Even when times got tough, they stuck with their plan. They stuck to who their guy was and that's what helped them win in the end."

The 2015 election was perhaps most unusual for the way in which it ventured into debates over foreign policy and immigration, prompting political conversations about values of the head and heart rather than value for the dollar. Were Canadians thinking as consumers when they debated what to do about Syrian refugees or about wearing a niqab in public? Probably not. Similarly, the political parties were finding that consumer information wasn't as useful as sociological data when it came to collecting data on voters and analyzing it. When political practitioners in the US shifted tack on this score, voter participation increased. The same thing happened in Canada in the 2015 election—nearly three million new voters and an abrupt halt to a decades-long slide in turnout: from 61 percent in 2011 to nearly 70 percent in 2015.

The long-cultivated relationship between politics and the consumer marketplace is too deep to be disentangled by one election, one prime minister or even pretty pictures. Harper and Trudeau were only the latest in a long line of prime ministers who had learned from the marketing practices in the consumer world and built upon them. Some of those practices put politics more in touch with citizens where they lived and worked; some fed the cynicism rampant about the transactional nature of modern politics.

David Ogilvy, that twentieth-century advertising giant, is probably best remembered for his warnings about the perils of underestimating your audience. He said, "The consumer is not a moron. She is your wife." Political marketing, when not held in check, veers dangerously close to the view of consumers as morons. In its extreme forms, it plays to people's emotions, not their thoughts. It operates on the belief that repeating a catchy phrase, even if it's untrue, will seal an idea in the mind of the unknowing or uncaring public. It assumes that citizens will always choose on the basis of their individual wants and not society's needs. Canada's 2015 election was a shopping exercise with two forms of currency: dollars and change. As much as Canadians were voting with their wallets, thinking as consumers, a large majority were also looking for change. For a real shift to take place in the culture of politics, though, citizens and politicians will be required in the years ahead to draw some clearer lines between their consumer and civic pursuits. Otherwise, only the scenery will change in the long story of shopping for votes.

ACKNOWLEDGEMENTS

This book has taken quite a while to write and almost equally as long to get to publication. It's a long story, so I have a lengthy list of people who helped me along this sometimes bumpy road.

First off, my immense thanks to Howard White and all the folks at Harbour Publishing (especially editor Silas White) who lifted this book out of the purgatory where it landed when Douglas & McIntyre faltered in 2012. They have done a very good thing—not just for me, but for the Canadian book publishing industry.

Trena White of the old D&M was the first to say yes to this project, though, and she brilliantly and deftly steered it throughout, making it a much better book with each of her suggestions. Chris Bucci, my agent at Anne McDermid and Associates, introduced me to Trena and kept things moving on this book when it sometimes felt they never would.

Within the book and in the accompanying notes, you will see evidence of the many people, of all political stripes, who agreed to be interviewed, sometimes repeatedly, for this story. I obviously could have not done this without them. This updated edition of the book came together with a lot of help from the people who worked on Justin Trudeau's campaign, as well as Prime Minister Trudeau himself. I am also grateful to the class of 2015–16 in Carleton University's School of Political Management, who offered smart analysis for the update.

My former editor-in-chief at the *Toronto Star*, Michael Cooke, made it possible for me to juggle this book with my day job as a parliamentary reporter. My other colleagues in the Ottawa bureau, especially bureau chief Bruce Campion-Smith, but also Tonda MacCharles, Les Whittington, Joanna Smith and Tim Harper, as well as Chantal Hébert in Montreal, not only put up with the absences and distraction, but actively encouraged the book and my interest in this whole subject. Same goes for former bureau colleagues Richard Brennan, Allan Woods and Chris Carter (the title of this book comes from Chris, who's now with the CBC).

I was away from the bureau, on a Canadian Journalism Fellowship, when I first got the idea for this book and chattered incessantly about it to the people around me at Massey College. It really started, in fact, when I wandered fortuitously that year into a class on "material culture," taught by Sarah Amato at the University of Toronto's Victoria College. So thanks to Sarah for the initial inspiration (and a fascinating class) and thanks to all the folks who shared 2008–09 at Massey with me, particularly former college master John Fraser, administrator Anna Luengo and Michelle Gagnon, who still manages to be my fellow fellow, even though we're back in our respective jobs and cities.

Michael Valpy, another denizen of Massey and an old *Globe and Mail* colleague, linked me up with Luke Savage, a former university newspaper editor (like me) who turned out to be the best kind of researcher an author could have.

My new friends in the field of political marketing, Alex Marland of Memorial University and Thierry Giasson at Université Laval, opened up a whole new academic world to me. Watch these folks:

they are the future of political science. Daniel Paré at the University of Ottawa and Andre Turcotte at Carleton University are also among the smart people who have helped me out in this field. I am also indebted to the bright students in Carleton's master's program in political management, class of 2015–16, who provided invaluable help when I was turning the hardcover edition of this book into the updated, revised paperback.

Robin Sears, Geoff Norquay and Yaroslav Baran at Earnscliffe Strategy Group are friends who are also hugely knowledgeable about politics and marketing. Robin, who has deep roots in a number of political parties, did a very valuable read of the manuscript before it was done and caught some things I'd missed. So did my great friend Shaun Poulter at CBC, one of the brightest guys I know. Greg MacEachern at Environics is a friend who is also family, and a sounding board over many years for many of the ideas presented here in this book.

Ann Lawson-Brehl, who's been my friend for more than two-thirds of my life, is a large part of this book because she's also a large part of who I am. Susan Harada, who's been my treasured friend for the past two decades, has helped me more with this book than she knows.

My parents, Vera and John, and my brother John and his wife Andrea Stewart, are powerful motivation to make the world a better place, because that's what they have always done for me. My stepson Jean-Michel, and his partner Andrea, are the kind of young people who give you hope about the future, too. My dad worked for an automobile giant and my mom owned a retail store in Milton, Ontario. In a way, this book connects the dots of my growing-up past to the political world where I chose to spend my career.

But the person to whom this book is dedicated is the man who makes everything possible for me: my beloved spouse, Don Lenihan. I could not have done this without Don's help, his brilliant mind and, most importantly, his love.

NOTES, LINKS AND FURTHER READING

Introduction: Dollars and Change

Prime Minister Justin Trudeau sat down with me on January 25, 2016, for nearly an hour to talk about his approach to political advertising, data and marketing. Much of this introduction draws from that conversation, in addition to many discussions over the years with his chief advisers Gerald Butts and Katie Telford.

Chapter 1: Let's Get Canada Shopping

Canada's early department-store culture, including Jack Brehl's observation on Eaton's catalogues, is described in Belisle, Donica. *Retail Nation: Department Stores and the Making of Modern Canada*. Vancouver: UBC Press, 2011.

The Bank of Canada's Currency Museum displayed the country's credit-card history in a 2012 exhibit: http://www.bankofcanadamuseum.ca/explore/exhibitions/past-exhibitions/a-la-carte/.

For more on the rise of the suburbs in Canada, see: Harris, Richard. *"Creeping Conformity: How Canada Became Suburban, 1900–1960." Themes in Canadian History 7*. Toronto: University of Toronto Press, 2004.

The Canadian Broadcasting Corp., as part of its People's History Project, assembled early coverage of the birth of the suburbs, available online: www. cbc.ca/history/EP1SCONTENTSE1EP15CH3PA3LE.html.

Valerie Joyce Korinek has also documented Canada's suburban pop culture in *"Roughing it in the Suburbs: Reading Chatelaine Magazine in the Fifties and Sixties." Studies in Gender and History 16*. Toronto: University of Toronto Press, 2000.

The Consumers' Association of Canada has compiled a chronicle of its history and achievements at: http://www.consumer.ca/en/history/.

An overview of Canada's rich advertising history is found in Russell Johnston's book: *Selling Themselves: The Emergence of Canadian Advertising*. Toronto; Buffalo, NY: University of Toronto Press, 2001.

The Massey Commission, as it was popularly known, issued its findings in the *Report of the Royal Commission on National Development in the Arts, Letters and Sciences, 1949–1951*. Ottawa: King's Printer, 1951.

For more on how psychology influenced postwar Canadian culture, see: Gleason, Mona. *Normalizing the Ideal: Psychology, Schooling, and the Family in Postwar Canada*. Studies in Gender and History Series. Toronto: University of Toronto Press, 1999.

To read more on Sigmund Freud's nephew and his influence on public relations, see: Bernays, Edward L. and Mark Crispin Miller. *Propaganda*. Brooklyn, NY: Ig Publishing, 2005. More on Freud, Bernays and their influence on political-consumerist culture can also be learned from an extensive BBC documentary: Curtis, Adam. *Century of the Self*, British Broadcasting Corp., 240 minutes. United Kingdom, 2002. Various segments of the documentary are available for viewing through Google Videos.

Advertising Standards Canada has an online history of mileposts and achievements at: www.adstandards.com/en/AboutASC/ourHistory.aspx.

Chapter 2: Sold Like Soap

To read more about soap and political salesmanship, see: Marland, A. "Marketing Political Soap: A Political Marketing View of Selling Candidates Like Soap, of Electioneering as a Ritual, and of Electoral Military Analogies." *Journal of Public Affairs*, 3 (2003): 103–15.

Dalton Camp's life in advertising and politics is chronicled in many books and newspaper articles, but most of the tales cited here are from four major sources, including Camp's own book, *Gentlemen, Players and Politicians*. Toronto: McClelland & Stewart, 1970, as well as: Stevens, Geoffrey. *The Player: The Life & Times of Dalton Camp*. Toronto: Key Porter Books, 2003; Duffy, John. *Fights of Our Lives: Elections, Leadership and the Making of Canada*. 1st ed. Toronto: HarperCollins, 2002; and Camp's many columns in the *Toronto Star* through the 1980s and 1990s.

Keith Davey, the legendary "Rainmaker" of the federal Liberal party, donated all his files and papers to the E.J. Pratt Library, Victoria College, University of Toronto. Many of the stories of the MacLaren ad campaigns and Lou Harris's research are drawn from Davey's papers, with much thanks to the family and the library for the several days of viewings. Also vital to this research was Christina McCall's signature work, *Grits: An Intimate Portrait of the Liberal Party*. Toronto: Macmillan, 1982, and Davey's own book: *The Rainmaker: A Passion for Politics*. Toronto: Stoddart, 1986.

The National Citizens Coalition has documented its origins, complete with reproductions of the first ads and memories of Colin Brown's son, at: http://nationalcitizens.ca/index.php/about-us/ncc-heritage.

Journalist and author Jonathan Manthorpe is given credit for naming Ontario's Conservative operation "The Big Blue Machine," and tales of its early success can be found in: Manthorpe, Jonathan. *The Power & the Tories: Ontario Politics, 1943 to the Present.* Toronto: Macmillan, 1974.

The Vickers and Benson ad firm is long gone now, but some of the creative minds who used to work there have posted recollections online at: http://vickersandbensonmemories.ca.

In addition, a treasure trove of Terry O'Malley's advertising files, complete with rough drafts of ad campaigns and his famous lists of proposed slogans, is held at Brock University in St. Catharines, Ontario. The author is enormously grateful to O'Malley and Brock's library archivist, David Sharron, for the opportunity to pore over these files and learn more about those "Mad Men" years in Canadian politics.

Chapter 3: Scientific Shopping

Philip Spencer's multi-part series on "political consumer" surveys appeared over several issues in *Canadian Forum* magazine from October 1940 to April 1941 and originals were consulted in Carleton University's periodicals archives. Spencer's articles are also cited in Daniel J. Robinson's *The Measure of Democracy: Polling, Market Research, and Public Life, 1930–1945.* Toronto: University of Toronto Press, 1999.

For more on Davey and the sources for his tales in this chapter, see notes for Chapter 2.

Martin Goldfarb was kind enough to sit down with the author to discuss his anthropological approach to politics and consumerism. As well, he has laid out much of his thinking in pieces written for the *Toronto Star* over the years and books he has co-written, including *Affinity: Beyond Branding*. Toronto: McArthur, 2010 (with Howard Aster) and *Marching to a Different Drummer: An Essay on the Liberals and Conservatives in Convention*. Toronto: Stoddart, 1988 (with Tom Axworthy).

For a blow-by-blow account of Pierre Trudeau's often stormy dealings with the media and the public relations business, see: Gossage, Patrick. *Close to the Charisma: My Years between the Press and Pierre Elliott Trudeau*. Halifax: Goodread Biographies, 1986.

Allan Gregg shared memories and insights in repeated interviews for this book, for which the author is grateful. Those conversations were further informed by reading multiple newspaper accounts of those years and books such as Hoy, Claire. *Margin of Error: Pollsters and the Manipulation of Canadian Politics*. Toronto: Key Porter, 1989, and Fraser, Graham. *Playing for Keeps: The Making of the Prime Minister, 1988*. Toronto: McClelland & Stewart, 1989.

Chapter 4: Market Tested

Margaret Thatcher's methods are laid out in detail in Margaret Scammell's groundbreaking book on political marketing: *Designer Politics: How Elections Are Won*. Basingstoke, England: Macmillan, 1994. To further that pivotal work, Jennifer Lees-Marshment has continued to add important insights to this relatively new field in political science. See her books: *The Political Marketing Revolution: Transforming the Government of the UK*. Manchester; New York: Manchester University Press; distributed exclusively in the USA by Palgrave, 2004; *Routledge Handbook of Political Marketing*. Routledge Handbooks. Abingdon, Oxon; New York: Routledge, 2012.

Canadian political scientists have been keeping a close eye on the changing shape of the electorate and shifts in voting behaviour and motivation, too.

Their findings are noted in repeated Canada Election studies and also in LeDuc, Lawrence. *Dynasties and Interludes: Past and Present in Canadian Electoral Politics.* Toronto: Dundurn, 2010, and Pammett, Jon H. and Lawrence LeDuc. *Explaining the Turnout Decline in Canadian Federal Elections: A New Survey of Non-Voters.* Ottawa: Elections Canada, 2003.

Very few political science books have focused on the machinery of campaigning in Canada. One of the rare ones is: Laschinger, John and Geoffrey Stevens. *Leaders & Lesser Mortals: Backroom Politics in Canada.* Toronto: Key Porter, 1992. Laschinger also generously talked with the author about the early days of direct marketing and the 1970s–1980s traffic between the political and consumer worlds.

First-hand chronicles of the early days of the Reform Party are provided in depth in Tom Flanagan's book *Waiting for the Wave: The Reform Party and the Conservative Movement.* 2nd ed. Montreal: McGill-Queen's University Press, 2009. Manning and Flanagan also agreed to be interviewed for this book, as did Jason Kenney, who also helped explain the founding days of the Taxpayers Federation.

Chapter 5: The Brand-Wagon

To see how well consumer and political research merged in the 1980s and 1990s, see: Gregg, Allan and Michael Posner. *The Big Picture: What Canadians Think about Almost Everything.* Toronto: Macfarlane Walter & Ross, 1990.

Liberal forays into branding and political marketing in the 1990s were discussed formally and informally with many members of the party through the years, but with Peter Donolo and Michael Marzolini, at length, for this book.

For more on Tony Blair's "New Labour" experiment, see: "Political Brands and Consumer Citizens: The Rebranding of Tony Blair." *The Annals of the American Academy of Political and Social Science* 611 (May 2007): 176–92, and also BBC's *The Century of the Self* documentary (see notes for Chapter 2.)

Jean Chrétien's testimony came before Justice John Gomery's inquiry into sponsorship and advertising activities: Canada. Commission of Inquiry into the Sponsorship Program and Advertising Activities. And John Howard Gomery. *Restoring Accountability*. Ottawa: Commission of Inquiry into the Sponsorship Program & Advertising Activities, 2006. Transcripts of testimony available here: http://epe.lac-bac.gc.ca/100/206/301/ pco-bcp/commissions/sponsorship-ef/06-02-10/www.gomery.ca/en/transcripts/default.htm.

A full article that sounded an early warning on how politics may not mix all that well with the consumerism and managerial values of the private sector: Whitaker, Reg. "Virtual Political Parties and the Decline of Democracy." *Policy Options* (June 2001), 16–22.

Chapter 6: And Now, a Word from Our Sponsors

An overview of Industry Canada's consumer-trends monitoring can be found online: www.ic.gc.ca/eic/site/oca-bc.nsf/eng/ca02091.html.

More details of the Delta Media focus-group findings were located using Access to Information requests. Statistics on household-spending patterns over the decades were obtained through conversations with researchers at the Conference Board of Canada.

For more on Canada's (relatively new) popular culture surrounding doughnuts, see: Penfold, Steven. *The Donut: A Canadian History*. Toronto; Buffalo: University of Toronto Press, 2008; Cormack, Patricia. "'True Stories' of Canada." *Cultural Sociology* 2, no. 3 (2008): 369–84; Buist, Ron. *Tales from Under the Rim: The Marketing of Tim Hortons*. Fredericton:

Goose Lane, 2003; Joyce, Ron. *Always Fresh: The Untold Story of Tim Hortons.* Toronto: HarperCollins, 2006.

Two new books, also dealing with doughnut culture and Canadian identity, were released after this manuscript was done: Cormack, Patricia, and James F. Cosgrave. *Desiring Canada: CBC Contests, Hockey Violence and Other Stately Pleasures.* Toronto: University of Toronto Press, 2013; and Hunter, Douglas. *Double Double: How Tim Hortons Became a Canadian Way of Life, One Day at a Time.* Toronto: HarperCollins, 2012.

Chapter 7: Market Leader

The story of the Conservatives' marketing switch is found in several books, particularly: Flanagan, Thomas. *Harper's Team: Behind the Scenes of the Conservative Rise to Power.* Montreal: McGill-Queen's University Press, 2007, and Wells, Paul A. *Right Side Up: The Fall of Paul Martin and the Rise of Stephen Harper's New Conservatism.* Toronto: McClelland & Stewart, 2007. The author is also grateful to Patrick Muttart, Tom Flanagan, Jason Kenney, Richard Ciano, Dimitri Pantazopoulos, Mark Cameron, Yaroslav Baran, Jim Armour, Geoff Norquay, Dimitri Soudas and other Conservatives (some who preferred to remain anonymous) who agreed to share their memories and insights in interviews.

Patrick Muttart gave an interview to Henry Olsen of the American Enterprise Institute for a 2011 article in which he was described as "perhaps the leading authority on working-class voters in the English speaking world." The article was posted online at: http://www.aei.org/publication/after-the-wave/.

To read more about former CBS correspondent's Lesley Stahl's observations with regard to the importance of imagery in Ronald Reagan's presidency, a good overview can be found online at: http://archive.pressthink.org/2004/06/09/reagan_words.html.

Chapter 8: Retail Rules

The transcript of Frank Luntz's talk to the Civitas group was supplied to the author, with much thanks to Elizabeth Thompson, the reporter who diligently sat outside and recorded the meeting. For more on the fresh marketing wisdom the US consultant was sharing with Canada's Conservatives, see: Luntz, Frank. *Words That Work: It's Not What You Say, It's What People Hear.* New York: Hyperion, 2007.

Advertising Standards Canada's bulletin from the 2008 election is available online: www.adstandards.com/en/standards/2008Advisory.pdf.

Stephen Harper's book introduction appears in: Henderson, Paul. *How Hockey Explains Canada.* Chicago: Triumph Books, 2011.

Chapter 9: Sliced and Diced

For a very thorough look at how micro-targeting changed Republican fortunes in the 2004 US election, see: Cillizza, Chris. "Romney's Data Cruncher." *Washington Post,* July 5, 2007. Online at www.washingtonpost.com/wp-dyn/content/article/2007/07/04/AR2007070401423.html.

Also see online archived interviews from PBS's *Frontline*: http://www.pbs.org/wgbh/pages/frontline/shows/architect/rove/2004.html.

The further US refinement of political databases, post-Rove, is thoroughly laid out in: Issenberg, Sasha. *The Victory Lab: The Secret Science of Winning Campaigns.* New York: Random House, 2012. Also see: McCoy, Terrence. "The Creepiness Factor: How Obama and Romney Are Getting to Know You." *The Atlantic,* April 2012.

To view an early PowerPoint presentation on the CIMS database, see online: http://www.thestar.com/news/politics_blog/2012/02/the-campaign-machine.html.

Mitch Wexler's article in the Canadian version of *Campaigns and Elections,* June 2010, pp. 45–48, is available online: http://content.yudu.com/ A1o5eb/CandEIssue2610/resources/48.htm.

The author is grateful to Wexler, as well as to Richard Ciano and Nick Kouvalis of Campaign Research, for repeated interviews and explanations of the micro-targeting business in Canada.

In the spring of 2013, Elections Canada released a report calling for tougher laws and codes of conduct around the use of political party databases and telephone communications with voters. It is called "Preventing Deceptive Communications with Electors" and is available online here: www.elections.ca/res/rep/off/comm/comm_e.pdf.

Chapter 10: This Little Party Went to Market

The New Democrats' embrace of political marketing is explained at some length in this article: Lavigne, Brad: "Anatomy of the Orange Crush: Ten Years in the Making." *Policy Options* (June–July 2012), pp. 93–101. Online: www.integritybc.ca/wp-content/uploads/2012/06/ AnatomyOrangeCrush.pdf.

The author also benefited from interviews and conversations with Lavigne, Anne McGrath, Brian Topp and Nathan Rotman.

An unusually candid post-mortem on the 2011 election, written by former Liberal party president Alf Apps, was a valuable resource for this chapter, as were conversations with previous party directors and presidents, former Liberal leader Michael Ignatieff, his former chiefs of staff Ian Davey and Peter Donolo, and Justin Trudeau (before and after his ascent to the Liberal leader's job in 2013).

In 2012, Canada's privacy commissioner released a study on political databases, carried out by University of Victoria professor Colin Bennett and

consultant Robin Bayley. The report is available online at: www.priv.gc.ca/
information/pub/pp_201203_e.asp.

The author thanks the NDP's Nathan Rotman and the Liberal party's Issie
Berish for extensive primers on their respective parties' databases.

Chapter 11: Ready

The video of the Conservatives' "just not ready" ad, formally called "The
Interview" can be found on the party's YouTube channel at: https://youtu
.be/c86-9HitWg0.

The Liberal ads mentioned in this chapter are also stored online on the
party's YouTube channel. The "Ready" ad is here: https://youtu.be/
UbI985_oN-k. The escalator ad, formally titled "Harder to Get Ahead" is
here: https://youtu.be/CdFxaKNd6xc. The Brampton-rally ad is also on
the YouTube channel at: https://youtu.be/wD5FAzvltpI.

Prime Minister Justin Trudeau's interview was obviously useful for this
chapter. But key members of his campaign team also were very helpful
in pulling together this update for the book, notably Gerald Butts, Katie
Telford, Dan Arnold and Tom Pitfield. I'm also indebted to Jack Bensimon,
David Rosenberg and Jill Engelman for an enlightening few hours at
Bensimon Byrne after the election.

To read more about "death in the middle" in the consumer world, see:
Silverstein, Michael J., and John Butman. *Treasure Hunt: Inside the Mind
of the New Global Consumer*. New York: Portfolio, 2006.

Some of the material on Trudeau in this chapter was also gathered while
I was writing an eRead for the *Toronto Star* on Trudeau's leadership
campaign. This book can be downloaded from the online Star Store at:
http://starstore.ca/products/justin-trudeau.

Katie Telford's "numbers tell stories" video can be found on the Liberal party's YouTube channel: https://youtu.be/MSN-sTgwcd4.

The New Democrats' Brad Lavigne spoke to me for this chapter, too, and his 2013 book remains an important story of how the party got within striking distance of power in the years before the 2015 election: Lavigne, Brad. *Building the Orange Wave: The Inside Story behind the Historic Rise of Jack Layton and the NDP*. Madeira Park: Douglas & McIntyre, 2013.

The Conservatives' former campaign chief, Jenni Byrne, is notoriously media-shy, but she published an op-ed article in February 2016 in which she hinted at serious disagreements at the strategy table about how to handle the NDP and the niqab during the 2015 campaign. Byrne, Jenni. "How the Conservative Party Can Avoid the Political Wilderness." *The Globe and Mail*, February 8, 2016. http://www.theglobe andmail.com/opinion/how-the-conservative-party-can-avoid-the-political-wilderness/article28616994/.

As for the question of whether Lynton Crosby was involved in the Conservative campaign, this author was not able to find any evidence that the Australian political consultant was in the country during the campaign, and at least two sources close to the war room said off the record that Crosby was not part of their daily strategy discussions.

Chapter 12: Shopping: The Sequel
Colin Bennett, a privacy expert from the University of Victoria, has a website where his academic and media articles can be found: www. colinbennett.ca.

INDEX